To Don and Lee,
I hope you enjoy this trek
across Tiger land —
all the best,
Eric Dinerstein

A SHEARWATER BOOK

TIGERLAND

AND OTHER UNINTENDED DESTINATIONS

TIGERLAND

AND OTHER UNINTENDED
DESTINATIONS

ERIC DINERSTEIN

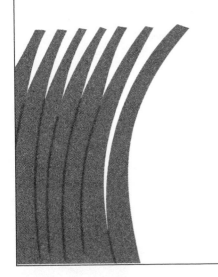

ISLANDPRESS / Shearwater Books
Washington • Covelo • London

A Shearwater Book
Published by Island Press

Copyright © 2005 Eric Dinerstein

SHEARWATER BOOKS is a trademark of The Center for Resource Economics.

Library of Congress Cataloging-in-Publication data.

Dinerstein, Eric, 1952–
Tigerland and other unintended destinations / Eric Dinerstein.
p. cm.
Includes bibliographical references and index.
ISBN 1-55963-578-9 (cloth : alk. paper)
1. Endangered ecosystems. 2. Conservation biology. 3. Dinerstein, Eric,
1952—Travel. I. Title.
QH75.D55 2005
590′.92—dc22
2005013822

British Cataloguing-in-Publication data available.

Printed on recycled, acid-free paper ✪

Design by John Costa, New Orleans

Manufactured in the United States of America

10 9 8 7 6 5 4 3 2

TO ELEANOR AND HOLLY

So I should not have to remind you
that little time is given here
to rest on a wayside bench,
to stop and bend to the wildflowers,
or to study a bird on a branch...

—Billy Collins, "The Parade"

CONTENTS

NATURE'S BELATED EMBRACE

BIOLOGISTS OFTEN BEGIN AUTOBIOGRAPHICAL SKETCHES BY describing an idyllic childhood spent in the company of bugs and salamanders. I confess to being an embarrassingly late bloomer as a naturalist. Instead of turning over rotting logs in bottomland forests or gazing into tidal pools, I stayed indoors, reading novels and watching old movies on television. I enjoyed a fling with dinosaurs and prehistoric mammals like most boys between ages seven and eight, but the truth is that growing up in suburban New Jersey, my exposure to natural history would barely exceed a few lines in a field notebook. During high school I vaguely remember seeing a whale of some kind washed ashore at Island Beach State Park and hearing the spring aria of what was likely a rose-breasted grosbeak on a rare walk through the woods. But compared to the bank vault of first sightings available to most biologists—bright butterflies on milkweed, the grace of a blue heron—I drew blanks. I was training to be the anti-Thoreau.

The gene controlling my delayed appreciation for nature is likely related to the brain chemistry of an epiphany. Yet the trigger mechanism remains elusive to me. Perhaps a sudden first encounter with a bald eagle, a Venus flytrap, a praying mantis, or a leaping salmon activates some regulatory enzyme. Maybe it can be traced to the periodic stimulation of the cortex by a string of unrelated small miracles: the stylized rumba of mating cranes, the underwater fashion show of tropical reef fish, or the saffron blur of a cheetah chasing down a gazelle. My only insight is that intimacy with the natural world is most palpable when one is solitary, moving slowly, and with the mind empty, free of the mental tail-chasing that passes for conscious thought.

My epiphanal moment occurred during my sophomore year in film school at Northwestern University. Friends talked me into moving to a farmhouse set on 250 acres of woods, abandoned pastures, and swamp near the town of Lake Bluff, Illinois, an inconvenient twenty-five miles from campus, and where I fell hard for a *Walden*-like lifestyle. While wandering along a stream, I accidentally spooked a sharp-billed bird that squawked in indignation and flew off. To this day, I don't know what exactly captivated me at that moment, but I did observe the escapee long enough to identify it in my field guide as a little green heron (a most accurate name, says a colleague, because it sports so little green in its plumage). Spring wildflowers began to catch my eye, and I can still picture my initial discoveries of trillium, wild iris, and columbines. Every new species of bird and wildflower was a revelation, as if I were actually the first naturalist to find it. The gravitational pull of campus life and student parties no longer drew me into Evanston; I began instead to listen for owls and the courtship flights of woodcocks over the horse pastures. The farmhouse in Lake Bluff was to be the first of a series of unintended destinations, the serendipitous zigzags in the geography of life that chart our destiny.

My reading list changed, too. The writers of the moment—Barth, Burroughs, Barthelme, Hawkes, Pynchon, and Robbe-Grillet—depressed me with their bleak visions and their near-total alienation from the natural world. There was still Nabokov and his butterflies, but finding other allusions to nature in his literary artifice was too much detective work. Thoreau's classic, an unwelcome reading assignment in high school, became my new companion. So did *The Marvels of Animal Behavior* by Thomas Allen, a compelling introduction to animal ecology and the field research of famous scientists. Each chapter illuminated evolution's hidden agenda in the lives of elephant seals, humpback whales, monarch butterflies, and other charismatic species. A chapter on social behavior in birds featured a photograph of the ecologist Gordon Orians (later to become one of my graduate school professors) knee deep in a cattail marsh. Surrounded by an all-male choir of red-winged blackbirds, he looked more like a rapt conductor of their territorial anthem of spring than an observer of their nesting patterns. I began to dream of the glorious life of a field biologist, while filmmaking seemed less appealing by the moment. The most talented graduates of my program at Northwestern had just been hired to shoot a commercial for a lightbulb factory.

At the start of my junior year—to the bewilderment of my faculty adviser and many friends—I traded in courses in film, philosophy, and literature for courses in math and the basic sciences—the core curriculum in academic torture, as one friend put it. The saving grace was Evolution and Phylogeny, taught by two young professors, David Culver, now chairman of the Zoology Department at American University, and Andy Beattie, now at Maquarie University in Australia. Whenever I felt overwhelmed by the hieroglyphics of calculus, physics, and chemistry, the elegance of Darwin's theories and the link to natural history sustained my faith in the possibility of my metamorphosis into a biologist.

The results of my first midterm shattered such hopes. My math professor took me aside after class and bluntly told me, "Young man, I don't see a future for you in calculus." Two years of dissecting the films of Fellini, Truffaut, and Bergman had left me ill prepared to find derivatives in the nanosecond that it took my classmates, freshman math prodigies. To be honest, I didn't have a future at Northwestern, either; nor did my two professors. Molecular biologists and geneticists already had seized the biology program and outcompeted the few ecologists for lab space, department funding, and ultimately tenure. Teaching natural history or even animal ecology had become passé.

I became a calculus refugee at the University of Idaho for a semester. I remember little about my course work, but I do recall spotting my first northern harrier as it flew low over the verdant Palouse grasslands on a secret reconnaissance of field mice populations.

I finished my undergraduate degree at Huxley College of Environmental Studies (part of Western Washington University) in Bellingham, Washington. At Huxley I found like-minded students and professors who recognized the intrinsic value of natural history. Ron Taylor, a former Idaho rancher who grew up in the purple sage and jagged shadows of the Tetons and then escaped to become a fighter pilot, taught me plant taxonomy and cowboy botany. Plant taxonomy is essentially an indoor pastime—you sit in a lab and identify flowering plants by carefully examining their reproductive parts, typically the number and arrangement of the stamens, pistils, and petals and the orientation of the ovary (superior or inferior). Taylor had the swashbuckling personality of a biologist who studies wolves or mountain lions, but he specialized in balsam root, a member of the daisy family. Plant taxonomy struck me as a discipline that should really be taught by an admirer of Georgia O'Keeffe (who, had she not followed her muse, would have found her calling in a university herbarium).

Cowboy botany, on the other hand, is strictly an outdoor pursuit. Out in the sagebrush country of eastern "Warshington," Taylor would rattle off the scientific names—Bam! Bam! Bam!—of flowering plants that he spied along the roadsides while barreling along in a campus van. Farther up the highway, I let loose my own Latin riff: "There's

Lupinus wyethii, Artemesia tridentata, Eriogonum thymoides, Castilleja chromosa, Balsamorhiza sagittata, and *Salvia dorii!*" (In order, that's prairie lupine, tall sagebrush, thyme desert buckwheat, desert paintbrush, balsam root, and purple sage.) I peered out the corner of my eye, looking for some sign of approval from the Clint Eastwood of plant taxonomists. He nodded slightly and continued to scan the riot of wildflowers on the horizon. I felt like a young gunslinger who had just put a slug through every glass bottle Butch Cassidy tossed into the air.

Encouraged by my adviser at Huxley, I went on to conduct a bird survey of a nearby wildlife refuge (home of more green herons) and to participate in a field study of black bears in Yosemite Valley. A year later, on a whim, I decided to apply to the Peace Corps under a program jointly managed by the Smithsonian Institution. If fortunate enough to be chosen, I thought I'd be bound for Colombia to study crop damage by some pest birds. Instead, I won the biological lottery. My post—the point of departure for the first chapter of this book— was to be the Himalayan kingdom of Nepal, a country that had just established a network of parks and wildlife reserves.

After an adventure of a lifetime, I returned from Nepal in July of 1977 with a near terminal case of culture shock, assuaged only by birding around Puget Sound and fleeing to the solitude of the Cascade Mountains. I was admitted to graduate school at the University of Washington but was eager to escape to the field again almost as soon as I started my studies. At the suggestion of friends and teachers, I enrolled in a tropical ecology course in Costa Rica sponsored by the Organization for Tropical Studies and taught by some of the world's top neotropical field biologists. At La Selva Biological Station, Gary Hartshorn explained how cathedral-like rain forests regenerate. While all eyes and binoculars were focused skyward to learn how to recognize the giant trees by their leaves, Gary gently detained with his rubber boot a baby fer-de-lance, a poisonous snake that had slithered across our path. In the Monteverde Cloud Forest Reserve, Bill Haber turned a field lecture on pollination systems and sexual reproduction of plants into an ecological interpretation of the *Kama Sutra*: how the decurved bill of a violet sabre-wing (a hummingbird) perfectly fits the flowers of an African violet vine; how only a single species of night-flying hawk moth has a tongue long enough (25 centimeters!) to reach the floral nectaries of the deep-throated corolla of the *Solandra* vine; and how the long-tongued bats lap nectar from the musky-scented flowers of an air plant. In Corcovado National Park and on Barro Colorado Island, Panama, Robin Foster taught me plant taxonomy that you will never find in a field guide: how to tell a certain tree by the color of its sap or from the telltale signs of peccaries, the pigs of the rain forest, that gnaw its buttressed roots; how to tell a fig tree from far away by the daggerlike projection (the spicule) at the tip of a branch; and how to identify almost any plant in the rain forest without access to the flowers by remembering the shape, arrangement, smell, texture, latex, or glands of the leaves. In one night of mist-netting, Frank Bonaccorso cured my severe case of bat phobia and transformed it into a lifelong fascination with those creatures. I left the course awed by those biologists and their easy familiarity with their natural surroundings.

In every place I visited after my experiences in Nepal and Costa Rica, I followed the same routine: I found a field biologist who was a walking encyclopedia of natural history and trailed that person like a cattle egret behind a water buffalo, gobbling up plant names, natural history insights, and every new bird identification pointed out to me. I reveled in the clutter of Latin names filling my head and began to make connections with what I had seen earlier in Asia. What is the expression? It is the recent converts who make the most fervent disciples? I had evolved from the anti-Thoreau to a latter-day naturalist.

And so the hobby became a career that has led me to some of the most intriguing destinations on earth for someone with an interest in natural history and conservation. With the exception of the first three, I conceived the chapters of this book during my travels as a

World Wildlife Fund (WWF) conservation biologist. As chief scientist at WWF, I have witnessed enough ecological Armageddons around the world, some documented here, to see firsthand how rapidly time is running out. Conducting conservation biology research and writing scientific papers are important parts of trying to save these areas. But the minuscule audience for such work needs no convincing that we must rapidly increase the scale and pace of conservation efforts around the world to slow down an accelerating extinction crisis. And writing a traditional scientific paper limits the author to a spartan thesaurus of dry verbs and bleached adjectives—hardly the language to inspire people to save life on earth, or capture the kind of fascination and love of wildlife that draws me to one place and another. If we are ever to persuade even a fraction of the U.S. population, let alone the world, that leaving behind a living planet is more than an empty slogan, we must restore a reverence for nature, as rapidly and in as many hearts as we can. Those of us schooled in natural history must help to illuminate for others the priceless handiwork of millions of years of evolution that is disappearing in a matter of decades, so that, educated and inspired, we may all act in the best interests of future generations.

Not all of the places I feature here are among the world's most diverse habitats, or ecoregions. Nor are they necessarily the most threatened places, even though the New Caledonia tropical dry forests may be the most endangered of such forests anywhere. It is the grandeur of the natural backdrop and the people fighting to save these places that move me in a profound way and that still keep me going when I see wild nature retreating or conservation on the defensive.

Each chapter introduces a range of people working on behalf of conservation, some of them internationally recognized scientists, others laboring in relative obscurity. But collectively they are some of the most compelling and dedicated individuals I have ever met. And their combined efforts prove a point: that against enormous odds, a single individual can make a difference in this world if he or she embraces the cause of safeguarding the future of the planet's millions of species so dependent on us for survival.

Each chapter also illustrates an important theme in the science of conservation biology that has broad geographic relevance. For example, in "An Inordinate Fondness for Bats," I stress the importance of maintaining vital migratory corridors for birds and mammals that move seasonally along tropical mountainsides. Although I focus on Costa Rica, where some of the best research has been done, this conservation approach applies to hummingbirds in the Andes, talking mynas in the Himalayas, and birds of paradise in the mountains of New Guinea. Similarly, in "Trespassers in Eden," I talk about the designation of no-fishing zones in the Galápagos Archipelago, a conservation measure designed to protect breeding areas for fish populations and the integrity of the marine environment. This strategy applies equally to the coastal zone of the Red Sea and the mangroves and reefs of the Indonesian archipelago, or the Florida Keys Marine Reserve, one of the first to experiment with this concept.

With species going extinct at the rate of one hundred per day, the chapters that follow could easily be advertised as a lament to the end of nature. Other writers have successfully mined that theme. Instead, this book offers a more hopeful vision of what success would look like in various ecoregions if the dreams of conservation-minded biologists came true. Given a strong political will, some of the conservation gains discussed here could be achieved within a year. Other critical priorities will take several years. Still others seem, at least today, like the hallucinations of a field biologist in the final throes of dementia: restoring the Galápagos Archipelago to an ecological state close to that experienced by Charles Darwin in 1835; restoring the Selous Game Reserve in Tanzania to its prominence as the premier wildland of East Africa; recreating an American Serengeti—a real national bison preserve—in eastern Montana. These highly ambitious visions may appear far beyond our grasp given the current political climate. But they wouldn't be the first impossible proposals that have become a reality. For much of its modern history, the state of Florida, for example, was so prodevelopment that species long identified with the state, such as the alligator, were prominent members of the endangered species list. Today, nearly half the state is under some form of conservation-based land management.

Many threats to conservation may seem too overwhelming to mitigate in time to save wild nature—overfishing in coastal seas and the open ocean, illegal logging in the tropics, the damming up of the earth's most biologically rich rivers and streams. Yet in some places all fishing is prohibited, even catch-and-release, to protect vital fisheries; logging bans are in place in some ecologically sensitive forests; and a movement is growing in the United States and Europe to restore free-flowing rivers by decommissioning dams that are no longer needed to provide power. In conservation, as in the world of politics, Berlin Walls do come down. We need to use science, advocacy, and our collective passion to hasten the coming of the day when, spurred on by enlightened local and national leaders, restoration of the earth's wild habitats and their natural inhabitants is central to the agenda of every government.

I had no idea that my first accidental encounter with the antisocial little green heron in Illinois would someday result in this book, let alone a career that has led me to many unintended destinations, some of which are described here. In the pages that follow, you will encounter many species of herons more exotic than that understated little green one: the colonial roosting black-crowned night herons of Nepal, which live among pythons, mugger crocodiles, and tigers; the diabolical black heron, a serial killer that shadows naive amphibians and invertebrates in the hippo pools of East Africa; and the endemic lava heron of the Galápagos, dancing its graceful seaside pas-de-deux with the elegant Sally Lightfoot crabs in front of an audience of marine iguanas, penguins, and sea lions. But even as my life list of the world's herons—and all the other species that have since caught my eye—continues to grow, I will never forget my first entry, the one that knocked me off the road to Hollywood and landed me instead in the jungles of Nepal. May other slow learners be led astray by their own heron experience and accept nature's belated embrace.

PART ONE

EARLY WANDERINGS

chapter one

TIGERLAND

THE QUIET, SERIOUS TIGER SPECIALIST WE HAD MET FOR THE
first time that afternoon motioned for the Nepalese driver to stop
the Jeep. Mel Sunquist was taking us along to check on the where-
abouts of his tigers, the first ever to be fitted with radiotelemetry collars. It felt great to be on the prowl this hot spring night in April
1975—just like the tigers, even more so because researchers are required to be out of the park by sundown. Engaging in this illegal activity only added to our excitement. My fellow Peace Corps volunteers
and I quietly stepped out of the Jeep and onto the dirt road that cuts
through Royal Chitwan National Park.

We were elated to escape the crowded, dusty bazaars of Kathmandu to tag along with a *tigerwallah* like Mel. Soon we would all
be posted as ecologists in some of the wildest and most remote places
in Asia. And after two months of relentless language training—

conjugating Nepali verbs and learning the local names for tiger (*baagh*), elephant (*haathi*), and sloth bear (*bhalu*)—it was high time to see a baagh for real. Standing silently in the receding heat of evening, we listened to the strange percussion of large-tailed night-jars and the distant alarm barks of spotted deer. I felt a million miles from home. Only a few months back, we had been faceless under-grads in the United States. Now, dressed in army surplus pants and t-shirts, we were a platoon of budding young American field biolo-gists stationed in the heart of Tigerland.

Mel switched on the receiver, raised an antenna over his head, and began slowly rotating it in a wide arc, a ballet movement used by hun-dreds of field biologists before him to locate their study animals, ex-cept that Mel was homing in on the largest terrestrial carnivore on earth. We felt no small amount of fear but tried our best to appear nonchalant. Mel's Nepalese coinvestigator, Kirti Man Tamang, was in the hospital back in Kathmandu, after being pulled out of a tree and mauled by a tigress only a few weeks earlier. Believing the conven-tional wisdom that tigers were reluctant tree climbers, Kirti had wedged himself into the crotch of a tree, waiting for the right moment to fire a tranquilizing dart. The tigress, evidently seeing Kirti as a threat to her three young cubs, defied conventional wisdom and scaled the tree. The thought of Kirti lying helpless on the ground, his legs badly shredded and an angry tigress standing over him, made me think twice about wandering far from the Jeep.

The tiger Mel sought was barely within range, so he tried the fre-quency of another. "I think we have a tigress very close by." His voice was animated, or at least as animated as his Minnesota origins would allow. Within seconds of his warning, a fierce struggle between the ti-gress and a large deer had us all scrambling back into the Jeep. The ti-gress in question had been right next to us, hidden from view by a wall of Chitwan's elephant grass, lying in ambush for, as we would later learn, a sambar, or Indian forest deer. Only the tigress's snarl and the beeps seeping from Mel's headphones signaled our proximity to this secretive predator.

Back at the Smithsonian research camp, over glasses of warm Coke spiked with local rum, we chattered away about our first adventure with the king of the Terai Jungle. But the night wasn't over. We shifted to a small clearing near the banks of the Rapti River, where we had pitched our tents. Nepali language instructors, all of whom were well-educated, charming Kathmandu dwellers, as new to life in the lowland jungles as we were, were paired up as tent mates with American volunteers. My favorite teacher was Narayan Kazi Shrestha, a bright, fun-loving man who eventually bestowed upon me the gift of fluency in another language and the self-confidence that comes with it.

But on this night, my tent mate was Surya Sharma, a studious, high-caste Brahmin in his early twenties and the son of a famous Nepalese judge. As we were drifting off to sleep, the sound of loud chewing and lip smacking stirred us awake. Surya peered through the insect netting. He reached over and clutched my arm. "Rhinos!" he whispered fearfully, using the English rather than the Nepali word (*gaida*), not wanting to gamble our lives on my Nepali vocabulary. We had been warned earlier that rhinos routinely trample and kill several tourists each year. I peeked through the fly mesh. Surya's grip tightened. I saw an enormous greater one-horned female rhinoceros accompanied by a calf. Eventually, they wandered off, but the interlopers left a lasting impression on both of us. For me, it was the first face-to-face experience with a creature I would eventually devote years of my life to conserving. For Surya, it was the abrupt end of tenure as a Peace Corps language teacher. When our program was over, he went straight to law school.

After our training period, I headed for the Royal Karnali-Bardia Wildlife Reserve, located 180 miles to the west of Chitwan. I had been handed an introductory letter to the Bardia park warden that detailed my mission, a single sentence hastily typed by Nepal's senior ecologist, Dr. Hemanta Mishra:

You are to census the tiger population in Bardia and to conduct other wildlife inventories as appropriate. [Translation:
*Get out of my hair and see if you can do something useful
out there.*]

Today, Bardia is easily accessed by an excellent all-weather road,
but in 1975 it was Nepal's version of the outback—a posting there was
considered a kind of banishment. Bardia is one of the most spectacular wildlife reserves anywhere, about the size of Shenandoah National
Park in the United States. It's bounded to the west by the Karnali
River, the wildest river flowing out of the Himalayas, which is filled
with crocodiles and Gangetic dolphins, where wild tigers and their
prey populate floodplain islands covered with forests of native rosewood and acacia. Bardia had never been properly surveyed for its
wildlife, and it seemed like a destination that would fulfill both my
earliest childhood fantasies of the exotic and my recent undergraduate
training as a wildlife biologist.

The standard joke among former volunteers is that in those days
the Peace Corps parachuted you into the bush with little more than a
Swiss army knife and a copy of JFK's *Profiles in Courage*. But being
dropped from an airplane into Bardia wasn't an option. With the monsoon fast approaching, the nearby grass airstrips were no longer ser-
viceable. Our only alternative was a four-wheel-drive Jeep. Together
with Will Weber, my Peace Corps director, and Cliff Rice, a fellow
volunteer slated to become my western neighbor as the ecologist of
the Royal Suklaphanta Wildlife Reserve, and a driver, we headed
south from Kathmandu. There was no road across lowland Nepal
then, so we would have to cross the border into India at Bhairawa and
continue westward on the Indian side of the frontier. But we soon
found our route blocked by a massive landslide, a natural disaster
common in the Himalayas especially during the monsoon. Impatient
westerners become unglued by landslides because delays are often
measured in days rather than hours. The Nepalese cope with such in-

convenience by drawing on their own brand of happy-go-lucky fatalism, simply remarking, *"Ke garne?"* or "What to do?" accompanied by a smile and a wave of the hand.

When we reached the landslide, travelers had been waiting for almost two days for the road to reopen, and a carnival-like atmosphere had developed. We came upon another westerner sitting forlornly in a tea stall that was catering to the temporarily detained. It was Dietrich Schaaf, a Ph.D. student from Michigan State who had been in Suklaphanta for a year studying swamp deer, a highly endangered variety of the world's thirty-seven species of deer. Encountering a few more westerners did little to cheer him up. He also seemed displeased to see Cliff, who held a master's degree and could claim a strong background in ungulate biology and behavior. In truth, Cliff was the only one among us who was academically prepared to take on his assignment. Unfortunately, what Cliff really wanted to do was study swamp deer, but Dietrich had already staked out that species as his alone—this was my first and far from last experience of territoriality among biologists.

Eventually, the last boulder was pushed down the mountainside into the Trisuli River, and we threaded our way through the rubble. We raced the onset of the monsoon across Uttar Pradesh, driving as fast as we could while swerving around imperturbable cows, horse-drawn buggies, ox carts, and countless people on bicycles. I vividly recall the image of slender young men and women of some untouchable caste, gracefully balancing tall stacks of bricks on their heads as they walked single file from a primitive outdoor kiln to a clump of mud huts. In 1975, carrying bricks in such a manner was a lifetime occupation for Gandhi's children. For the first time, I questioned whether my assignment was a frivolous venture in a region overwhelmed by crushing poverty.

Once we crossed back into Nepal below the town of Nepalganj, we met with the conservator of forests, who traced our route west to Bardia. There was only a dirt track, he said, and the rains had started already. I tuned out the rest of his warnings, pretending not to comprehend what I didn't want to hear. Several hours later, after winching ourselves out of several streams, we gave up and headed back to Nepalganj and the conservator's office. I would have to wait for a Forest Department elephant to carry me and my belongings to Bardia.

After Will and Cliff left for Suklaphanta, I walked over to a large building that turned out to be a U.S. Agency for International Development guesthouse. It was empty except for the caretaker, an ex-Gurkha soldier. I asked if I could stay there. He couldn't let me without a letter, he replied. Anything you wanted in Nepal, down to the smallest request, required an official letter, a *chitti*. And when you handed the chitti to a government officer, even if it boasted enough stamps of authenticity to guarantee your passage to Nirvana, he would hold it away from his face in feigned puzzlement, as if your request were preposterous or written in Cyrillic or Chinese, rather than in Devanagri, the script shared by Nepali and Hindi.

Should I obtain a chitti, the ex-Gurkha said that the cost for a room at the guesthouse would be about $50 per night, almost half my monthly stipend. Now what? I thanked him and turned to leave when he asked in an innocent voice, "Do you know geometry?" He went and fetched a hardbound primer, a relic from the British Army education program. If I would teach him all about isosceles and right triangles and other such objects, he would let me stay for free while I waited for my elephant. I silently thanked Mrs. Luella Beebe, my tenth grade geometry teacher, for sparing me a night of camping out with cobras and banded kraits in a patch of scrub jungle at the edge of town.

Two days later, my elephant arrived, an old female, accompanied by her two sullen drivers. It takes several days to travel the fifty miles to Bardia, and this was a slow elephant. We had to set off immediately. I strapped my small shipping trunks on top of the elephant's saddle and took a seat between them. No sooner had we gotten under way than the rains began again, and the elephant had trouble moving quickly through the mud that masqueraded as the seasonal dirt track between

Nepalganj and Bardia. Fortunately, when we reached a forest development project camp on the second day, a Danish and Nepalese forester team kindly offered to take us in while we waited for the deluge to end.

I had come prepared for such circumstances; in my backpack was a copy of *Huckleberry Finn*, and I was rereading the section where Huck and Jim were floating down the Mississippi, escaping from "civilized" society and slavery. I tried to picture my elephant ride as a Mark Twain journey in a land of adventure. But unlike Huck and Jim, I had a close destination and a research program to initiate. The thought of being stuck on this side of the Babai River, looking across at the Bardia Reserve until the end of the monsoon, made me nervous. What was the alternative—return to Kathmandu and wait until the rains stopped in September? Whatever happened to me over the next two years, I told myself, I could treat each new challenge as a source of worry and defeat or as a new adventure. No matter what life in Nepal's jungles held for me, I vowed that I would always choose the latter.

After the rains stopped, I soon had a chance to test my new resolve. We saddled up our haathi and headed west. Within a few hours, we reached the banks of the Babai, and, to my dismay, the river was a deep brown torrent. Across the surging water beckoned the rosewood and acacia forests of Bardia. The drivers were determined to cross without delay. The mahout, sitting behind the elephant's head, urged her down the riverbank. She stalled at the water's edge, perhaps gauging the speed of the current or the stupidity of the humans sitting on her back. The mahout would have none of it. Whacking her with his stick across her broad forehead and muttering curses, he drove her forward. Within seconds, the elephant was up to her knees and elbows, then shoulders, and before I could tell the driver that we might want to reconsider our plan of attack, we were swept away.

For a brief moment, only the tip of the elephant's trunk and my head were above water. Elephants are surprisingly buoyant, however, and powerful swimmers, and the drivers, who held on to the saddle ropes, soon had us back on the riverbank. I immediately opened my steamer trunks to assess the damage. Fortunately, I had been advised to pack all of my clothes, books, and camera gear in plastic bags or within waterproof biscuit tins and Tupperware, and everything but the shorts I was wearing had stayed dry.

I looked up the riverbank and noticed a small open-sided thatch hut, where a group of men were playing cards and drinking tea. I asked in Nepali if they had seen what happened. "You tried to cross in the wrong place," they laughed. "Just wait a few hours. The Babai River is not like the mighty Karnali. It only drains the low mountains behind us. So when the sun shines, the river level will drop, and you will cross the Babai in this place in front of where we sit. *Aram garnos.*" (Another national expression, which roughly means "chill out.")

Over tea, the villagers' questions unfurled in a sequence I would soon grow accustomed to: "Are you American? How old are you? Are you married? What is your salary? How much land do you farm? How many cattle and buffalo do you own?" The villagers had no problem with my bachelorhood, even at the advanced age of twenty-two. But they were dumbfounded that I didn't grow my own rice back home, and that my parents kept no water buffalo or goats in their Miami condominium.

Eight hours after our misadventure, we made it across the river without further incident and arrived at reserve headquarters, a cluster of two whitewashed brick buildings and several thatch-roofed huts. I was met by Krishna Man Shrestha, the newly appointed park warden. The drivers removed my steamer trunks and, before I could even wave goodbye, turned the elephant back toward Nepalganj. I handed the warden my official two-page letter of introduction from Dr. Mishra, thankfully kept dry in its Zip-Loc bag. The warden put on his reading glasses and began glancing back and forth from the letter to my face. He never altered his expression—a distinct frown made more severe by scars from a childhood battle with smallpox. I told him in respectful Nepali that I was assigned to be the new survey biologist for the reserve and looked forward to working with him over the next two years.

Decades of service in the government bureaucracy had honed Krishna Man's skill at establishing hierarchy. The pecking order was about to be applied, even to an extraterrestrial like me. He pointed at a tiny two-room thatched hut on stilts and declared that I could share it with an army sergeant who was temporarily stationed in Bardia. What was I going to do for food, and how would I eat? Had I brought any rations with me? I hadn't thought that far ahead. And I was quite hungry, having consumed nothing all day except the tea and biscuits offered by the Nepalese villagers who witnessed our failed attempt to cross the river. The warden told me that I could share meals with him for a few days, but then I would need to find a cook and figure things out on my own. The nearest bazaar was on the Indian border, more than ten miles away.

I unloaded my few belongings onto the two shelves in my cubicle. The sergeant was off on holiday, but there were plenty of other occupants, I soon discovered. At dusk, the thatching emitted a cacophony of chirps and squeals. By nightfall, it was alive with rats and a nursing colony of Indian pipistrelles. Five years later, I became enamored with bats, but this, my first experience with them, was terrifying. I nearly panicked when the juvenile pipistrelles dropped on my mosquito net while learning to fly, or flitted through the narrow room, tight furry fists glued to leathery wings. The rats held their own in this hut of horrors, chewing on anything I absentmindedly failed to store away each night in my steamer trunks. My mosquito netting doubled as a barrier to keep nocturnal rats and bats from scrambling over me like a piece of furniture. By candlelight, I wrote in my journal sentiments sure to be found in those of many other young volunteers, brave attempts to dispel premature adult despair with naive youthful optimism: *Just make it through the first month, and the rest will be easy.*

On the third morning, a tall, handsome Nepalese man clambered up the stairs of my hut to marvel at the new carnival freak from America carried in by elephant. In one breath, Gagan Singh told me that he was a game scout for the reserve and, not to worry, he would find me a cook, and together he and the cook would go to the bazaar, buy the pots and pans I needed to set up a kitchen and a month's worth of food rations (rice, lentils, potatoes, onions, sugar, salt, and tea), and carry it all back to Thakurdwara, the park's headquarters. When he returned, he would help me get settled, guide me around the reserve, and show me where the tigers lived. To the rest of the world Gagan may have been a dark-skinned, low-caste Sunwar (the low-ranking goldsmith caste) who had grown up in the forest and hadn't studied beyond the third grade. But he was a true jungle savant, and to this unnerved twenty-two-year-old foreigner, he was Gunga Din.

Gagan returned late the next day, as promised, accompanied by a young man from the Tamang hill tribe named Prem Bahadur, both of them carrying on their backs enormous loads of food and kitchen goods. Prem would be my cook, and, over the next two years, Gagan became my everything else: tiger tracker, jungle tutor, local anthropologist and language instructor, older brother, and best friend.

Even with Gagan's enthusiasm, I still had some doubts. I had never fully adapted to the humid summers of New Jersey and Illinois; now I was living on the northern edge of the Gangetic plain, where humidity was invented. I couldn't recall seeing Johnny Weissmuller sweat in his film portrayals of Tarzan, even when swinging through the steamy jungle to rescue Jane from a tight situation, or scratch at ugly welts raised by biting insects. Thus influenced by Hollywood, images of sweltering heat, skin rash, and stinging ants were abrupt intrusions into my wildlife fantasy. I was to make some adjustments.

By the end of my first month, I had settled into a routine of fieldwork and exploration of the reserve. But in my hovel, things had taken a turn for the worse: Besides the rats and bats, the roof leaked like a colander during every monsoon downpour. So I began to develop plans to build a native-style house at the edge of the jungle once the monsoon ended in October. Gagan helped me select the best site, close to the banks of the river, about five hundred yards from my current residence. I envisioned a veranda where I would watch langur monkeys leap through the fig trees on the other side of the Khoraha and observe Indian otters glissading down the riverbank. A leopard or jungle cat in my front yard would be perfect. It was time for some privacy, after enduring the scrutiny of my neighbors, who took note of my every move as if *I* were the object of biological research. My thatch-roofed palace, constructed in native style by the local animist tribe, the Tharu, would be ready by the rice harvest.

Gagan could recognize plants in his local taxonomy incredibly fast. He never required the flowers or fruits for identification; a single leaf was enough. He could tell me what the spotted deer fed on and what leaves the langur monkeys consumed. He explained how the pod of the Raj briksha (*Cassia fistula*) had powerful medicinal properties. Chew one end of the pod to cure constipation, the other to stop diarrhea (although now I can't remember which end is which). He knew better than most foresters which trees were best used for different purposes. When we were caught in a monsoon shower, he showed me how to fashion a disposable umbrella from the broad leaves of the tantari tree (*Dillenia indica*), as well as toilet paper taxonomy, a skill vital for every field biologist or anyone who has ventured onto the back roads of Asia. Why use paper when there were the soft leaves of the pipuri (*Casearia tomentosa*) or the absorbent and pleasantly scented foliage of durshiya (*Colebrookia oppositifolia*), a member of the mint family?

After our hot walks through the jungle, Gagan convinced me to take a shortcut home through the Tharu villages. He would accept for both of us the hospitable Tharus' invitations to rest inside their cool houses and have something to eat. Striking young women dressed in brilliantly colored blouses and bedecked in silver earrings, necklaces, and bracelets would serve us homemade Tharu specialties. Usually, there were boiled jungle greens laced with chili peppers, oral stun guns. Sometimes it was dried fish ground up with salt and chilies served in plates fashioned from tree leaves. I would try to extinguish the bonfire in my mouth with bowl after bowl of *jarrh*, their home-made rice beer. It was safer than drinking the water put before me, but not by much. Gagan could consume such vast quantities of jarrh that if rice beer consumption were an event in the Pan-Asian games, he would bring honor to his country.

In July of 1975, Gagan and I began a walking tour of Bardia to as-sess its wildlife. Some westerners I met in Kathmandu had told of hunting sambar deer along the edge of the reserve a decade earlier, but ecologically speaking, Bardia was a blank spot on the world's bio-logical map. Tigers were still present, we knew, but how many and how serious the effects of poaching on their numbers remained a mys-tery. Rhinoceros, on the other hand, had disappeared from Bardia's floodplain at least a century earlier as a result of uncontrolled poach-ing. Gagan and I decided to begin by exploring the northern edge of the park at Chisapani and then head east to the Babai River, the site of my accidental baptism on the ride into Bardia. We followed the banks of the Karnali River from Thakurdwara about fifteen miles north to the Chisapani gorge, where the river spills out of the mountains into the Terai, the flat, low-lying plain at the base of the Himalayas. Along the steep slopes were goral and serow, two goatlike antelopes more characteristic of the higher mountains to the north, and the base of these hills were supposed to be alive with king cobras. As we were to discover, there were also wild dogs and striped hyena, their denning areas graveyards littered with the bones of whatever herbivore had been unfortunate enough to become their dinner.

The Karnali drains a huge watershed of Nepal's western Himalayas. The river drops quickly, emerging cool and clear at the gorge (Chisa-pani means "cold water") before it heads across the Indian border to its eventual rendezvous with the Ganges. The park guards stationed at Chisapani welcomed us warmly and prepared a special dinner in our honor. The upper Karnali is famous for the abundance of the Indian subcontinent's prized native sporting fish, the giant masheer or sher (*Tor tor*), a glorified carp. The guards bought masheer and some impressive-looking catfish from the local fisherman, who still lived inside the reserve. We were served hunks of bony carp on a low mountain of white rice, with liters of *rakshi*, the foul but highly popular distilled rice wine to wash it down.

The infinitive of the verb "to be drunk" in Nepali is *rakshi lagnu*, literally "to be affected by rakshi," but even before the cocktail hour was over, our hosts had lost the ability to conjugate the verb in any language. Avoiding the sour-tasting liquor, I greedily ate the chunks of fish, using my right hand as the Nepalese do instead of a fork. After swallowing a number of mouthfuls, I felt an irritation in my throat. I swallowed again. A fish bone had become lodged in my gullet. The mirthful chatter ended abruptly, and Gagan quickly taught me the Nepalese method for dislodging fish bones: Make a fist-sized ball of rice and swallow it without chewing to force the bone loose. I tried that, along with the standard Western approach of coughing my guts out, but nothing happened. I grew anxious. Would I have to walk the sixty-five miles to Nepalganj to have some doctor debone me like a piece of sturgeon?

I barely slept that night, and by morning the fish bone hadn't migrated an inch. Despondent, I took a walk to the riverbank. I saw an empty thatch-roofed platform at the edge of a field, a place where old men typically sit in the monsoon to tell stories, mend fish nets, and watch the river go by. Moments after I sat down there, a grizzled grandfather, wearing only a loincloth and a Nepali hat called a *topi*, lowered himself next to me. I greeted him in traditional Nepali, "*Namaskar, Bajhe*" (literally, I bow to the god in you, Grandfather). When he realized that I could understand him, he launched into his life story: about growing up in that village and catching the masheer, about the tigers that came out of the forest and sometimes killed his buffalo and cattle, and about how hard life was for his family. I finally said to him, "Bajhe, I would love to hear your story, but I have a fish bone stuck in my throat, and it's killing me." "Why didn't you say so?" he replied and hobbled off. He returned a few minutes later with a small pouch. Inside were some dried lali gurans (*Rhododendron arboreum*) petals. "This happens to us fishermen all the time. Just suck on these dried petals, and the fish bone will quickly pass."

Within an hour, the bone had dislodged itself. To this day, I can't explain what happened. Rhododendron leaves contain a compound called andromeda toxin that is quite poisonous to livestock. Perhaps some of that toxin is found in the petals, as well, and it stimulated the mucus membranes of my throat to work overtime. Perhaps it was all the power of suggestion. Who cared? I could swallow again without pain. I sat back and listened to the old man's stories for the rest of the morning.

The next day, Gagan and I resumed our trek through the heart of Bardia. I decided to use the road and trail network to carry out my tiger census. Old junglewallahs know that tigers prefer to move along dirt roads and trails to patrol and mark the boundaries of their territories. One rarely encountered tigers out in the open, so I would have to employ an indirect method to estimate their numbers. Indian foresters and wildlife officials have traditionally used the footprints of tigers, known as pugmarks, to count them. Some Indian wildlife officials claim that such counts are quite accurate if trained observers conduct the census. After measuring about a dozen sets of pugmarks, I began to have my doubts about the validity of this approach. I observed, as have others, that the size and shape of the footprint changed markedly depending on the substrate and varying effects of the monsoon rains. In these and many other instances, it wasn't clear whether you were seeing the traces of different tigers or those of the same tiger many different times. The pugmark study was a washout. It was just as well. Lying in the dirt to trace tiger tracks and then spending all evening calculating analyses of variance was dreadfully boring and a far cry from how I pictured spending my days in Bardia.

There had to be a way to census tigers other than using pugmarks, so I consulted my bible, *The Deer and the Tiger*, George Schaller's classic 1964 research account into the wildlife of India's Kanha National Park. Schaller has inspired more field biologists on more continents than any other living scientist. His love of natural history, his ability to endure hardship in the field, and his gift for quickly capturing the essence of a species' biological niche are world renowned.

The Deer and the Tiger forced me to change my thinking: Perhaps studying the ecology of their prey was more important than studying tigers. Because tigers are such magnificent animals, biologists often become afflicted with research myopia and spend a disproportionate effort documenting the ecology of the glamorous carnivores, while neglecting the study of their seemingly more pedestrian prey. Work by Mel Sunquist on the nutritional requirements of female tigers revealed that it takes about two barking deer per week to fuel a breeding female tiger. If prey intake falls below that threshold, tigresses stop having cubs. Thus, we need information on the patterns and population dynamics of the tiger's prey, and *The Deer and the Tiger* provided a model of how to go about studying not only barking deer but also spotted deer, hog deer, sambar, swamp deer, wild boar, and other species that find themselves on the tiger's menu.

Scientists learned relatively early the deceptively simple ingredients of tiger management: Set aside a sufficient area of suitable habitat with enough surface water and stop the poaching of native ungulates, or hoofed mammals, and tigers. Do this and tigers will come roaring back from the brink. They are resilient and wily, but if the species on which they feed are greatly diminished, they're in big trouble.

I tried several approaches to studying tiger prey before settling on what proved to be the most romantic. The most common method is to estimate the density of deer species by systematically clearing the droppings on a randomly located series of study plots and then counting the new droppings that accumulate over a set interval. There is an entire literature devoted to what a friend of mine calls turd biology, or turdology for short. A turdologist in Nepal must be able to distinguish the discrete clusters of small round droppings of hog deer, the more elongate pellets of spotted deer, the wider cylinders of sambar, the even larger offerings of swamp deer, the vitamin-shaped tablets of hares, and the bonbons of wild boar. Then there are the droppings of tiger prey that return to the same sites (called latrines) to defecate: the minute, comma-shaped pellets of barking deer and the Junior Mints left by nilgai antelope, the largest antelope of Asia. Our routine was as follows: First, Gagan and I cleared plots of any droppings we found. Second, we revisited those plots at regular intervals to count and remove the pellet groups left behind by obliging ungulates that had no idea that, with each defecation, they were contributing to our understanding of predator-prey dynamics.

If measuring tiger tracks was astoundingly dull, crawling on hands and knees to pick up turds was a close second. To clear plots more quickly and survey a larger number of sample areas, sometimes Gagan would recruit Tharu friends by suggesting that we were going to pick up gold nuggets off the jungle floor. He was a notorious practical joker. Once, when we had finished clearing a pellet census plot in one of Bardia's largest grasslands, he trained his binoculars to the northeast and proclaimed that the weather was so clear he could see all the way to "Kat-a-man-doo," as the Tharu pronounced the name of the capital. Kathmandu was slightly beyond the range of Gagan's binoculars, about 210 miles to the east, as the crow flies. It didn't stop the curious Tharus from eagerly lining up to take a look, many trying out binoculars for the first time. When they realized Gagan's trickery, they howled with laughter, even though the joke was on them. The Tharus may have lacked sophistication, as evidenced by the names they assigned to modern inventions—an airplane was a *cheel-gari*, or "eagle car," and a helicopter a *put-put-tiya*, the sound it made on the rare occasion that one flew over their village—but I began to think that perhaps it is in just such places, off the flight paths and power grids, that people can better maintain the endearing capacity to laugh at themselves.

The pellet counts yielded useful results on population densities of tiger prey, showing that axis deer were by far the most abundant ungulate, followed by barking deer, wild boar, and nilgai. Hog deer and swamp deer were still rare. But the quality of the data didn't change the tiresome nature of the activity. More appealing were afternoon safaris spent counting tiger prey from the back of a Toyota pickup. From March through May, after fires burn through the grasslands, the Terai jungle resembles the savannas of northern Tanzania. During the hot season, we would drive slowly in the late afternoon to conduct total counts of the herds of deer and boar that come out to graze on the grass shoots or feed on fallen fruits.

Our most remarkable discovery was the rapid response of the deer population to improved conservation measures. The presence of the Nepalese Army, which assumed responsibility for the protection of the reserve in 1976, changed the behavior of both the wildlife and the poachers virtually overnight. When I first arrived in Bardia in 1975, about a year before the army came to stay, I commonly heard gunshots, and the easily spooked wildlife rarely ventured out in the daylight. But immediately after the army began patrolling, the gunshots ceased, and by the next year, the wildlife moved about without fear, even during midday. By the second year of my study, we had trouble counting the vast herds of spotted deer that formed during the late afternoon grazing hours, and I was delighted to rediscover a small herd of swamp deer that had survived and come out of hiding, like refugees from a root cellar after an episode of ethnic cleansing. As the poachers retreated, the nilgai antelope also staged a comeback. While their numbers were definitely increasing, as indicated by the large number of calves accompanying cows, they just seemed much less spooky, and therefore visible. Unlike the recovery of endangered rain forest species or the fragile arctic tundra, for example, conservation in much of South Asia does not require generations of patience; the rapid healing powers of the annual southwest monsoon quickly cover human transgressions.

My period of reconnaissance was over. Six months into my tenure, I had marked out an intensive study area near Thakurdwara where I would concentrate my fieldwork on the deer and the tiger of Bardia. But I wanted to leave room to explore other parts of the reserve whenever I felt youthful wanderlust. And truth be told, I was becoming a bit lonely for some Western company. The least desirable aspect of the Peace Corps in Nepal, and probably elsewhere in Asia, was that it was largely a polyandrous arrangement for male volunteers (*polyandrous* describes the peculiar situation found in shorebirds and Tibetan cultures where several to many males share one female). The ratio of men to women was about fifteen to one, and most women volunteers were restricted to the Kathmandu Valley. For men assigned to remote outposts like Bardia, the odds of gaining an audience with the king were much better than dating a female Peace Corps volunteer (PCV). When male volunteers posted in the hinterlands of the Terai or the Himalayas came to Kathmandu, they trolled the area known as "Freak Street" or the neighborhood of Thamel, hoping to impress barefoot, half-stoned hippie chicks with their silver-tongued Nepali and insider's knowledge of the culture. The more notorious volunteers flew to Thailand on R&R and frequented Pat Pong, Bangkok's district of carnal pleasures. Bardia would never be confused with Florence, Italy, where young men my age could sit and admire the parade of gorgeous art history majors gliding by the Uffizi each afternoon.

So it was with great surprise that in January of 1976, I heard about a young American woman staying at an engineering camp across the river from Chisapani at the base of the gorge. She was visiting a group of engineers undertaking a feasibility study of a dam across the Karnali. I decided to return to Chisapani. I'm not sure what my chances were, a single PCV against a phalanx of hydro engineers, but I was determined to try. Gagan came with me as my Sancho Panza.

After a forced-march pace up to Chisapani, we reached the gorge. A dugout canoe service was the means of transport on all of the big rivers, including the Karnali. In 1975, more Nepalese were probably fluent in English than knew how to swim, yet there they were, sitting cross-legged in the bottom of unstable dugouts, praying that the gods would see them safely to the other side. The current at the gorge was strong and the water quite cold, this being the middle of winter, but we managed to make it across safely. Gagan and I walked up to the engineers' camp, where we met a lovely young woman sitting amid a brotherhood of overprotective hydrologists. By coincidence, she happened to be the younger sister of the Peace Corps doctor, and she was Canadian, not American. As the only two westerners there in our early twenties, we hit it off. However, Gagan and I had needed to give an official excuse to the warden for going on this junket, and so we went scouting for goral, a goatlike antelope that lived up the gorge, and to look for signs of gharial crocodiles. We returned after two hours, and I talked with my new friend until the light started to fade. We agreed to meet up again in Kathmandu (which we did, but she left Nepal soon after).

I walked back to the river crossing elated to have spoken to a Western woman for the first time in months. Unfortunately, time had gotten away from us, and the dugout canoe service had stopped running. One of us would have to swim across to fetch it. Gagan could only dog-paddle—I was still teaching him the crawl and breaststroke. I am no Mark Spitz, but it was my fault that we missed our ferry, so I volunteered. The current was less of a concern to Gagan than the crocodiles. Gharial reach lengths of fifteen feet or more, but they are harmless unless you are a carp or a catfish. The real worry was the more common and aggressive mugger crocodiles that on occasion have pulled small children under in lakes and rivers in India. I had studied enough physiological ecology of reptilians to hypothesize that the water in the Karnali was too cold for muggers to be active at sunset. At least, that's what I kept repeating to myself as I waded into the current and began swimming to the other shore.

Gagan and I kept up with the pellet plots and deer observations but saw no tigers, even though their tracks appeared on all the roads and trails. I decided that we should move farther up the Karnali, out on the floodplain islands in the middle of the vast riverbed, to look for tigers and swamp deer. Bardia is a prime example of one of the few remaining areas in Asia where tigers still occupy vast floodplains or river deltas. An outpost—the Sundarbans—has attracted an international reputation because the tigers that live there have become man-eaters. In that vast honeycomb of mangrove swamps and river delta on the border between Bangladesh and India, tigers routinely swim between islands during high tide in search of food. All too frequently that includes unfortunate villagers. Many theories have been offered to explain this frightening behavior. The simplest explanation is numeric: The relative scarcity of natural prey in mangrove swamps is supplemented by the high density of humans who invade daily to fish, collect honey, and cut wood for charcoal. The Sundarbans may have the highest ratio of human density to native prey density in any area of the tiger's range.

Our chance to explore the upper Karnali came on a float trip in early spring of 1976, organized by Frank Poppleton, a Food and Agriculture Organization (FAO) employee assigned to head an aid project attached to the Department of National Parks and Wildlife. Frank was a graduate of the old school of East African game wardens and a commanding presence: well over six feet tall with a shock of white hair, brilliant blue eyes, khaki shorts, pale green knee socks, and desert boots. Unfortunately for him and other white colonials residing in East Africa, their days were numbered with the coming of *uhuru* (African liberation). So their last refuge became the FAO and assignments to wildlife programs in the developing countries of Asia.

One early morning, Krishna Man (the park warden), Poppleton, Gagan, another game scout, and I set off from Chisapani in a Zodiac raft. Floating the Karnali River from below the gorge at Chisapani back to a landing near the park headquarters affords a survey of lovely islands covered entirely by rosewood trees, acacia, or a mixture of the two. These legumes are the first tree species to colonize the floodplain because they fix nitrogen with their roots—taking it from the air and enriching the soil for those plants that come after—and are able to grow with their roots partly submerged in water during the monsoon period. They also provide prime habitat for deer, thereby attracting tigers.

One of the goals of our river expedition was to locate gharial. Gharial help crocodilians lay claim to being the ugliest reptiles, and perhaps the most ancient. Their long, narrow snouts filled with about fifty pairs of sharp teeth, their beady eyes, and the giant knobs at the end of the noses of adult males are unlikely to inspire plush-toy designers. However, if you are lucky enough to see one raise its prehistoric snout out of the deep brown murk of a monsoon river, you are the rare naturalist who has experienced a firsthand glimpse into the Jurassic period, 200 million years ago.

At the time of our float trip, there were probably no more than two hundred gharial left in the wild, and Chitwan and Bardia were two of the last places they could be found. Unlike the more terrestrially adept Nile crocodiles or American alligators, gharial are hopeless on land. Their weak forelegs make it hard for them to climb more than a few feet up the riverbanks to deposit their eggs, so they bury them close to the water's edge. In protein-starved South Asia, gharial eggs were not only easy to collect but also a sought-after item by poor villagers, to eat themselves or to sell to brokers. And if the villagers didn't rob the exposed nests, an unexpected premonsoon flood could wash away the eggs and that year's reproductive effort. For the past fifteen years, scientists had been collecting gharial eggs, hatching them in a captive breeding facility inside Royal Chitwan National Park, and releasing the juveniles into the rivers when they had grown large enough to fend off adjutant storks and other predators. Even so, their future was far from secure. They had to locate a river stretch with enough fish to survive and breed, and that was becoming increasingly difficult in Nepal and India, given the pressure local fishermen exerted on all the major rivers. Places like Bardia, strictly protected from fishing and croc poachers, were the last hope for avoiding the total extinction in the wild of this ancient reptile.

On a sandbar in the middle of the river, Gagan's sharp eyes located a gharial. And then another. It was too early in the year to observe nesting behavior, but their presence so near Chisapani gave us hope. Today, gharial have made an encouraging comeback and have been reintroduced in other rivers within their former range, thanks largely to the dedicated efforts of long-time gharial researchers Tirtha Man Maskey, now director-general of Nepal's national parks, and Ram Pritt Yadav, the senior warden of Chitwan for most of the past two decades. Their efforts to build a holding facility, collect and incubate the eggs, and rear young gharial until they can be released illustrate what a few dedicated individuals can do to save a species from extinction.

After another short stretch on the river, the vast floodplain of the Karnali opened before us, and something briefly surfaced ahead of the boat that would never appear on a wild African river. It then reappeared fifty feet away. We soon spotted another creature not far from the first. I only glimpsed a long snout attached to a gray lump, but the sound it made required no further confirmation. We had come upon a pair of Gangetic dolphins. There are only six species of freshwater dolphins in the world; the Amazon and the Orinoco are home to two species, one as pink as a flamingo. But freshwater dolphins reach their maximum diversity in Asia, where the Indus, the Ganges, the Irawaddy, and the Yangtze Rivers each has its own distinct species.

We tried to paddle closer to the dolphins, but they kept their distance. Unlike that of the gharial, the number of Gangetic dolphins has continued to plummet over the last two decades, after the Indian government built dams restricting their movements. It's a tragedy that, in 2005, the population has dwindled to a few stalwart dolphins occupying only the Karnali in the west and the Kosi in the eastern part of Nepal.

Gangetic dolphins and other freshwater dolphin species lack the charismatic personalities and legions of western admirers rushing to defend their cause. Physically, the Gangetic dolphin bears only the slightest resemblance to a spinner or bottlenose. Asian freshwater dolphins are practically blind, relying on echolocation to find their way and to catch fish in the muddy rivers of the monsoon. I used to walk the two miles from Thakurdwara to the Karnali during the warmest days of May to cool off in the water and to try to approach the small population of dolphins that swam nearby. I never succeeded in doing so, but the sight of them rolling through the current is etched in my mind, particularly because Gangetic dolphins are the first species I encountered in the wild that will probably go extinct in my lifetime.

About an hour later, I noticed that Gagan had a strange expression on his face. Something was not right with him. Normally the toughest of junglewallahs, he seemed to grow more uncomfortable by the minute, but, being of such low caste, he was too embarrassed to ask to go ashore for a break. Finally, his good sense and physical discomfort overcame his social inhibition. When we reached the first of a score of floodplain islands with a dense tree cover of rosewood and acacia, Gagan leapt out of the boat and headed for the nearest thicket, the rest of us following suit. Three minutes later, he came charging back, pulling up his shorts as he ran toward us. He had practically trod on a sleeping tiger.

We followed Gagan single file to the site of his encounter and quickly climbed some rosewood trees for a better view. I looked to see that everyone was at least fifteen feet above the ground, the memory of Kirti Tamang's near fatal mishap fresh in my mind. After a few minutes, we grew bored watching the large male stretched motionless in the grass below us. It seemed too risky to chance the tiger waking up while we descended from the branches, so we decided that the safest course was to rouse it. We shouted, "Get up, king of the jungle!" and clapped our hands loudly. The tiger must have been awake through the whole episode and just biding its time to make a run for it. With a great roar, it exploded from a prone position and leaped what seemed like fifteen feet in one bound, fortunately in the opposite direction of where we perched. We scampered back to the raft and the safety of the river. After nearly eight months in Bardia, I had seen my first tiger.

I was to see other tigers without initiation by Gagan's indigestion. One of the techniques Schaller used was to observe the behavior of ungulates and their predators from tree platforms, known in Nepali as *machans*. Gagan loved to construct things, and when I told him of my plan to erect a series of machans, in each of the habitats in my study area, he willingly agreed to design and build them. He recruited two Tharu friends for the task, as well as my new cook, Kanchha. Within a short time, we had erected thirteen machans scattered within four miles of my house. They were simple structures: The floor was fashioned from a few wood planks lashed to tree branches by vines and rope; the roof was the starlit night sky. I was to become perhaps the Peace Corps' first semiarboreal volunteer.

My life quickly settled into a new routine: a quick dinner at 3:30 p.m. in order to be out walking and reach a tree platform within the hour. On the way to my favorite machan, I would pass the prized perch of a jungle owlet in a grove of acacia. I sometimes nodded to this bold little fellow, a night watchman of Bardia, as I headed out to assume the late shift. In the spring, I would occasionally stop to witness the wild mating dance of the peacocks. One of the most wary of local residents, peacocks roost at night on the outermost branches of the kapok trees, where even the agile leopards can't stalk them. But when a male peafowl performs his spring étude in a jungle clearing, he lapses into a choreographed frenzy of vibrating feathers, an easy target for a hungry predator. I have picked up the discarded costume of tail feathers often enough in the spring to know the mortal risks of wild courtship dancing.

When I reached my machan, I would take off my backpack and remove a length of rope, tying one end to a belt loop in my shorts and the other to the pack frame. After climbing up to the platform, I hauled the backpack up after me. Then I would arrange my foam pad and sleeping bag, drink some water, and wait until the sun started to sink and the deer and boar emerged from the shadows. Around 5:00 p.m., the first herds of spotted deer would begin filtering into the grasslands from the forest edge. Spotted deer, also known as axis deer or chital, are the most abundant deer in the subcontinent and certainly rank among the most beautiful of all cervids. The fawns of most deer species are spotted at birth, but this species and fallow deer are the only two that keep their spots into adulthood. Spotted deer males have enormous antlers, reportedly the largest in relation to their body size among deer. They are also the favorite prey of Bardia's tigers.

During more than one hundred overnights in machans, I took detailed observations of spotted deer, watching their breeding behavior and noting what they ate as they grazed and plucked leaves below me at dawn and before dusk. Prior to my study, the only cases of a biologist spending so much time studying Asian ungulates in this manner over such a long duration had been Schaller's work in Kanha and the work of John Eisenberg and his colleagues in Sri Lanka. Of course, there are no tigers in Sri Lanka, but leopards gladly took over the role as top carnivore in that system. To help me interpret what I saw, I overcame my initial shyness and struck up a correspondence with John Eisenberg, an encyclopedia of mammalogy, and Richard Taber, one of the world's leading deer biologists, who became my graduate adviser at the University of Washington. But I was still too intimidated to write to Schaller.

Based on my observations and data from the exhausting pellet count studies, the tree platform observations, and drive counts through the open savannas, I published a series of papers on the ecology of tiger prey and their habitats in Bardia when I returned to graduate school. The first paper focused on the habitat types that provided a home for tiger prey, and what factors influenced the gradual progression of vegetation changes, called plant succession. The second paper looked at the demography and reproductive biology of the prey populations and how the prey base for tigers might increase. The final paper charted the relationship between the different habitat types, the food they produced for tiger prey, and the numbers and biomass of the prey, *biomass* being a term used to describe the amount of prey, measured in pounds or kilograms, in a given area. But the scientific language of the papers failed to capture a powerful observation that grew stronger with each passing day: I was witnessing the recovery of a national park. The deer had increased in large numbers, and the tigers prowled without fear of humans. Their behavior had changed from the time of the beginning of my study to this point close to the end of my two years in Bardia. The prey species of tigers seemed to be more diurnal than in the early days, especially the spotted deer. Tigers began moving more out in the open. Gagan and I were the only ones wandering the park now, except for a few guard patrols. On a return trip to Bardia in 1986, I observed that tigers were more visible there than in any other part of Nepal, and I would like to think that the protection we afforded them in the mid-1970s helped contribute to their total loss of shyness a decade and more later.

I have many vivid memories of my nights in the tree platforms. Once, a giant flying squirrel landed on the trunk of the tree just above my head. We surprised each other, but it quickly glided to an unoccupied tree nearby. On many occasions, I heard alarm barks of spotted deer as tigers and leopards patrolled the roads bisecting the grasslands. One evening, a herd of deer began barking about a half mile away. I couldn't see anything, and the light was fading rapidly. More spotted deer sounded their warning as the intruder continued its journey along the road that passed right under my tree platform. The tiger was headed my way. I could feel it. The alarm calls were emanating only a short distance from my tree, and I strained to see the shape of a large felid, but it was too dark by that time to see anything. The alarm calls ceased; one minute went by and then another. Then the deer began barking again, this time several hundred feet on the other side of my tree, before they went back to grazing. The next morning I climbed down to see the tiger footprints in the road just below me. The spotted deer had heralded its arrival, but without a night vision scope, all I could do was triangulate the tiger's movements by the proximity of the alarm calls.

Not all of my fieldwork was confined to the reserve. There were unconfirmed reports of a surviving population of blackbuck antelope in the Bardia area. In the Hindu mythology, blackbuck pulled Krishna's chariot across the sky. The spiraled horns, vivid black foreheads, shoulders, and backs, and white underbelly give the males a striking appearance. At one point, blackbuck were the most abundant ungulate in India. A resident ornithologist in Nepal described a train trip he took in the 1950s across the northern plains of India, where he saw herds of blackbuck as one might have seen groups of pronghorn antelope on the northern Great Plains of the United States during the 1800s. The comparison offers other parallels: Both blackbuck and pronghorn were chased by cheetahs, the pronghorn by the now extinct North American species, and the blackbuck by the extirpated Asiatic cheetah, which supposedly still lingers in Iran. The black and white markings, so appreciated by nature lovers, became a popular target for army soldiers and private citizens. In India, land clearing added to the decimation of blackbuck populations. By the time I arrived in Nepal, there were more blackbuck on game ranches in Texas than in all of India and Nepal combined.

Gagan and I walked to the area where blackbuck had been seen. We found seven individuals living in a cultivated area, taking shelter during the day in a vast patch of marijuana. If you turn over soil in the western Terai to plant a garden, the dominant weed that spreads across the clods of earth is *ganja*. Fields allowed to go fallow become thickets of marijuana. The villagers living near the blackbuck herd were poor farmers from India who, as devout Hindus, wished no harm to the *krishnasagar*, as blackbuck are known in Hindi and Nepali. They only wanted them to stay out of their croplands.

Gagan organized the farmers to flush the blackbuck from the marijuana jungle so that I could photograph them. Proof of the small herd, I thought, might help attract the funding to set up a small reserve or even to pay for a translocation to Bardia once the population expanded. I began to plan a quick publication in a scientific journal, but how would I describe the blackbuck's habitat? As a 7-foot-high overstory of *Cannabis sativus*, or for what it really was, a field of Nepalese reefer? I could see the headlines now: "Young American biologist finds endangered Nepalese antelope living in field of pot!" I did eventually publish a short article in an obscure local journal, and in Nepal we managed to have the plot formally protected and the farmers compensated for income lost from the fields.

Peace Corps volunteers at the end of their service ask themselves the perennial question: What difference did I make? Most volunteers in Nepal can point to something tangible they accomplished: a suspension bridge they constructed, a water supply system installed, groves of fruit trees planted. I like to think that I helped put Bardia on the map biologically, that my surveys helped lead to reserve extensions (Bardia is now three times the size it was in 1975, when I first arrived), and that I contributed in some small way to preserving one of the great nature reserves of Asia and the world.

Like most volunteers who are honest about their experience, however, I realize that I probably took away more than I ever gave over those two years. I had my first taste as a survey biologist. Professionally, the experience cemented my desire to go on to graduate school to become a wildlife biologist and eventually to return to Nepal. When I crossed the Babai for the last time as a Peace Corps volunteer, heading back to Kathmandu and America, I knew in my heart that my departure was only temporary. A former volunteer had warned me that I might go back to the United States, but I would never leave Nepal. Twenty-six years and countless visits later have proven him a sage. But it was this destination, Bardia, that gave me a new dimension on international wildlife conservation, not from flipping through a *National Geographic* in a dentist's office, but living it, and figuring out firsthand what it takes to save something as grand as a tiger.

After one of my last nights in a Bardia treehouse, I looked down in the morning to see large herds of spotted deer grazing below me. A tiger came walking by and spooked them, sending up a chorus of alarm barks. I was delighted to be in a balcony seat, watching this drama play out below as it had a million times before: the stalking tiger, the alert deer, the race for cover. For the first time in my life, I felt like a jungle guardian. Even though this wasn't my country or my personal reserve, I had spent more time out with these wild animals than any westerner before me. And for the first time, I considered how jungle guardians, here, in the Amazon, or in the heart of the Congo Basin could help protect these magnificent places, even if all alone, if only they possessed dedication and strength of will. My connection with nature felt so strong at that moment that if I were to have died the next day, at the ripe age of twenty-four, I would not have felt cheated of a meaningful life. And if that were my fate, I hoped my ashes could be scattered here, so that something from my body—a calcium fragment, a bit of nitrogen—would find its way into a fig tree, a langur monkey, or perhaps even a tiger.

The most powerful lesson, though, and one that has buoyed me in later years, was the result of my very first experience in Bardia. Or rather, the one on its eastern boundary when my elephant, her two drivers, and I were swept away trying to cross the Babai River. Somehow we got back ashore and later crossed that river, and I lasted the two years and did what I could to contribute something meaningful to conservation, even if I never actually followed Dr. Mishra's instruction to census the tiger population. Many times since, I have remembered that promise to myself, that if I managed to get across the Babai on that elephant, I could handle any challenge that life had in store for me. I had learned a priceless lesson that all of us must discover in our own way: When life knocks you off your horse, or your elephant, get back on and cross the river.

chapter two

AN INORDINATE
FONDNESS FOR BATS

FROM THEIR SINGING PERCHES NEARLY HALF A MILE AWAY, THE penetrating calls of the three-wattled bellbirds cascaded down the mountainside. *BONK! BONK! BONK! BONK!* The exuberant males lifted their white heads and filled the azure sky with sound, their black facial wattles wagging with each outburst. This early June morning was perfect, so calm—a stark contrast to the relentlessly billowing mist that drapes the landscape from December to May, when the moisture-laden Atlantic trade winds spill over the continental divide and descend into the cloud forest, beading every leaf, frond, and feather. *BONK!* While the trade winds blow, the bellbirds spend a silent exile in the lowlands of Costa Rica and Nicaragua. Now they have returned with great fanfare to breed on the outskirts of the Monteverde Cloud Forest Reserve, Central America's most famous protected area.

Afternoons here at this time of year are often punctuated by the sound of thunderheads pressing up from the Pacific lowlands. Sometimes these cloudbursts pounded across my tin roof at dusk, scuttling another night of my fieldwork. Other days, the rains passed through Monteverde in the early afternoon, leaving the night sky dense with stars and the bustling traffic of tropical fruit bats. With these variations from day to day, part of my job as bat catcher on this cloud-wrapped mountain depended on mastering the Zen of weather forecasting. Six months into my field study, and I was still a novice. I walked outside and listened, trying to decipher the codes of the more experienced local forecasters. Aside from the bellbirds, the calls of emerald toucanets—dazzling miniature toucans—seemed to grow more agitated with the rising humidity. Bright yellow frogs churning about in nearby breeding ponds picked up their late afternoon chant. Did the intensity of their calls signal an imminent deluge? It was now almost 5 p.m., and I had to make a decision. I could sit under my dry porch and watch another breathtaking sunset over the Gulf of Nicoya, or I could gather my equipment and walk into the advancing gloom with a good chance of catching nothing but rain.

"Let's go!" urged the fidgeting graduate student over my right shoulder. "Stay home and sip Cointreau," advised young Baudelaire reclining to the left. The high stakes of my Ph.D. project motivated me to grab my headlamp. I needed to risk periodic downpours to gather enough data to contribute something new to the biology of tropical bats. Besides, even if I captured only one individual tonight, it might be a new bat species for Costa Rica or even Central America and worthy of a note in a scientific journal. Such was the draw of working as a biologist in a poorly studied tropical cloud forest in the summer of 1981: A walk in the woods or, in my case, stringing up a mist net could provide a eureka moment in natural history.

For tropical fruit-eating bats, dusk marks the beginning of rush hour. Peak feeding lasts about two hours, during which the bats flit about the forest, loading their tiny stomachs with the juices and soft flesh of ripe figs, pungent black pepper fruits, miniature wild toma-toes, and other aromatic delicacies. The nets biologists use to catch bats are called mist nets because they are constructed of thin nylon monofilament, a kind of synthetic gossamer. They are virtually invisi-ble to birds, and the mesh spacing is wide enough to fool the sonar of commuting fruit bats. Most bat species navigate by echolocation; they emit a type of high-frequency sonar that bounces off objects in front of them and on its return is processed by their brains. Bats can in-stantly convert that information into a visual navigation map of the night world. In flight, bats actually detect the "holes" formed by the mesh of the nets but naively assume that they can slip through them, only to tumble into a gentle flap of nylon. My relationship with the bats was strictly scientific and noninvasive: trap, disentangle, measure, collect fecal samples, and bid au revoir to each individual captured. But if the thin nylon strands became soaked with rain, even inexperi-enced juvenile bats avoided the nets entirely, rolling over or under them like veteran stunt pilots.

Tonight I must have been too early to begin netting for bats be-cause a blue-crowned motmot, one of the last of the diurnal birds to retire, plopped into the net. We regarded each other with mutual sur-prise before I freed it and proceeded to check the trapline. A pau-raque, a nighthawk of the tropics, lay tangled in the second net. Birds two, bats zero. The pauraque flashed its wide-mouth threat display as I released it. This defensive act seemed rather tame compared with the unsettling leer of and eerie, high-pitched screams emitted by cap-tured vampire bats—an experience that still unnerved me, despite having handled many in the tropical dry forest below Monteverde.

I was removing a black scarab beetle that had become entangled when I noticed another object glowing in the light of my headlamp. Flailing helplessly in the net was an inch-long solid gold scarab beetle. I dropped my field gear and set to freeing it, working each strand of nylon off leg, antennae, and wing with the care of a neurosurgeon. When I had removed the beetle, I held it to the light of my headlamp.

It was as if the House of Bulgari had been commissioned to create a limited edition of the perfect insect. Every part of the scarab was bedecked in gold, from the end of its clubbed antennae to the tip of the abdomen, an exquisite brooch come to life and now walking freely in the cup of my hand.

It turned out to be a rather dull night for bats. But the encounter with the rare golden scarab (*Plusiotis resplendens*) had reminded me of an oft-repeated anecdote in the history of biology. Asked by theologians what could be inferred about the mind of the Creator from a study of his works, the British scientist J. B. S. Haldane dryly replied, "an inordinate fondness for beetles." Entomologists estimate that about 330,000 species of beetles amble, burrow, chew, oviposit, and roll dung balls, making beetles the most species-rich of all animal orders, higher than flies, wasps, and grasshoppers, and more yet to be discovered. Had Haldane known much of bats, he might have mentioned that the Creator also seemed enamored of *them*; they are second only to rodents as the most abundant group of mammals on the planet.

My own fondness for bats was totally unexpected. Like every child, I had drawn bats on Halloween. But Bela Lugosi's ghoulish countenance and nocturnal undertakings made me want to sleep with a crucifix under the pillow, even though I was born into the Jewish faith. Despite my early fear, I never even saw a live bat until I joined the Peace Corps in Nepal, where in short order I became a bat killer. I routinely smashed or harassed Indian pipistrelles, petite bats that frightened and annoyed me when they nested in the rafters of my thatch-roofed hut. One day, I went into the jungle with a colleague to set up a mist net for catching birds. In broad daylight, a short-nosed fruit bat had the misfortune of getting tangled in our net. My friend shared my batphobia. So I bludgeoned the harmless fruit bat with my walking staff. We tossed the limp body into the bushes, hoping that an alert jackal would consume the evidence of our crime against nature.

I still feel great remorse at that incident. But my aversion to bats persisted for another four years. Of course, my distaste for bats hardly made me unique. Despite the economic and ecological importance of bats, a fondness for them is rare. They are feared and persecuted virtually everywhere. To a large extent, the bat's unpopularity is based on falsehoods: Bats get tangled in your hair (false), they all carry rabies (almost always false; better to steer clear of common carriers such as raccoons, foxes, and skunks), and they live on blood (usually false, only three out of twelve hundred species do so). Rather than more study to reveal their fascinating adaptations to life, bats are in dire need of a public relations campaign. Even news of a now abandoned hypothesis that Old World fruit bats are closely related to primates—and by extension, *Homo sapiens*—did little to rehabilitate their bad reputation. There are a few societies, such as the Tibetans, that value bats as good luck symbols, and the Batman films have helped on the popular culture front. But in Western culture, nothing will ever undo the damage done by Count Dracula, or the enigmatic rocker Ozzy Osbourne, who in his demonic period reputedly bit off the heads of live bats during concert performances. No matter how many people have recently come to appreciate them, thanks largely to the efforts of groups like Bat Conservation International, bats clearly have a way to go before rivaling giant pandas as the most lovable mammals on the planet.

I shared many of these prejudices and fears. To even think that I would someday become a bat biologist would have sent a shudder down my spine. Perhaps stories like mine, of outright aversion and fear, later evolving into fascination and even inordinate fondness, hold lessons for phobics. For all those who panic at the sight of snakes, spiders, lizards, sharks, dogs, or bats, read on—there is hope.

The quickest way to appreciate bats, at least intellectually, is to look at the superlatives. Of the 5,000 mammal species known to science, almost 1,200 are bats. By comparison, there are only 39 species of cats and 80 kinds of whales and dolphins. Despite the dramatic attempts at hang gliding by flying squirrels, galagos, and the so-called flying lemurs, bats are the only mammals that truly fly. In the tropics, bats fill the night sky and are invariably the most diverse group of mammals found at any site. Most intact rain forests along the equator harbor upward of 40 species; a site in Paracou, French Guiana, tops the charts with 78 species. Such high totals are hardly surprising. One of the well-documented patterns of biogeography, the science of the distribution of plants and animals, is that species diversity increases toward the equator. This pattern is as true for beetles as it is for mammals. In the 1970s, however, the noted tropical bat biologist Theodore Fleming made a remarkable discovery. He observed that if bats are excluded from consideration, a list of mammals from a tropical site in Costa Rica or Panama is no different in species richness from a site in Northern California or most locations far from the equator. Some mammal groups—voles, burrowing mammals such as pocket gophers, and some hoofed mammals such as wild goats and sheep—are actually less diverse in the tropics than at higher latitudes. Thus, "Why are there so many species of mammals in the tropics?" is not the right question. Instead, we should be asking, as Fleming did, "Why are so many species of bats found there?"

One explanation for Fleming's insight is that there are many more ways to make a living as a bat based near the equator than in Buffalo, New York. In the New World tropics, bats eat all sorts of food items: fish, frogs, birds, mammals, lizards, scorpions, flying insects, fruit, pollen, nectar, and, in the case of the three species of vampire bats, blood. In all of the United States and Canada, except an area near the Mexican border, bats feed almost exclusively on flying insects.

Here on the slopes of Monteverde, upwards of thirteen species of fruit-eating bats coexist along the mountainside. I reckoned that such incredible diversity of species must be tied to what they were eating and where, and my research project was designed to unravel the mystery of how this rich animal community fit together. The afternoon after my golden scarab encounter, I gathered my field gear and walked up the mountain for another night of netting at the edge of the reserve. I dropped my bags and set to work stringing up mist nets along a trail. My goal was to capture at least twenty individuals per night, three hundred bats per month. At the end of a year and a half, I would surpass three thousand captures, a target that should provide enough data to determine the structure of bat communities with some certainty.

I wish I could say this approach was completely original. In the sciences, every era has its sexy new idea. When I first became interested in bats in 1980, the theory of "resource partitioning" was all the rage. Tropical species live in a diverse but hostile world. Hummingbirds, fruit bats, anole lizards, any large group of closely related species that lived in proximity were thought to become increasingly specialized in the resources they drew on. The theory suggested that the increased specialization would lessen competition among similar species. It's not that they were being ecologically courteous; it was a way to survive and leave more offspring in a dog-eat-dog rain forest. For fruit bats, the mechanism for separation could be eating different species or sizes of fruit, feeding in different habitats, or even perhaps feeding in the same habitat but at different heights in the forest canopy. The more species that had similar habits, the more finely they must divide the resources, at least according to the theory. One aspect that intrigued me was whether the size of fruits eaten corresponded with the bat's size. Another was to determine whether closely related species lived at different elevations along the mountainside. If I could detect such patterns, I could shed light on Fleming's tantalizing question.

In retrospect, it amazes me how rapidly my transformation to bat lover occurred, once I was properly introduced. The relationship was less than a year old when I started making these solo forays into the night to commune with bats. A turning point in my career as a biologist, and the one that forever rid me of my prejudicial stance on bats, was my acceptance a year earlier into the Organization for Tropical Studies (OTS) course in Costa Rica, an eight-week total immersion in tropical biology for U.S.-based graduate students. From sunrise to past midnight, seven days a week, it was one intellectual stimulant after another, fueled by rice, beans, coffee, and rum. Luckily for me, among the many charismatic lecturers in the course was Frank Bonaccorso.

With his black curly hair, Fu Manchu mustache, and irreverent spirit, Frank was full-time bat biologist, part-time standup comedian. Currently the chief curator of mammals at the Museum of Natural History in New Guinea, he has championed the study of mammals in a country noted for its tree kangaroos, spiny anteaters, and, of course, extraordinary fruit bats. His unique approach of mixing *Saturday Night Live*–style humor with field research made him the perfect guest instructor, and his love of bats was contagious. In three nights out with Frank at the La Selva field station in the Atlantic coastal lowlands, he transformed my rather ordinary fear of bats into a growing admiration for them and stimulated the mammal trapper in me with his strategic stringing of mist nets and the macho thrill of learning to remove the bats without being nipped (we let Frank handle the vampires).

My real change of heart must be attributed to the sheer delight of coming face to face with a cast of unforgettable creatures. We captured charming Honduran white bats with clown-like yellow ears and leaf noses that, within minutes, lay tamed in our hands, chewing contentedly on pieces of banana. I fed sugar water from an eyedropper to docile, long-tongued, nectar-feeding bats, the hummingbirds of the night. And then there were close encounters with the carnivores, such as the crafty fringe-lipped bats that tuned into the calls of amorous male frogs and snatched them midperformance. But to me the most elegant were the variety of fruit-eating bats, many with bold white stripes down their backs and on their faces.

Frank's discourses on the ecology of bats were delivered through formal lectures often spiced with humorous natural history anecdotes. He regaled us with descriptions of the marvelous New World bats we would meet if we followed in his footsteps, such as the industrious tent-making bats. The I. M. Peis of the bat world, these bats create their own shelters under a *Heliconia* leaf or banana frond by cutting the mid-rib veins and allowing the halves to collapse into a bivouac within which a family could roost safely out of sight. We might also befriend the bulldog bats that scoop fish out of the water like an eagle; the carnivorous false-vampire, the largest New World bat, which snatches birds and small mammals while they sleep on tree limbs; the delicate sac-winged bats, among the smallest species, weighing less than a nickel but with a social system identical to that of African lions—the dominant male closely guarding his harem of breeding females from jealous competitors.

Now totally smitten by these nocturnal winged mammals, I decided early on to focus on the fruit-eaters, just as Frank had. I had already been a closet botanist and suffer the weird affliction of needing to know the Latin names of the plants around me wherever I travel. If I elected to study bats that drank nectar from night-blooming flowers or plucked ripe fruits from the rain forest, I would be able to develop my credentials as a mammalogist but still have an excuse to learn as much as I wanted about tropical botany. I had found the perfect marriage of natural history in what biologists call plant-animal interactions.

After the first ten days at La Selva, our group headed off to the tropical dry forests along Costa Rica's Pacific coast. Frank had to leave, but before he departed, I was able to discuss my rapidly growing interest in fruit-eating bats and explore some ideas for a thesis topic. He generously left me all of his mist nets, his hand-sewn bat bags for briefly holding captured bats until release, his Pesola scales for weighing bats, and other paraphernalia of bat catching. He also imparted a final bit of clarification of my neophyte status. Mimicking the voice of the martial arts master from the television show *Kung Fu*, Frank addressed me thus: "Grasshoppa', when you catch wrinkle-faced bat, only then can you call yourself Bat Man." The wrinkle-faced bat, the most bizarre looking of all species of the order Chiroptera, is rarely encountered, despite its wide range, from southern Mexico to Venezuela. Its face has been described as the most grotesque visage in nature, an unflattering series of fissures and creases in a head too large for its small body. I couldn't wait to become one of the lucky few scientists in the world who had captured the Quasimodo of fruit bats.

Wrinkle-faced bats might be impossibly rare, but other types of fruit bats flew into our mist nets with such regularity that I soon realized I could carry out an ecological field study on them in a reasonable amount of time. The sheer abundance of bats in tropical forests was something I was about to learn the hard way. Our next stop in the course, the Palo Verde Field Station, cemented my desire to study bats, but not without some late-night drama. The daily routine at Palo Verde was the same as at La Selva. First, out all day learning the names of the local plants and animals and the ecology of the site, then a quick dinner followed by one or two lectures delivered by a changing roster of distinguished researchers in tropical biology. I usually skipped the lectures to pursue my new evening passion of mist-netting bats, but when I learned that Daniel Janzen, a demigod of tropical biology, was speaking, I formulated a plan. I would slip out a few minutes before he started his talk and unfurl the three mist nets I had set up across a shallow stream near the field station. I would hurry back to catch the lecture, and afterwards sprint into the forest to check the nets.

After setting the nets, I snuck into the lecture hall just as Dan Janzen took the stage—bearded, dressed in field khakis, supremely confident. He began his lecture while chewing on a chicken leg he had grabbed a moment earlier as part dinner, part prop. He started by framing the evolutionary backdrop to his new theory. Since their first appearance back in the middle of the Cretaceous period about 100 million years ago, flowering plants have evolved the structures called fruits, designed to attract fruit-eating animals, in order to disseminate their seeds. This relationship has become so prevalent among tropical flowering plants that over 90 percent of them encase their seeds in fleshy fruits. In biologists' parlance, plants evolved such reproductive strategies to enhance their fitness. Nothing revolutionary here, I thought. Where was the bomb thrower I had heard so much about?

Then Janzen posed an intriguing evolutionary puzzle. He listed a number of tropical trees and shrubs that produce very large, hard, indehiscent (not opening when ripe) fruits, whose entire fruit crop, at least these days, goes uneaten. Instead, the fruits drop to the ground under the parent tree where they rot or are attacked by insects and pathogens. Isn't it odd, he asked, and a poor evolutionary strategy for a plant like the calabash tree, for example, to put so much energy into producing such tough, massive gourds that are ignored by the region's birds and mammals? Janzen's answer to this riddle was simple and brilliant. Nature was not inefficient in design; rather, he insisted, the fruits of some plants had evolved to be eaten and dispersed by now extinct prehistoric mammals such as giant ground sloths and gomphotheres that once flourished in Latin America. Plant traits such as the production of large hard fruits that we see today, in other words, are relicts from an earlier era when mammoths and their kind roamed about and smashed fruits between their giant molars. And then the Janzenian finale. He announced that ecological studies of plant-animal interactions without consideration of history, and in this case, the extinct megafauna of the American tropics, were misleading at best; the reproductive strategies of at least some of the plants in the forest today were shaped by species that are no longer here. And if we didn't explain what he dubbed these neotropical anachronisms, we would never understand how tropical forests actually evolved and functioned.

I sensed the buzz in the room. Some biologists loved to swat at Janzen's ideas and try to prove him wrong. As for me, I had never been so enthralled by an academic lecture—pre-PowerPoint, no overhead transparencies—just a stream-of-consciousness discourse, punctuated by occasional bites into a chicken leg, that turned my understanding of plant-animal interactions upside down. Despite my intellectual engagement, my internal alarm began to sound. I had left the nets untended for far too long—they would be filling up with bats. Yet I couldn't break away; I had to hear what the smartest people in my course thought of this novel hypothesis.

The right hand of a precocious graduate student from the University of Georgia shot up. "Your theory of megafaunal dispersal doesn't make sense, and besides, it's untestable." I was shocked by her temerity and her bravura. What she was doing, besides confronting Janzen, was offering a popular view at the time, that evolutionary hypotheses could not be proved or disproved and therefore amounted to speculation. Janzen proposed a novel way to investigate the problem, by making use of domestic horses and tapirs, the only large mammals left today in Costa Rica. His idea was to see if those big herbivores could ingest fruits and pass the seeds no smaller contemporary fruit-eater could handle. If they could, his observations would at least be consistent with the idea that large mammals played a role in shaping fruit traits.

After a few more questions, Janzen started to end the Q&A session, but the Georgia Bulldog wouldn't let go of his cuff. I stopped to listen at the screen door. For a moment, I thought the chicken leg might go flying across the room. Instead, Janzen merely turned icy. I, however, was greatly inspired by his megafaunal seed dispersal hypothesis, which he had developed in collaboration with paleoecologist Paul Martin. In fact, their work, which came to be more widely accepted, would greatly influence my own study of rhinos as megafaunal seed spreaders in Nepal some years later.

In the warm fragrant night, I raced back to the stream with Jim Cohen, a fellow OTS student from the University of Florida. Jim shone his headlamp beam over the nets and uttered a barely audible, "Holy shit." Tangled in the nylon was what seemed like an entire colony of vampires and Jamaican fruit bats. Our three nets must have been set across a major flyway or near a roost, resulting in massive gridlock. In the upper shelf of the nets, bats hung upside down (or right side up from their perspective), patiently waiting to be released. But the bats in the bottom shelf of the net were struggling to stay above water. The sheer weight of the bats in the lower tier had caused it to sag into the river. We rushed to their rescue, releasing the lightly tangled individuals first and ripping the strands of nylon off the Jamaican fruit bats that had managed to wrap themselves like mummies. We left the vampires for last.

Jamaican fruit bats are perhaps the most common of all neotropical fruit bats. Brawny and a bit pugnacious, they have an intense personality. They appear well adapted to a fig diet, with a body plan of what seems like 50 percent wings, 30 percent flight muscles, and 20 percent jaws for ripping open figs or carrying them off whole. We had gloves along to protect us from their jaws, but the gloves were cumbersome; it was easier to free the bats with bare hands. Once the bats grabbed on to you, they didn't want to let go, but Frank had taught us to blow gently in their faces to make them release their grip. While we were untangling the bats, biting insects swarmed to the lights of our headlamps and attacked our faces. I imagined that Frank had somehow engineered this indoctrination to test the depth of our desire to become bat men.

Once we had emptied the first fifty-foot-long net, we turned to the smaller nets, which were also heavily studded with bats. In the middle of the last one, we could hear the alarm calls of the Jamaican fruit bats. Something enormous had just landed and seemed to be attacking a helpless individual. We rushed over to see what it was. There, struggling to free itself from the nylon while simultaneously grabbing its dinner, was a false-vampire bat. Its wingspan reached three feet, about the size of a northern goshawk, but ecologically, it's the harpy eagle of tropical bats, the largest aerial carnivore of its kind. I marveled at its giant ears and its huge carnivorous jaws and teeth; it reminded me more of a griffon or a small dragon than a bat. I put my gloves back on and grabbed the animal just as he grabbed me. Thankfully, the huge bat was barely tangled, and I had him out in seconds, stopping to stare deep into his eyes while he scolded me for interrupting his dinner.

There were probably no more than sixty bats in the nets, but it seemed more like six hundred in the two hours it took us to free them. Jim and I returned to the research station and collapsed on two picnic tables outside the cinder-block building. In our panic to free the bats flopping in the lower rung of the net, we had abandoned the protocol Frank had taught us at La Selva: Remove each bat, put it in its own cloth bat bag and tie the loose end, weigh the bat, measure its forearm with a dial calipers, and check for fecal samples in the bag after you release it. If it was an adult female, we were instructed to see if she was pregnant, by gently palpating her abdomen, or lactating, by gently pinching her teats (in bats conveniently located in the armpits). Still, we had survived my worst fear—handling a net full of vampires on the first night without Frank as our chaperon—and we had netted the largest bat in the neotropics our first night out in Palo Verde. This elevated us to rock-star status among the other OTS students. They couldn't know that in the next year and half, I would catch only one other false-vampire bat among the more than four thousand individuals I captured in Costa Rica.

There was no longer any question in my mind of whether to study bats, the only question was where. OTS showcased the most attractive venues in Costa Rica. By the end of the course, we had explored the moist lowland forests on the Atlantic slope (La Selva); the tropical dry forests (Palo Verde); a spooky, mist-drenched habitat of montane grasslands known as paramo (the Mountain of Death); the cloud forest of Monteverde, reminiscent of Tolkien with its dramatic elfin woodlands battered by winds and bathed in a damp dimness; and the Pacific lowland moist forests in Corcovado National Park—the wildest piece of real estate left in Costa Rica. When I returned to Seattle after the finish of OTS training, I had to break the news to my graduate adviser at the University of Washington, and, worse, to my mother, regarding my newfound passion. I wasn't going to study an ungulate for my Ph.D.; I had enlisted in the ranks of bat biologists. Once my pride in asserting a sense of academic independence had waned, I had a few sobering thoughts about how I was going to pull this off. Bats weren't a traditional subject for study in a wildlife program in 1980. Virtually all of the graduate students in my program studied deer, elk, or something with four legs and a four-chambered stomach. Moreover, my major professor, Richard Taber, was the world's most renowned deer biologist and had never studied bats or specialized in tropical mammals. A generous and kind adviser, he offered all the encouragement he could but suggested I might want to consider transferring to a graduate program where more faculty members were interested in tropical mammals.

I decided to accept the situation as but one more challenge and remained in Washington. Some students are given a detailed map and sextant by their professors to guide them through their dissertation research until they smell land on their own. I would have to steer toward my doctorate like a Polynesian sailor: no compass, relying on the stars, and on overcast nights, lying down in the bottom of the outrigger to feel the drift of the currents. But I realized I still needed help from somewhere and began to seek out researchers elsewhere who might share ideas and keep me from running aground on an intellectual sandbar.

I managed to secure funding from OTS to return to Costa Rica to conduct a three-month pilot study of bats in Monteverde. I'd like to say that I chose Monteverde because no one had studied fruit bat ecology there or anywhere else in tropical forests above five thousand feet in elevation. At least, that's what I told my colleagues in graduate school. However, the truth is that a bad dose of chiggers and scores of small black flies in Corcovado had made me look at Monteverde in a new light—a tropical forest nearly free of pestilence. In the tropics, a mile up from sea level is this side of paradise. The cool temperatures at higher elevation are a welcome relief from the intense heat and

humidity below. The chilly nights keep at bay virtually all that is poisonous or noxious in the lowlands. In a cloud forest, you can lie down
on a trail in the middle of the night, as I often did between checking
my nets, and never worry about fer-de-lances, bushmasters, eyelash
vipers, Africanized killer bees, bot flies (which lay eggs in your scalp or
more private parts of the anatomy), mosquitoes, giant stinging ants, or
chiggers—nothing to worry about save a dry season population of relatively benign house scorpions.

But it wasn't really biology or physical comfort that finally decided
me; it was my first long walk through the cloud forest of Monteverde
in late December of 1980. African violets grew on trees, as did or-
chids, ferns, and bromeliads. In fact, characteristic of cloud forests,
most plants grew on other plants, twisting layers of color and foliage.
Birds, amphibians, and insects came in a riot of colors: resplendent
quetzals, three-wattled bellbirds, toucans, golden toads, glass frogs,
bright morphos, and dazzling clear-winged butterflies. If there were
outstanding bats here, all the better.

Monteverde also housed a whole colony of gringo biologists who
had made the same location decision. The best-known expatriate biologist was George Powell, a tall, bearded, angular biologist who was
one of the first ornithologists to work in Monteverde, conducting
fieldwork for his graduate degree at UC Davis. In his travels through
the Cordillera de Tilarán, the range in which Monteverde is nestled,
and elsewhere in Costa Rica, he worried that the rapid conversion of
cloud forest habitat to coffee and cattle pastures had reached a crisis
stage in Central America.

While still a graduate student, George used his meager savings to
buy out several homesteaders in the area. The cloud forest above
Monteverde had been protected informally by the community of expatriate American Quakers that settled there in the 1950s. After leaving the United States in protest of the Korean War, Quaker pioneers
had turned the lower slopes of Monteverde into an active dairy farming community and conserved the upper slopes to maintain their wa-

tershed. George persuaded the residents that the watershed should be set aside as a fully protected reserve. The Tropical Science Center, based in the capital of San José, worked with George in that effort, and he raised funds from the World Wildlife Fund, the Explorers Club of New York, The Nature Conservancy, the German Herpetological Society, and many individuals concerned with nature conservation. Each group was swayed by the arguments of this passionate defender of cloud forests. For George, saving one of the last refuges for the resplendent quetzal in Central America had become far more important than his own dissertation project.

George eventually did earn his Ph.D. while acting as the founding father of the Monteverde Cloud Forest Reserve. But he was nowhere to be found when I arrived. He was off in the Brazilian Amazon, studying the effects of deforestation and forest fragmentation on the local extinction of birds. Occasionally, I walked by his empty house on the way up to the reserve. Quetzals continued to nest in tree cavities in his backyard, as they did in the late dry season, waiting for the return of their protector.

I started my pilot study in Monteverde in early January of 1981, six months before my encounter with the golden scarab. It was already the dry season, so named because from January to April there are no daily thunderstorms to speak of, although the drenching mist propelled by the Atlantic trade winds continues to blow fiercely over the continental divide. Between the mist of the dry season and the thunderclouds of the wet season, the upper reaches of the Cordillera remain bathed in cloud cover and cool wet conditions for much of the year, thus earning the name cloud forest.

Farther down the Pacific slope, the mist dissipates, and there are near-daily displays of rainbows. The rainbows arch over the most beautiful forest I have ever seen, one dominated by trees in the wild avocado family, the Lauraceae, of such noble height and architecture that they make for stunning wooded landscapes. The leaves cluster like green pompoms at the end of the trees' waving boughs, and in the windy season, they beckon and moan when they rub against each other. Their miniature avocados attract some of the most extraordinary fruit-eating birds on the planet.

With so many fruiting plants and so many fruit-eaters, Monteverde attracted other graduate students interested in studying plant-animal interactions, as well, including Nat Wheelwright, a friend and fellow graduate student studying the ecology of fruit-eating birds. Nat and I often compared field notes because birds and bats are thought to eat quite different types of fruits, so much so that the differences have been codified into sets of preferences for certain fruit traits, known as syndromes. Birds have good color vision but no sense of smell, excepting some vultures and many seabirds. Consequently, fruits "designed" to be dispersed by birds tend to be brightly colored and have little fragrance when mature. In contrast, fruit bats are color blind but possess a keen sense of smell; bat-dispersed fruits thus tend to be dull colored but strong smelling upon ripening. And, of course, thanks to Janzen, we realized there was a group of plants designed to be dispersed by giant prehistoric mammals, the megafauna dispersal syndrome. In the 1980s, bird and bat fruit syndromes represented a way of looking at the biological world in which everything fit neatly into place, each element perfectly adapted for its role in the grand play of evolution in the tropics. Nat taught me to look at this performance with the jaundiced eye of a critic, however, especially because we found birds and bats eating many of the same fruits. He was also prescient in not placing great emphasis on the ecological straightjacket of syndromes. Recent studies show that many birds have an excellent sense of smell. Starlings, for example, boast a rodent-class olfactory. Another elegant theory shelved by natural history.

I started mist-netting bats with the help of my girlfriend and fellow Washington graduate student Jill Zarnowitz the day we arrived. Jill had just started work for a master's degree on cavity-nesting birds in the Olympic Mountains of Washington, but in the winter months, she graciously took time off from her field project to help me get started with mine. A tall, pretty woman, she had a lifelong love for nature that easily eclipsed my own. She had lived for a year in a cabin in the wilds of Alaska and radio-tracked wolves through a winter in the Apennines. She seemed right at home in our tiny casita sans indoor plumbing.

If we needed anything, we went directly to our landlady, Stella Wallace, the unofficial mayor of Monteverde. On one of our first visits with this dairy farmer turned painter, Stella remarked that we should meet her son-in-law—none other than the acclaimed bat biologist Dr. Richard LaVal. Ten years earlier, this tall, lean, red-bearded mammalogist had looked at the composition of the entire bat community of Monteverde to compare it with other lowland sites. In my first three months in Monteverde, Richard proved as invaluable as Nat in steering me in the right direction. We compared notes about where he had captured bats ten years earlier, and I tried to set up a netting protocol that complemented his earlier work. My design was to sample all of the elevational bands of forest, from the edge of the cliff where Monteverde drops abruptly to the Guanacaste lowlands, to the sheltered premontane forests, the more exposed cloud forests, and finally the stunted forest at the continental divide. By mist-netting in each of these habitats on a monthly basis, I would be able to determine if bat species were stratified by the four elevationally defined forest types found along the mountainside. Amazingly, the difference in elevation from the drier forests along the cliff edge to the wind-blown, cloud-strewn stunted forest on the divide was only about one thousand feet over a distance of two miles. But the climatic changes, influenced by the blustery trade winds, were so dramatic that the forest types were of strikingly different character.

Capturing bats was the easy part—identification was another matter. Bat taxonomy, and all mammalian taxonomy, is largely based on dentition. The number of teeth a mammal has, the presence or absence of canines, the shape of the molars, and other dental quirks and eccentricities determine the species. Of course, to place a bat into its proper genus often doesn't require a look into its mouth; a measurement of the forearm or the shape of its tail or nose leaf may be enough. But once you are in the right genus or in closely related genera, you really have to know the pattern of dentition—for instance, whether it has one pair of lower outer incisors or two, or incisors with two bumps on the top or three. Sometimes you need a hand lens to see these features clearly. Fortunately, I had Richard, whose head held a taxonomic key to the bats of the neotropics. Whenever I had a question, I would bring my captures down to his house for him to identify and enjoy a cup of tea.

I spent nearly half the month sampling in the habitats Richard hadn't covered in his study: in the Monteverde reserve itself and up at the Ventana—the window or pass on the continental divide. In late January 1981, Jill and I went up to the Ventana for a windy night of batting. We found a sheltered spot along a narrow trail, out of the misty gale. We had space for only a couple of nets and set them where the vegetation formed a tunnel, decorated on the sides by sprays of wild fuchsia, exuberant vertical gardens of wild begonias, and giant elephant-ear-leaved stems of gunnera, an odd plant that stores blue-green algae in its stems. If the bats wanted to avoid flying along the windy crest, maybe they would use this access route in the lee of the continental divide. We caught only fifteen bats that night, but, remarkably, each one was a different species. To reach 100 percent diversity within a single sample of fifteen is an extraordinary event, for bats or for any other vertebrate species. Typically, in any community of animals, most species in a sample are rare and a few tend to be extremely abundant. Yet my subsequent samples from the Ventana continued to yield low numbers of any one type of bat along with astonishing diversity. Perhaps the Ventana was the portal through which the Atlantic and Pacific and the northern and southern Mesoamerican bat faunas mingled, the Grand Central Station of flying mammals.

That first night in La Ventana, the greatest surprise came from two of the last bats to hit the net. They looked vaguely familiar, but I couldn't quite place them. The first was an insect-eater with bright chestnut-maroon fur. I quickly removed it and checked the other net. It was another insect-eater that closely resembled the first, but with a golden-yellow pelage. Excitedly, I recognized the two as hoary bats of the genus *Lasiurus* but far more flamboyant than the hoary bats back home. The other thirteen species we released right away, but Jill, whose fondness for bats had been instantaneous, kept the two cherished captures warm in their separate bags in her field vest to show to Richard the next day.

The next morning I rushed over to Richard's house. With great anticipation, I handed him the two bags; when he opened the first, his eyes grew wide in amazement. Before us, now awake after its nap in the comfort of the bat bag, was the chestnut hoary bat, *Lasiurus castaneus*, a new record for Central America. The pelage on the back was rich reddish brown over yellow fur. On the belly was another study in yellow fur over black. I had never seen so lovely a bat. Then the next bag's occupant was coaxed out, the yellow *Lasiurus ega*, a new record for Costa Rica and a rare capture for Central America, as well. It was my first chance as a biologist to say Eureka.

Before long, I had added ten species to the list for Monteverde, several for Costa Rica, and one for Central America. Between new and familiar species, my personal belfry was fast filling with fascinating bats, from dainty nectar feeders to the larger fruit-eaters.

That first night in Ventana was back in January of 1981. Now it was June, and I was immersed in my dissertation research. Evenings like the gold scarab one aside, my routine each night was the same. When the bats landed, I would gently remove them from the nets and place them in a bag to collect their fecal donation to my study of fruit bat–plant interactions. Fortunately, bats have relatively short gut retention times. What goes in passes through in about fifteen minutes. To learn what bats ingested became a botanical detective story. Because tropical fruits are so aromatic that even the wild black peppers and the wild tomatoes have unique fragrances, I reached the point where I could recognize the fruits the bats were eating not only by the types of seeds they were passing but by the smell of their offerings. What I discovered was that the fruit bats embraced the same philosophy as the acclaimed creator of the New American Cuisine, Alice Waters: Eat what's local, dine on what's in season and most nutritious, and select produce at its peak of ripeness.

By now, removing bats from mist nets had become something I could do in my sleep. I became familiar enough with bat taxonomy to recognize species as soon as they flew into the net, even bats I had never captured before. I began to develop a supplementary technique for bat identification based on their aroma. While I have never seen this method described in any scholarly publication, I believe it's possible to tell bat species by their unique perfume, perhaps from scent glands they use to mark females and each other. When I captured a bat that was new to me, I would dutifully perform the standard technique: weigh it and measure its forearm. But I also brought it up to my nose and gave it a good sniff. Hints of overripe melon and papaya with civet-like undertones identified the dwarf fruit bat. Scents of ripe fig, chocolate, and old leather gave away the more robust white-lined fruit bat. Nose of spicy black pepper with a guano finish described the short-tailed fruit bat. I wondered how a wrinkle-faced bat might smell—perhaps like fermented mango and banana.

Another six months went by, and now I was a year into my field study. On a raw night in January 1982, a group of new graduate students from Princeton University arrived, led by their professor, the acclaimed John Terborgh. Terborgh's knowledge of tropical biology— from primates to birds to plants—was legendary, equaled only by his physical toughness. Friends later told me that Terborgh could live under any conditions in the field and never complain, his brilliant intellect clothed in a polite Virginia demeanor. On this trip, he was accompanied by an inquisitive first-year grad student named David Wilcove, who peppered me with questions. I felt a bit uneasy with David's enthusiastic inquiries, because my thesis project was becoming less conclusive every night.

I was beginning to get discouraged about being able to demonstrate that bats separated out by the four bands of forest I was sampling on the mountainside. Beginning with my pilot study, I had marked bats with ball-chain necklaces threaded through aluminum numbered bands so I could follow their movements at different altitudes. Closely related species actually seemed to overlap quite a lot. The ecological dogma of that time, as I mentioned earlier, held that members of animal communities used resources in different ways because of competition. Competition determined which species you might find and in what proportions. The problem was, that now seemed untestable. To really get at the question of how bat communities are structured, I first needed to create replica Monteverdes. Then I would need to manipulate the number of ripe fruits available to see if bats used resources differently when fruits were abundant or scarce, while carefully controlling the numbers of bats in each area. Even then, it might be hard to determine whether bat communities differed because of current competition or because they competed in the past and experienced a major selection event—an event in the life of an individual or a population that affects its survival, and through which only a subset of the population makes it, presumably because of possessing an essential trait or traits. The number of pieces in the neat jigsaw puzzle I had set for myself had multiplied, and I had no idea what the final picture might look like.

I discussed with Nat a talk I had with Terborgh and Wilcove on the intellectual challenges of fieldwork while he and I walked up to a pasture surrounded by majestic wild avocados. Our objective was to observe quetzals and other birds feeding on new fruits. This particular wild avocado species had beautiful small black fruits set in a red cap that made it easy for the quetzals to find them. Nat had the idea of observing trees to see which species of birds came to take their fruit and in that way determine diets and the relationship between size of bird and size of fruit. Nat placed mesh screens below feeding perches where quetzals typically returned after sallying forth to pluck fruits.

The resplendent quetzal would regurgitate the seeds too large to pass through its gut, and those would collect on the mesh screens, giving Nat a better indication of their diet and the size of fruits eaten.

Suddenly, a stream of green and red streaked across my binoculars' field of view, and for the first time I saw the adjective "resplendent" as a verb. The quetzal fed for a while and was then joined by an emerald toucanet. Nat pointed out that even if he found that these birds ate different fruits, or I found that the three species of yellow-shouldered fruit bats I was studying ate different fruits, all it would show is that they differed in their natural history. There was no clear evidence to support or disprove the theory that competition forced diet separation. Nat raised another example of fuzzy theory. When we were in school, much of the literature in the area of plant-animal interactions focused on seed dispersal, and many theories had been concocted to explain why some species were better dispersers than others for particular plants and to show that everything was neatly evolved. Nat explained that what most biologists were actually measuring, however, was fruit removal—who eats what—not which birds disperse the seeds to which sites or, most important, how well those seeds germinate and how many resulting young plants survive. Without such information on plant fitness, wasn't much of what passed for evolutionary theory, especially in the area of community ecology and plant-animal interactions, merely glorified natural history?

I left Nat at midday to have solitude with his quetzals and walked down to get ready for another night of netting. There is a calming sense of ritual to field research. For me, the ritual was grabbing my headlamp and gear and carrying bat netting poles up the mountain. For a marine scientist, I imagine it's checking the scuba gear before the next dive; for large-mammal biologists in Africa, maybe it's fiddling with the GPS unit before the next overflight of the Serengeti. But sometimes doubt about the eternal order of things creeps into the peaceful rituals. In my case, what if my hypothesis turned out to be obvious or just plain wrong? What if walking up and down this mountainside in search of patterns among the fruit bat community was conceived under the rubric of a misguided theory? What if it's nothing more than a tropical free-for-all out there?

We were learning the sometimes painful process by which science progresses: from observation to hypothesis to prediction to test—to a return to the drawing board, if necessary. By making observations, erecting hypotheses about what we observed, shooting down those hypotheses, and replacing them with others that more accurately describe what's going on, we inch closer to the truth. But in my darkest hours, I began to view natural history in a new way: as the bucket of ice water poured down the back of the armchair theoretician who skipped the observation step in the sequence.

Almost since the publication of Darwin's *Origin of Species* in 1859, what was known as the adaptationist paradigm had been a dominant school of thought, and it was in full swing in the second half of the twentieth century. In evolutionary ecology, you always looked first for the adaptive significance of some feature or behavior, be it bright feathers, teeth or claws shaped a certain way, the construction of a flower, the wing patterns of a butterfly, or the hunting technique of an aardvark. The idea was that there was a good evolutionary reason for everything. In the heyday of that era, if you asked an evolutionary biologist the question "Why did the chicken cross the road?" he or she would reply, "To increase its reproductive fitness. On the other side of the road was more food, fewer chicken predators, fewer competing chickens, better shelter, or a more handsome rooster." The problem was, you really didn't know whether road crossing by the fabled chicken was under strong selection pressure. Was it possible that chickens that failed to cross the road in time left fewer offspring or no offspring at all? Unless one could demonstrate a selection event in the life history of the chicken, "Because it felt like it" was the simplest, most direct answer. I suppose this is an overstatement, but not every behavior of animals can be considered adaptive. Animals make mistakes in their choices just like we do. Sometimes it's just because of insufficient information. Sometimes the consequences of crossing the road aren't significant. Maybe it's best to say that natural selection has favored impulses and behaviors that have good evolutionary intentions in an imperfect world.

A week after my diurnal bird study with Nat, I went out for an evening of batting with Richard LaVal. That night, he and I discussed the value of repeating field studies in an area and separating the repetitions by a decade or more. In the late 70s and early 80s, still the heyday of tropical exploration, replication was not the best career move. There seemed so much to study and so few field scientists, if you said you were repeating so-and-so's transect of bats or birds or amphibians, you'd get questions like "What if you find the same thing?" Now the repetition of ecological field studies, and even the collection of long-term data, is considered vital. A friend of mine studied marine iguanas in the Galápagos for four years. In the first three years, everything was ducky, and he wondered what limited marine iguana populations. The next year, a severe El Niño storm hit, the waters warmed, the algae eaten by the iguanas disappeared, and there was a major population crash. The lesson here is fundamental for ecology: The relatively short duration of most field studies misses not only cyclic events but also the rare events that may actually structure animal communities.

Previously conducted baseline studies allow us to better understand what is going on, even if we may be too late to change anything. Richard and I wondered if someone repeating our studies a decade or two later would find similar patterns or a shifted world. In subsequent years, Richard found the latter. Repeating the netting program we developed for ten to twenty nights a year since 1982, Richard discovered some interesting changes. Between 1997 and 2003, he encountered four species of lowland bats not recorded in Monteverde during our previous studies. The lowland yellow-shouldered bat, rare in 1981, had become seasonally abundant. Vampires, which were never encountered in 1973 and were sparse in 1981, had become regular members of the bat fauna. For birds and mammals, range shifts or expansions may or may not have little bearing on species conservation, depending on their abundance and adaptability. But shifts in climatic regimes could be catastrophic for the future of amphibians and other dwellers in tropical cloud forests.

Today, one of the hottest research topics is how plant and animal populations are responding and adapting, or not adapting, to climate change. It's now considered good science to go back and resample transects from two or three decades ago to detect any response—that is, if the natural habitats are still there. Baseline studies enable us to draw correlations between shifting climate patterns—such as rise in ambient temperature, longer or more intense dry seasons, and re-duced or increased precipitation—and the movements of animals. In the event of climate change, cloud forest species with tight environ-mental requirements for breeding are predicted to shift their range along the elevational gradient to find the right horizontal slice along the mountainside to reestablish themselves.

Thus, climate change poses a serious stress for those species that don't travel well, or as in the case of some invertebrates, don't travel at all. With global warming under way and the dry season more pro-nounced, it seems that species once common in the dry forest below the mountain have established residence on the lower part of Mon-teverde. The keel-billed toucan, a lowland bird, now breeds in Mon-teverde. Quetzals have begun nesting farther up the mountainsides. Other examples abound. For low mountains like Monteverde, where the highest point is barely over two thousand feet above sea level, there may be no room to move up the mountain, and the environmen-tal conditions that create cloud forests in the first place may literally evaporate. This could be critical for species that need the thin band of cloud forest as their sanctuary.

Climate change may also be behind the already catastrophic de-cline in Monteverde's amphibians. The same night Richard and I were out batting in Monteverde, amphibians were calling or hopping all along the stream next to our nets. We even caught a few fringe-lipped bats on patrol for tasty singing frogs. But somewhere in the deep recesses of the cloud forest, the last golden toad on earth, one of the rare endemic species Monteverde was created to protect, may have taken its last moist breath. By the early 1980s, the species had completely disappeared.

By the middle of 1982, about eighteen months into my fieldwork, I began to realize that I wouldn't have the data to demonstrate the ecological separation of bat species that I had hoped to show. So I took another angle, putting my newfound knowledge of bat fruits to good use. I wondered how bats that ate nothing but watery, sugary fruit could somehow find the nutritional sustenance to produce and suckle two babies a year. In the lowlands, fruit bats often expand their diets to include fat and protein-rich insects during one or both periods of pregnancy and lactation. One would think that in a colder, more stressful environment and higher altitude, the vegetarian lifestyle would fall out of fashion. To answer my new question, I analyzed the nutritional quality and abundance of the fruits and found that peaks in carbohydrates, fats, and proteins corresponded with peaks in availability for the fruiting species the fruit bats really keyed in on: a smorgasbord of wild tomatoes, wild black peppers, and a guava-like fruit called *Eugenia*. I fed such fruits to captive bats held in flight cages and determined their feeding preferences. The bats were marvelous shoppers, picking the ripest, most nutritious fruits nearly every time. My field study showed that peaks in lactation seemed timed to coincide with the period when fruits were most nutritious and most abundant.

My stint in Monteverde is long finished. I'd like to say that my research findings shook the world, or at least the bat world, but I'm not sure that I made much of a ripple. My interest in tropical conservation had been set ablaze, however. For that reason, one of my biggest disappointments was being unable to hook up with the founder of the reserve, George Powell, while I was there. George is a bit of a ghostlike figure, slipping in and out of places like the Peruvian Amazon, where he works now—and one of the most accomplished yet least heralded conservation biologists around. Most people have never heard of him, because his humility precludes advertising his achievements, but he accomplished more for conservation while still in graduate school than many biologists achieve in their entire careers. While part of our meager graduate fellowship money went for beer on Fridays, George Powell used much of his to start the purchase of the Monteverde Cloud Forest Reserve. His ability to see the big picture kept him two steps ahead of us. While we were still studying, or getting lost in, the intricacies of cloud forests, he began advising the group RARE, a conservation organization, on how to save cloud forest species. While we debated the latest theories about evolutionary biology, he was off studying the effects of fragmentation on local extinction and helping to chart new directions in the yet unborn field of conservation biology. While we focused on what animals were doing inside the Monteverde Cloud Forest Reserve, he was already radio-tracking quetzals and bellbirds to find out where they disappeared to for half the year and designing a network of parks linked by altitudinal corridors to better conserve their year-round ranges. He was prescient in pursuing this research program, because ornithologists now believe that up to half of Costa Rica's rich bird fauna are seasonal altitudinal migrants. Moving up and down mountainsides is a way of life for the charismatic bellbirds as well as the smallest hummingbirds.

George certainly chose an independent route. Skirting the shoals of academia after receiving his Ph.D., he charted his own career course, linking rigorous field biology with conservation. One of his great contributions has been in the area of designing comprehensive protected area networks. He was one of the first biologists to point out that Costa Rica's vaunted park system, held in high regard by the world, needed to become far more extensive and representative if Costa Rica were to maintain its reputation as a leader in global conservation. Most of Costa Rica's parks were on poor soils in the wet lowlands, where agriculture was impractical, or on the highest volcanoes where no one lived or farmed. Missing from the design of a network of reserves were middle-elevation forests linked by forest corridors to the lowlands. By demonstrating how species like quetzals and bell-birds relied on such corridors, George helped design an effective park system in Costa Rica that has served as a model for the rest of the world.

George's path made me begin to realize that as much as I loved asking questions about bats and plants and exploring the world of tropical biology, it wasn't enough. For some, the world of academic ideas is so intoxicating that there is no choice but to breathe the rar-ified atmosphere of the university life. Learning from George's exam-ple and that of others like him, I realized that I wanted to contribute something immediate and tangible to the world. My professional cocktail was going to require mixing equal parts biological research and conservation.

My fondness for bats has never left me. Nor has my growing commitment to help save the rain forests in which they live. My chance to reunite with my fellow bat men and bat women came in 1990, when I attended my first International Bat Biology meeting. Just as bats account for a whopping percentage of the class Mammalia, the number of biologists who study or are interested in bats exceeds those studying the other orders of mammals, except rodents. The meeting was held in Austin, Texas, the headquarters of Bat Conserva-tion International and, fittingly, home to one of the world's largest ag-gregations of free-tailed bats, which roost under a bridge in the heart of the downtown.

I presented a paper, not on my Monteverde bat study from ten years previous, which was merely another brick in the wall of tropical natural history, but on a topic that united my old world as a bat biologist and my new one studying the distributions and concentrations of plants and animals on the planet, essentially an attempt to see if bat species richness could predict overall biodiversity in a region. The large hall was filled with several hundred of the top bat systematists, ecologists, and behavioral biologists; I was a newcomer to this group of scientists. My nervousness at presenting to this audience was somewhat dispelled by Frank's reassurance that the meetings were quite collegial and often irreverent (after all, these were people who studied bats). Hijinks were common.

I saw that I was to follow a raft of papers on the subject of echolocation in insectivorous bats and figured I better do something that would wake up the crowd, or at least deflect their suspicions of my dubious credentials as a bat biologist. I began by announcing that I had discovered six new species of bats not yet described by science. There was an instant hush. The late Karl Koopman, then dean of bat taxonomists, who was sitting in the front row, and other leading scientists awoke from their siestas. Their ears perked, and I swear their noses started to twitch, like echolocating bats trying to get a fix on what is in front of them. "All of the six species are in the leaf-nosed bat family," I continued. "I didn't bring any photographs, but I do have my own drawings of these bats and the characteristic features that distinguish each as a new species." I could see them grow suspicious, leaning forward in their seats. Who was this guy?

I flashed on the screen one fanciful drawing after another, describing each of the spoof bats as I went. Gradually, the audience sensed the joke I was playing and joined in. No upstart had scooped them on a real new species, after all.

I followed this farce with my dry talk about the correlation between bat diversity and biodiversity across the ecoregions of Asia, which did receive some comment but not the interest my opening had. In hindsight, what I really would like to have done was something even more unconventional. Just as on some religious revival show, I could have offered a confession of being born again as a bat lover. I could have ended my fifteen-minute presentation by doing something no one had probably ever done at a bat meeting: reciting a poem, titled "Bat." A gem written by the Irish poet Eamon Grennon, it tells about learning from a bat how to move through life as an astute human being. In the poem a man finds himself trapped, panic stricken, in a bedroom with a live bat. He opens a window to allow the bat to flee, and the nature of his observation changes as the bat searches for an escape hatch; his emotions pass quickly from outright fear to fascination and admiration. As the bat finally discovers the portal to freedom, the witness observes:

> Gone for good. It's the sheer
> stoic silence (to my ears) of the whole operation
> that stays with me, teaching me how to behave
> in a tight corner: hold your tongue, keep moving, try
> everything more than once, steer by brief kisses and
> the fleeting grace of dark advances, quick retreats,
> until you find lying in your way the window, open.

As for me, I had found the open window that appears in all of our careers, if we only look. I discovered it by navigating like a bat and trying everything at least twice before turning away from a safer route. I found it by nurturing my fondness for bats, an interest that saved me from a career as a dissatisfied deer biologist trudging through the muskeg of Alaska. I discovered my appreciation for their place in the world as regenerators of rain forests and developed a desire to protect them and all the things around them, which became the foundation of a career in conservation. I am forever grateful for having followed the way of the bat.

Finally, I became a card-carrying bat man, as the old master had challenged me. Not in my first month or in my first 500 captures, but after 1,426 bats had graced my nets, I finally captured a wrinkle-faced bat. Actually, I caught 8 of them, but none was more exciting than the first. I uttered a deep-throated Eureka! when I looked up at a tawny-colored bat with a mug of odd wrinkles that stared shyly back at me in the net on a warm July night. This was no Quasimodo or freak of nature. It was *Centurio cenex*, the shar-pei of the bat world and as charming an animal as ever graced a wildlife calendar.

chapter three

KINGDOM OF THE SNOW LEOPARD

THE SNOW LEOPARD LAY MOTIONLESS BUT ALERT ON A WIDE, exposed ledge above a pile of giant boulders. From his windswept lair he surveyed his domain, a pair of pale green eyes taking careful inventory. His smoke-gray coat, accented with swirls of black spots and large dark rosettes, blended into the monochrome backdrop of the surrounding rock wall. A minute passed, then another, with no sign of life from below. Suddenly, the tip of his tail swished in excitement. I brought the camera up to my eye and held my breath. Below him, another leopard drew into a crouch, poised to leap up the rock face. As if flung from a catapult, the lower cat vaulted onto the first and the two tumbled together in play. I depressed the shutter a split second too late. All I would have to show for my vigil was an empty frame of bare rock or perhaps the blur of a tail. Before I could regroup, a child wearing an oversized Seattle Supersonics jersey raced over, shouting for his mother to come and see the spotted pussycats. My Himalayan reverie vanished on the spot.

Turning from the snow leopard exhibit, I crossed over to the administration building of Seattle's Woodland Park Zoo. I had an appointment with Helen Freeman, the director of education, and I was late, detained by my attempt at stalking snow leopards. We were going to discuss the possibility of me joining her on a trip to South Asia to look for this elusive predator in the wild. Inside, a tall, striking woman in her mid-forties greeted me. She spoke quickly and assuredly while ushering me into her office. Her bright red hair was the perfect complement to her enthusiasm and energy.

After a few pleasantries, Helen drove straight to the point: "I know it's rather short notice, but permission just came through from the Indian government. If we don't leave soon, it will be winter and the mountains will be impassable. So you are interested in joining me to look for snow leopards, right?" She uttered the invitational paragraph in a single breath. "Absolutely," I replied. She could have said we were to search for abominable snowmen or Himalayan marmots— mountain-dwelling groundhogs—and I still would have said yes. I was a newly minted Ph.D., and for the past few months I had been involved in a lackluster study of small mammals in the Douglas fir forests of Washington State, just biding my time until I started postdoctoral research in Nepal. But eight months felt too long to wait with wanderlust gnawing at my insides. Ever since my two and half years there as a Peace Corps volunteer, I was itching to get back to Asia. "The timing is perfect," I told her.

Helen was the world's foremost authority on the behavior of snow leopards in captivity, and her commitment to their conservation was unflagging. Now she was determined to initiate a field study to learn more about the snow leopard's biology and its habitat and to disprove its reputation as a serious predator of livestock. This trip, if all went well, would lay the groundwork for me or others to follow to begin an intensive study. There was only one hitch for Helen: She had never been to the rooftop of Asia, the only place the species is found in the wild. Even on this short expedition, if we could be lucky enough to get a glimpse of this iconic lion of the snows, we would have a place to start our fieldwork, but the odds were stacked against us. In 1983, the number of biologists who had seen a wild snow leopard could stand on the summit of Mount Everest with room to spare.

Helen's rise to prominence in snow leopard conservation circles and her interest in field biology were rather unorthodox. She hadn't run traplines for muskrat as a teenager, nor had she tracked wolves and moose in Alaska after college. She had been a traditional housewife blessed with a generous husband named Stanley and two teenage boys, living in a comfortable suburb just across Lake Washington from Seattle. Her undergraduate degree was in business administration, but when her youngest son entered kindergarten, she went back to the University of Washington to get an advanced degree in animal behavior. Her adviser and mentor was the noted behavioral ecologist John Alcock. She was already working at the zoo when she was asked to help set up a volunteer program and a class in animal behavior to be run jointly by the zoo and the university. This was the early 1970s, about the same time the first pair of snow leopards, named Nicholas and Alexandra, were donated to the zoo. The pair was so stressed when they arrived that Helen decided to make some behavioral observations of her own. Perhaps ways could be found to help them adjust to captivity.

She grew to love the pair, and through them, the whole species. Perhaps it was their magical far-away gaze, their regal detachment from the world beneath the high boulders of their enclosure, or their acrobatic beauty; or perhaps all of those characteristics punctuated by their endangered status. Her observations of the czar and czarina and subsequently other snow leopards born at the zoo became a full-fledged study and, ultimately, a thirty-year commitment to try to save them. Almost single-handedly, and with the full encouragement of her husband, she founded—from her basement—the International Snow

Leopard Trust, the first international nonprofit organization devoted exclusively to the conservation of an endangered cat.

My interest in snow leopards had an entirely different evolution. My Peace Corps post in the lowlands of Nepal was far below their altitudinal range, but I did get to know snow leopard biologists. My fellow volunteers and I rented the bottom floor of a rundown house in Kathmandu for a place to crash while in town to collect our paychecks and enjoy some R&R. The apartment became a gathering place for other impoverished wildlife scientists, including Rod Jackson and Gary Ahlborn, the first biologists to fit wild snow leopards with radiotelemetry collars, which allowed the scientists to track them using an antenna and receiver from several kilometers away.

Rod, born in South Africa and schooled in England, resembled a blond Roman Polanski. He overflowed with passionate intensity for his mission to save snow leopards, and he possessed a grit reminiscent of the great solo alpinist Reinhold Messner. His sidekick Gary was a laid-back Californian and a stalwart field man. Their research area was situated in one of the most remote recesses of Nepal, west of the hauntingly beautiful Dhaulagiri Himal, the world's fifth highest mountain. Just to reach the site was an expedition in itself, forcing the duo to cross high passes in deep snows. There were other risks, too. Once, when they had captured a snow leopard in a leg noose to fit him with a collar, Rod was bitten through the hand as he tried to inject a sedative. Gary bandaged up Rod's bloody paw, but Rod had had no tetanus or rabies vaccination and was forced to make the three-week trek out to a health facility and back again. Gary remained behind in the Langu Gorge with the avalanches and the constant numbing cold, determined to keep the project moving forward until his colleague returned.

The zeal this species has inspired in Rod, Gary, and Helen is understandable. Among the large cats—the tiger, lion, leopard, jaguar, and puma—the snow leopard was the last to be officially described (in 1775), portrayed in illustrations, or photographed. There are plenty of beautiful cats among the thirty-nine species in the Felidae family, but the three leopards—clouded, common, and snow—may be the most visually stunning. Cloaked in the most beautiful fur of any cat, the reclusive clouded leopard is the Greta Garbo of the lot; it lives a solitary life in the remote jungles of Asia, from Nepal to Borneo. The common leopard, which ranges from South Africa to Java and north to the Russian Far East, is the most ubiquitous. With its orange-tawny pelt speckled with rosettes, it rivals the clouded leopard as one of the most beautiful mammals ever to walk the earth. Some also would include in this category the melanistic form of the common leopard, the phantom-like black panther of Southeast Asian rain forests.

However beautiful the other leopards may be, the snow leopard is in a class apart. It boasts a more developed chest and a more muscular frame, with obvious differences in its appendages and fur. To me, it resembles a common leopard that's spent a lot of time at the gym. Randall Eaton, a carnivore biologist, once described wolves as a pair of jaws in track shoes and snow leopards as a pair of jaws in snowshoes. The snow leopard's gigantic forepaws allow it to secure a grip on rocky inclines or to pad down the steepest terrain without sinking into the snow. These cats are also accomplished leapers, regularly vaulting eighteen feet in one bound. A long, thick tail helps the animal maintain balance while climbing and during downhill slalom runs in hot pursuit of its favorite prey species, the blue sheep. To top off this list of adaptations to the rigors of alpine living, the snow leopard's smoke-gray fur is thick and luxuriant, measuring two inches on the back and five inches on the belly.

There are other wild cats of the snows, to be sure, such as the lynx and the puma, but they lack the aura of snow leopards. The snow leopard's home is part of its mystery. There is a spiritual element so deeply ingrained in the snow leopard's dominion that every fragrant bough of dwarf juniper, each blossom of monkshood, primrose, and poppy, and even the boulders seem infused with transcendent meaning. Tibetan prayer flags flutter over many of the lower mountain passes used by snow leopards, where the stone cairns created by salt traders, religious pilgrims, and yak herders serve as miniature religious shrines. The sparkling vistas of the high Himalayas present more than just a nice Kodachrome backdrop for the researcher or an epiphany for the religious pilgrim up from the Indian plains. The mountains offer the promise of redemption. The Tharu people of lowland Nepal bury their dead so that the first view the soul would encounter upon rising from the body would be the Himalayas to the north, a panorama that would purify the soul and ensure a higher rebirth.

Remarkably, few biologists have studied snow leopards, despite the allure of the species and its spectacular surroundings. As of 2003, only four major field studies of snow leopards had been published. There are some obvious reasons, beginning, of course, with the remoteness and difficulty of the terrain and the rarity of the species. Snow leopards are thinly distributed, with maybe one individual every forty square miles; furthermore, their secretive behavior foils easy detection. Only recently, with the advent of infrared camera traps, molecular techniques that identify individuals from hair and feces, and satellite telemetry collars to track them over their enormous home ranges, has it been possible to deepen our acquaintance with this shy monarch. The total historical range of the snow leopard was likely more than one hundred thousand square miles across the mountains of Asia, but by the mid-eighties it had been reduced to about half that area.

Political barriers have proven even more formidable to conducting research than the snow leopard's rugged home. Much of its preferred habitat lies along the politically sensitive borders of twelve nations in the high mountains of central and South Asia, where frontiers are often disputed, sometimes violently. Not surprisingly, these areas have remained off-limits to all but a few foreign researchers. Only the most dedicated and persistent, like Rod Jackson, have had the fervor and the patience to obtain the necessary permits. Helen and I were headed for the upper parts of Kashmir, and we were lucky indeed to have a chance to search for snow leopards there on short-term visas, thereby avoiding the paperwork required for a longer stay.

Finally, to want to study such a species of the deep snow and remote mountains requires a special breed of biologist: equal parts explorer, mountaineer, and scientist. Gourmands need not apply. To work in the high Himalayas you must be able to subsist indefinitely on the Tibetan diet of dried meat, ground barley kernels, and rancid yak butter tea.

Among exploration biologists, the master in snow leopard study is George Schaller, or GS, as he is referred to in Peter Matthiessen's award-winning book *The Snow Leopard*. Schaller's career is almost legendary; he has conducted the first in-depth field studies of many of the world's most charismatic large mammals, including mountain gorillas, tigers, lions, and giant pandas. He has also studied in detail many of the large hoofed mammals of the high mountains and steppes of central Asia, such as blue sheep, Tibetan antelope, and takin. After all of his work in far-flung destinations, Schaller's first love has remained the cold high places of Asia, where few humans stray and plenty of extraordinary wildlife such as wild yaks, musk deer, and Marco Polo sheep still roam.

Although Schaller and Matthiessen traveled together, the two had entirely different objectives. Schaller went in search of blue sheep, the major prey item of snow leopards where their ranges overlap, and possibly to glimpse the cat. He reckoned that because the Buddhist religion forbids the killing of animals, the environs of the holy lama of the Shey monastery would provide a sanctuary where the interaction of predator and prey could be studied without the influence of humans. Matthiessen, a devout Zen Buddhist, was on a spiritual pilgrimage. His wife had recently died of cancer, and the trip was a chance to release some of the grief from his heart and to find greater understanding of our rightful place in the shadows of these great mountains.

Perhaps a conversation or study with the lama of Shey monastery would offer him the salve and the restored balance we all seek after suffering a deep loss.

Helen and I were on the Pan Am flight to New Delhi when I learned that I was her third choice for the job. She had wanted GS, above all, to be the biologist on this trip, but he was busy studying giant pandas in China. Then there was Rod, but he was engaged in negotiating his way back into Nepal, Tibet, Pakistan, or wherever he could convince a government official to grant him permission to track snow leopards. That left me. I would have been my third choice, too. I had done my share of trekking in the Himalayas and mountain climbing in the States, but when it came to wildlife studies, I was a *Terai-wallah*, a person of the hot humid lowlands, where no self-respecting snow leopard would ever venture. On the plus side, I spoke fluent Nepali, decent Hindi, some Urdu, and a bit of Tibetan. So even if I couldn't tell Helen with confidence, "An adult male snow leopard passed this way two days ago, judging by the age of the footprint," I could at least order her a nice curry in several languages.

On the long flight over, I managed to reread the rather limited literature on wild snow leopards. Much more was available on their prey, including Schaller's collection on Himalayan ungulates, *Mountain Monarchs*. The book provided some wonderful insights into the behavior of little-known species such as blue sheep; Himalayan tahr, a kind of goat-antelope; and the spectacularly horned markhor goats. With over seventy species of antelope, Africa is often considered the center of diversity for lowland hoofed mammals. The Himalayas, on the other hand, are the center of diversity for mountain ungulates. Over forty-two species are native to the youngest, highest mountain chain in the world, far more species of upland ungulates than in any other montane system. I read on. The high diversity in hoofed mammals is paralleled by some bird groups such as the brilliantly plumed gallinaceous birds. The monal pheasant, the blood pheasant, the western and the Blyth's tragopan are all avian marvels. But the greatest diversity and endemism—a word used to characterize those species whose range is limited to a small geographic area—by far is in alpine flowering plants. Most trekkers and mountaineers never see this carpet of color, because most species flower in the cloudy monsoon, when few foreigners come to explore the high meadows above the leech-infested rhododendron forests. But the number of flowering plants in the Himalayan chain surpasses that of the alpine floras of the Sierras, the Andes, the Caucasus, the Carpathians, the Snow Mountains of New Guinea, and the Alps. Four genera in particular— primroses, poppies, louseworts, and rhododendrons—have undergone remarkable events of speciation in the isolated valleys and slopes of the high Himalayas.

Helen asked if I had been to Tibet, perhaps the last stronghold for the snow leopard. I answered in the affirmative, and technically, I had. I once trekked to a national park in the Nepalese Himalayas that abutted the Tibetan border. As many Peace Corps volunteers had done before me, I stood on a mountain pass that formed part of the vast unmarked political boundary, or at least so I was told. I put one foot over the line and then the other. I stood for a while peering into the homeland of His Holiness, the Dalai Lama. There was no Chinese border guard there to stop me, no one to admonish my breach of protocol, except for a small flock of red-billed choughs, a kind of high-elevation crow. I had no visa to sanction my intrusion, so I stepped back into the diplomatic safety of Nepal. I have no record in my passport or any photographic evidence of my "Seven Minutes in Tibet." But I had been there.

The long flight to Delhi in economy class, featuring no leg room, was a prelude to the discomfort we would face in Indian jeeps and taxis over the next few weeks. Helen, allowing no time for jet lag, had arranged a tight schedule of meetings straight off. We were advised by the top officials to go to Srinagar and meet up with Mir Inayat Ullah, the head of the wildlife department for the states of Jammu and Kashmir. We could also try to visit Ladakh, the Tibetan region of northernmost India, to look for snow leopards.

Over the next few days, we met a dozen or so officials from different departments, who all expressed interest in our mission but offered little more than excellent tea and sympathetic gestures. A high-ranking Nepalese friend, whose country, unlike India, has never been colonized, once reminded me that the British invented bureaucracy, but the Indians perfected it. My youthful impatience was starting to grate on Helen, but she persevered and played the good ambassador for both of us. Looking back, I wish that I had possessed the maturity to be of more help. Two years later, my professor in graduate school, Richard Taber, asked me in front of his current crop of students, "Eric, what were the things we didn't teach you in graduate school that proved essential for your work in international conservation?" Without hesitation, I responded, "Diplomacy and patience."

With my energy somewhat depleted, we finally boarded the Air India jet for Srinagar, the enchanting capital of Kashmir. Srinagar was a center of the Moghul Empire and the summer capital for the states of Jammu and Kashmir. Romantic colonialists went there to escape the heat and dust of the Indian plains and the sticky confines and mosquitoes of the monsoon. In 1983, it was also a leg of the Hippie Triangle— along with Kathmandu and the gentle azure coast of Phuket, Thailand, a key caravan stop on the flower-child route across Asia. For Helen and me, it provided a welcome break from the stifling red tape of Delhi wildlife politics and brought us a step closer to seeing a snow leopard.

At the airport, I noticed a broadly smiling man dressed in an expensive-looking blue suit standing in a group of smartly dressed younger men. The older gentleman had a bold red handkerchief folded neatly in his breast pocket and not a hair out of place. I thought he might be the mayor of Srinagar or some other high official. But this was Mir Inayat Ullah, the wildlife director, who stepped forward, greeted us warmly, then showed us into a waiting jeep. I tried to pay attention to his guided tour of the outskirts of Srinagar as we made our way to his office. His sharp-featured assistants accompanied us and hung on his every word, their perfectly trimmed mustaches twitching when their boss made an amusing remark. Their neatly combed hair and carefully pressed jackets and trousers made me wonder if Director Ullah enforced a strict dress code. In my REI-issue wardrobe and hiking boots, I felt way underdressed.

Ullah was a maverick in his own way, though. To him, the world of Delhi was an irritation to be ignored as much as possible. The grand vision of this well-connected Kashmiri was to make his state the next major nature destination in Asia. It seemed that he had already arranged our entire itinerary. We would take a quick trip to nearby Dachigam Wildlife Sanctuary to see the hangul, the endemic subspecies of red deer native to Kashmir. Next, we would take a drive through the country back to Srinagar for an afternoon of shopping and rest. Then we would go on a four-day trek to look for snow leopards in Zanskar, a high, remote mountain range bordering Kashmir and Ladakh. Unfortunately, business in Srinagar would detain the director, but his top assistants in their smart sport coats would be with us for the entire journey. With our fortunes in the hands of Director Ullah, we sat back in our chairs, at ease for the first time on this trip, as he pressed fragrant Kashmiri tea, lovely cakes studded with citrons and sultanas, fresh walnuts, and overflowing Kashmiri hospitality upon us.

On the way to our hotel, Helen gave me some background on this invitation and on our host. Obtaining permission to go to Jammu and Kashmir had taken nearly two years of legwork. The contact with Inayat Ullah came through a mutual friend of Helen's. Even with the invitation from Inayat Ullah and the government of India, it took almost another year to get approval—for just a three-week trip.

Our hotel bordered the famous Dal Lake, above which rose ancient Moghul forts and temples. The sun was dropping over a majestic palace perched on a hill above the south rim of the lake. In the chilly air, Helen and I decided to take a turn around a historic Moghul garden a short distance from the hotel. It was early fall, and petals were fluttering off the rose bushes. The crimson and orange foliage of the sweet gums planted along the perimeter of the garden glowed in the late afternoon sunlight. On the lake shore, ornately carved wooden houseboats sat empty. The hippie armies that filled them in the summer had shifted like shorebirds to southern India to spend the winter. We seemed to be the only visitors. The view of the floating village of houseboats, the sun setting over the temples, and the distant peaks filled me with serenity.

The next morning we set off early for Dachigam Wildlife Sanctuary to hike into the reserve to look for hangul, Himalayan black bears, and maybe even musk deer. This was to be a warm-up for the more arduous trek that would begin the following day. We were introduced to the most senior park guard, who had guided George Schaller during his stay in Dachigam. Our timing couldn't have been better; the hangul were rutting, and the bugling of the randy males echoed off the high valley walls.

Our guide knew Dachigam's secrets, like where to spot the Himalayan black bears fattening themselves on acorns. He pointed to a dark speck on the hillside that my binoculars revealed to be a foraging black bear. Another rummaged a few trees away. Above the steep hillsides of oak and other broad-leaved trees, he told us, snow leopards used to wander into the upper reaches of Dachigam. I wondered if any had ventured down to the lower reaches, where we were, to look for the hangul. In fact, I learned from Helen only later that this range issue was part of Ullah's agenda in bringing us here. First, he wanted us to check out lower Dachigam and its suitability for snow leopards. Second, he wanted to receive some animals himself. Helen was chair of the North American Species Survival Plan for captive snow leopards, and Ullah wanted a pair for exhibit in lower Dachigam.

In midafternoon, we headed back to Srinagar for a final meeting with Ullah before the following day's expedition. We drove through apple orchards filled with women clad in brightly colored skirts, blouses, and headscarves who were busily harvesting fruit. The living canvas before me was more captivating than any pastoral scene found in the impressionist wing of an art museum. I was enchanted by the play of color and light: the swirling skirts of the women, the bright red fruits set off against the green foliage of the apple trees, and beneath it all a sun-speckled carpet of purple crocuses, the source of Kashmir's saffron trade.

"So, you liked Dachigam?" inquired Director Ullah in the warmth of his office. One of his pet projects was to bring back to the reserve representatives of all of the native species of Kashmir to live safely. "So, do you think Dachigam can become the center of our nature tourism industry?" Now that we had seen a piece of this Shangri-la, Ullah began telling us in greater detail his vision, in which wildlife reserves would rival handmade carpets, embroidery, and houseboats in attracting tourists to his state. Before we could answer, another heavily laden tray of fragrant Kashmiri tea, sumptuous cakes, and other treats appeared. I couldn't get enough of the aromatic infusion. Ullah noticed my growing addiction. "So, you are fond of the tea?" I responded positively and inquired how it was prepared. "Very easy and very fast," he assured me. "Take one teaspoon of loose tea with some crushed cardamom pods, a cinnamon stick, and a pinch of our saffron. Throw it into four cups of water and allow it to boil. Reduce the heat and let it steep for five minutes. Now, here is the trick." I leaned forward, as if a secret handed down from the Moghuls was about to be revealed. "Put a teaspoon of powdered almonds in the bottom of each cup, and pour the hot tea over it. Sweeten the tea with honey as you like, and you have the nectar of Kashmir." Helen and I drank one restorative cup after another. Ullah beamed in delight.

That night I packed my gear for the trek. It was the beginning of winter in the mountains, and Helen had already caught a cold. I hoped that she would have the stamina for the steep trail ahead. Our trek was supported by a small platoon of porters who would carry our

gear, food, and firewood. I had brought a fitting companion for this adventure, Graham Greene's *Journey Without Maps*, an account of his
wanderings across the wilds of Liberia in the 1930s. I would have to
read by flashlight or flickering candle, as there was no electricity.

We drove for several hours out of Srinagar to reach the start of our
journey into the mountains. Our route began to climb right from the
trailhead. I wondered at what point we would cross the topographical
contour demarcating the ecological separation of the common leopard from its upland cousin. In 1983, conventional wisdom held that a
pugmark, or animal paw print, below 9,000 feet was always that of a
common leopard; between 9,000 and 12,000 feet, the owner of the
footprint could be a common leopard taking the high road at the upper edge of his territory or a snow leopard descending into the forest;
above 12,000 feet, and certainly above timberline, was the exclusive
kingdom of the snow lion. Today, we know that snow leopards descend
to relatively low altitudes and can be found at 2,000–4,500 feet in
Mongolia and China. GS and his Chinese colleagues found signs of
them in the wide, flat valleys between mountain ranges. I'm sure the
elevation at which you find them is partly influenced by prey availability. Snow leopards innately prefer the rocky outcrops, deep snow, and
broken terrain of the majestic high country. But if good dining exists
below, they don't mind the occasional foray to the lowlands.

Recent data from Bhutan shows that at times snow leopards may
coexist with tigers as well as with common leopards. Pralad Yonzon,
one of Nepal's first Ph.D. field biologists, took the first picture of a
tiger at 9,000 feet elevation in Bhutan using an infrared camera trap, a
point-and-shoot camera triggered by an infrared beam. In the eastern
Himalayas, tigers routinely walked up to timberline to feed on mountain ungulates like takin, deer, and serow, a kind of goat-antelope. This
intrusion into their hunting areas must make the much smaller snow
leopards most uncomfortable. Where they overlap, tigers routinely
kill common leopards if they can catch them, and naive snow leopards probably meet the same fate on occasion. Tigers probably never

ranged as far west as Zanskar, so where we were going, the local snow leopards just had to worry about wolves and herders chasing them from their kills, and, of course, the shadow of poachers.

I walked in front with several of Ullah's lieutenants and some forest guards. Helen was in the middle followed by a string of local porters. Ullah's men were still wearing their sport jackets but had switched to sneakers or light boots for the trek. Like most wildlife officials I have met in Asia, they never considered carrying their own packs; it was a sign of high status to hire a porter to do that work. They walked in single file with their transistor radios glued to one ear. An international cricket match was under way. India was playing against the team from the West Indies, if I remember correctly, and the great Kapil Dev was in fine form. Showing us snow leopards was the assignment from their boss, but it was not to interfere with the higher calling of cricket.

We stopped for tea at a village, and I tried a few words in Urdu. The villagers either couldn't understand my accent or spoke another language. A gang of small children swelled in the doorway, smiling while the mother and father served us steaming mugs of tea. I asked one of our guides how many children the couple had. I often do a quick sample whenever I am nearing a wild place to at least guess what the human pressures on the land may be at the time or in coming decades. I recalled what a Nepalese biologist once told me about mean household size in his native country: "The average size of a Himalayan family is eight: the father, mother, five children, and the anthropologist."

We trekked on for another few hours and then stopped for lunch, a quick meal of tea and puffy unleavened bread. Helen's cold was getting worse with the exertion, and her voice sounded a bit hoarse, though she said she felt fine. Outside on the trail, the porters and Ullah's men were having a small conference. The trail was getting steeper, and the sky had turned a leaden gray. Snow seemed in the offing. The porters wanted to be paid in advance, or they threatened to quit. Our leaders convinced them that that was not an option, and they reluctantly continued. How different they were from the porters

I had traveled with in the Nepal Himalayas. The dispositions of Tamangs, Magars, and other Nepali hill tribe groups would win anyone over. They could go all day in flip-flops or barefoot along snow-covered trails, carrying hundred-pound loads while loudly singing native folk songs. I always trudged behind with a much lighter load, trying to catch my breath in the thin air. Evenings with Nepali porters were a welcome treat after a day of traversing some of the steepest terrain in the world. Nepali is a language designed for telling jokes and stories and for nights around the campfire. But here in Kashmir, the porters were much less inquisitive and much less cheerful.

Sometime in the afternoon, a porter motioned me over to where he was crouching. At first I though he was urinating, for that is the posture many men in this part of the world use to pass water and maintain the illusion of privacy. But no, he wanted to show me something. I felt mild trepidation as I approached. Underneath his wool shawl, resting in his hands, was a traditional wicker basket holding charcoal embers. This was his own portable heater, and he was offering it to me. I thanked him and, being a first timer, made sure I didn't get the basket close enough to set my pants on fire. Within a few seconds, my whole lower half and chest were warm and comfortable even though the ambient temperature was close to freezing. I thanked him and wished him great health and strength for the journey ahead. The porter, Abdullah Masjid, merely smiled and told me to keep the basket. He would find another.

We stopped for dinner in a small village where we were to spend the night, the last settlement below the national park boundary. Above us was a nature reserve, where we would begin our search for leopards. Which park it was I wasn't even sure. *Journey Without Maps* was apt, indeed. None of Ullah's men had brought a map of our route, and the guards who were leading us had no need; they knew the network of trails by heart. Even now it is quite difficult, if not impossible, for foreigners to obtain official maps of border areas. After dinner, I tried to initiate a conversation with the wildlife officers about snow leopards and the park we were about to visit. But a recap of the day's cricket action took precedence, so I went to sleep. I woke several times to Helen's racking cough from across the room. I began to wonder if we should consider turning back.

We woke to a chilly dawn. The sun had abandoned us, and snow was a certainty. The only question was whether we would cross a mountain pass several miles above us before much snow had accumulated. I thought about asking Helen about the wisdom of proceeding, but she gave me the look of someone who wasn't about to back down and retreat to Srinagar. Onward.

Before we had been walking for an hour, it began snowing in earnest. At first, I felt exhilarated by the beautiful flakes sticking to the branches of the conifers. The pitchlike fragrance reminded me of hiking in the mountains of Colorado and Wyoming, but the mountain bird life was much more interesting here. There were beautiful tits (akin to New World chickadees) of several types lighting up the branches like animated Christmas decorations. And there was the possibility of coming across remarkable tragopans or cheer pheasants on our path.

It began to snow harder. Behind me, I couldn't see Helen's bright red parka anymore, but I kept walking, knowing she wouldn't want anyone to wait for her. The wildlife department officers were ahead of me, still in their sport coats and still with transistor radios plastered to their ears. Soon the reception would start to fade, and Kapil Dev and the Indian cricketers would be on their own, bowling without the fervent support of our companions.

I thought of something George Schaller had said to Peter Matthiessen on their expedition. Matthiessen was having trouble with his footing in the steep terrain of Dolpo. Schaller advised him to lift only one appendage at a time, either left foot, right foot, or walking staff, but not two of the three at once. How exciting it would have been to travel with GS, I thought. My own first encounter with him, two years earlier, had been at an international conference on deer biology, management, and conservation at the Smithsonian's Conservation and Research Center. There are thirty-seven species of deer in the world, and at least as many famous deer biologists were in attendance: Valerius Geist, the Russian-born ungulate expert; Tim Clutton-Brock, the British-born sociobiologist; John Eisenberg, the dean of American mammalogists; Dale McCollough, an elk specialist; my own professor, Richard Taber; and a host of other academic luminaries. It was my first big-time scientific conference, the one where you try not to stare at the name tags, jaw dropping as you attach the famous name to the face. There were rumors that Schaller was lurking somewhere, but I didn't know what he looked like. I was so nervous about my own presentation, scheduled as the first talk after the lunch break, that I spent most of the noon hour making trips to the men's room.

I entered the bathroom and took possession of the open urinal next to a relatively tall man with closely cropped graying hair. Something told me to summon my peripheral vision and peer at his name tag out of the corner of my eye. It was GS! I tried to remain calm and allow him time to wash and dry his hands. Then I summoned my entire reservoir of nerve for the next three years to timidly introduce myself. He was friendly and said he had enjoyed reading my trio of papers about the wildlife of Bardia National Park in Nepal. For nonbiologists, my reaction may be hard to fathom. It was like meeting Michael Jordan in a men's room attached to a basketball gym and having him say that he saw you out on the court earlier and that you could play some. I'm sure George doesn't remember our first meeting, but it's in my mental scrapbook. Forever. On its own page.

During the next two hours, the snow fell harder and harder. Perhaps it was snowing all over Kashmir. We kept climbing higher, and I soon realized we were heading into near whiteout conditions. I had been in whiteouts before, and I knew we had better find shelter soon. We were coming close to the pass, so I decided to wait for Helen. I waited for five minutes and then ten. Finally, she came along riding a small mountain horse being led by a porter, who had graciously stayed back to keep her company. She didn't look well but managed a game smile. For the first time, the heat and dust of Delhi seemed mildly appealing.

We made it over the pass, which could be discerned in the blizzard only when we suddenly started to descend. Then, just below the pass, we found shelter in a maharajah's old hunting lodge, much worse for wear but evidently used by herders on their way to summer pastures high in the Zanskar range. Under the rough shelter, Helen crawled straight into her sleeping bag. At one point along the narrow trail that day, she said, with a steep wall on one side and a drop-off on the other, her stirrup (a piece of metal and a braided rope) had got caught on a tree root jutting from the cliff. It yanked her sharply back and sideways, halfway out of the saddle. But instead of rearing or throwing her over the cliff, that little horse stayed put and let her work her foot back out. "I am very grateful to that horse," she confided, then turned over to sleep.

In the room next to ours, the porters built a small fire to keep warm. The heat from the wet logs stayed in their room, but all of the smoke drifted into ours. As I tossed about, I began to worry increasingly about Helen's health. Her racking cough made it difficult for her to sleep, and we had no medicine of any real value for her condition. The best treatment was to get down from the mountain.

We woke to a crystal clear morning, blue skies, and drifts of snow against a wall of evergreens. Helen was too focused to ponder the serenity of the landscape. She climbed out of her bag and onto the donkey, ready to move. Her face was pale, but she was determined to carry on. She wasn't GS, his iron constitution allowing him to push into remote places that few field biologists ever enter. But she had his iron will, and I felt a newfound admiration for her.

We were headed down the mountain paths and by the end of the day would reach the first settlement. One of the forest guards, breaking a trail through the snow ahead of the group, whistled for us to come forward. He had come upon a leopard's footprint, but at that elevation it was difficult to tell which species it was. Deep snow was not a problem for snow leopards as it was for us. They typically follow animal trails and are often quite active after a heavy accumulation. I wondered if the next hour would be our best, and perhaps last, chance to see one. We were somewhere near 10,000 feet, I guessed, still below timberline, but not by much. For all we knew, one could have been watching from a nearby boulder, tracking us with her unblinking green eyes. Helen had seen a pugmark on the way out that morning, too. It had looked to her very much like it was made by the forepaw of a snow leopard. "You were out of hearing, so I decided to take it at face value and be thankful that I may have crossed the path of a snow leopard," she reported.

Trudging through the knee-deep snow proved tiresome for us and the donkeys. But in a few miles or so, the snow would have melted and the trail would revert to the familiar crunch of bare soil. A snow leopard researcher and friend of mine once took a much longer walk in the snowy mountains around Juneau, Alaska. Joe Fox had preceded me in the Peace Corps in Nepal. But unlike me, who sweated out my two years in the lowlands, Joe sought higher ground and more physically challenging assignments. He was the Nepal Parks Department's volunteer for the newly created mountain parks: Langtang, Shey, and Lake Rara in the western Himalayas. He was a hit with the Nepalese for his sense of humor and unpretentious manner. With his bright red beard and hair and even brighter spirit, he was the life of the party. Upon returning to the States, he went to Alaska to study mountain goats. In 1980, he made the front page of every newspaper in Alaska, not for his scientific findings, but because of a life-altering event. While out radio-tracking his mountain goats, Joe had ventured too close to a steep, slippery snowfield. Before he knew it, he was sliding out of control down the precipice. With no way to arrest his fall, he went over the cliff, falling 1,500 feet. He landed in a snowbank, suffering only a broken arm, a dislocated shoulder, and a few bruises. The walk out must have been painful in the deep snow—he was miles from any road—but knowledge of his luck helped him along. Joe's good fortune—to fall on a deep pillow of snow, get up, and hit life's reset button—is an oft-told tale by those whose lives are full of similar risks.

Joe had always been interested in snow leopards and was deeply hopeful that Helen and I would obtain permission to launch a field study somewhere in India. As it turned out, getting permission to start up Joe's snow leopard study in Hemis National Park in the Indian state of Ladakh was one of the positive outcomes of our trip, and the result was one of the most thorough studies ever done of snow leopards. It was part of a collaboration Helen had fostered between the Jammu and Kashmir Wildlife Department, the Government of India, the Wildlife Institute of India, and the U.S. Fish and Wildlife Service International Affairs Office. One of the many interesting aspects of Joe's study was the competition he found between the snow leopard and the other large predator of the high Himalaya—the wolf—in the alpine meadows.

By now, our route was descending rapidly, and we clearly were not going to encounter wolves, marmots, or snow leopards. We were headed down the backside of the mountain, opposite the way we had ascended. I took some comfort in knowing that not a single snow leopard was seen on GS and Matthiessen's trek to the Crystal Mountain, or in the first four months of Rod and Gary's study in the Langu Gorge, or in Joe Fox's entire first stint in Nepal's Himalayan Parks. Like tigers in the lowlands, or Javan or Sumatran rhinos, this was a species that did not often show itself to strangers. A biologist had to devote everything—or be unbelievably lucky—even to gain a glimpse.

We returned to Srinagar by way of a guard post, where we had a refreshing lunch. Helen seemed better but still weak. After a night's rest, we were taken on a tour of the Gulmarg area, which, though better known for its ski resort (a rarity in the Himalayas), was a gateway to one of the disputed boundary areas between Pakistan and India. Much has been written about the surreal atmosphere surrounding the world's highest war. On the edge of a glacier, above 18,000 feet, Indian and Pakistani troops occasionally lob mortar rounds at each other, exchange fire, and then retreat shivering to their bunkers, only to repeat the madness all over again when they are given the command. One has to wonder what lunacy, other than pride, would possess officials in Delhi and Islamabad to send so many troops up to this godforsaken stretch of ice and rock. The confrontation over the forbidding glaciers and avalanche-prone mountain slopes reminded me of the war fought over the Falkland Islands between Great Britain and Argentina, a conflict that Jorge Luis Borges aptly described as "two bald men fighting over a comb."

Between the two opposing camps is a no-man's land that no sane yak herder or lost mountaineer would dare cross. The only year-round residents are pikas, rabbit-like creatures of the high mountains; the whistling marmots; and maybe a snow leopard or two.

Wildlife often flourishes in demilitarized zones around the world (such as the haven for endangered cranes and other rare species between South and North Korea) because would-be poachers and other human trespassers are considered infiltrators and shot on sight. Once the animals realize the armies are not aiming at them, they quickly reclaim the area and flourish.

The creation of policies to protect snow leopards was a key part of Helen's agenda, as much as setting up a field research program. The next day, we discussed one of her proposed programs with Ullah, and later, in Kathmandu, we would share the idea with Nepalese officials. It involved protecting key breeding areas for snow leopards in mountain valleys free from livestock grazing. A second program involved places where snow leopards came in contact with grazers: Compensation schemes could be established for domestic livestock killed by snow leopards, she suggested. In theory, payment should rarely be necessary, given the snow leopard's proclivity to stay away from human settlements. But, in reality, there is not a single alpine valley in the Himalayas, even in national parks, that is not grazed to some extent in the summer by yaks, buffalo, sheep, or goats. Given this high level of contact, even if wolves may be a greater menace to domestic animals in some areas, occasional predation by leopards is a near certainty. In Mongolia, for example, GS reported that horses and domestic yaks, especially the foals and calves, are heavily pursued by leopards. Rod Jackson and Madan Oli, a Nepalese biologist, found that snow leopards in Nepal commonly feed on sheep and goats when they get the opportunity. Not surprisingly, herders retaliate, killing snow leopards.

To poor villagers, livestock predation is but one more cruel test of survival in an unforgiving environment. Helen and the International Snow Leopard Trust were thus pushing the adoption of compensation schemes to livestock herders in lieu of retaliation against the leopards. Of course, for such schemes to work, officials must be able to verify that snow leopards were responsible for livestock losses and ensure that herders weren't inadvertently encouraged to penetrate deeper into near-pristine snow leopard habitat. The compensation schemes are now in place and working.

Long term, the best solution I see for snow leopards in the poor nations of Asia is to make the cats worth more to local people alive than dead. Trekking across the snow leopards' range can be big business. If a percentage of the park entry fees and hotel concession profits were reserved for conservation, the money necessary for compensation, as Helen has proposed, could be generated locally. Money, even in small amounts, speaks loudly. As soon as villagers realize that they would receive a percentage of the profits from the trekking industries, their attitudes could change overnight; this is an approach that has worked successfully with tigers in communities bordering reserves in lowland Nepal.

Still another threat that puts snow leopards under great pressure is the value of their fur, which is sold in the bazaars in and around many Asian capitals, including Srinagar. An even greater concern is the use of snow leopard bones as a substitute for tiger bones in traditional Oriental medicines. With the growth in tiger farms in China to meet this demand and pressure from conservation organizations to find effective substitutes for tiger and snow leopard bones, this threat may diminish in coming years.

Helen and I walked through the narrow streets of Srinigar's old bazaar. Above us, old men sat in windowsills embroidering traditional scarves. In tiny wooden stalls, beautiful hand-sewn clothes and crafts were exhibited for sale. Aggressive carpet salesmen cajoled us to come have a look at their wares. A good price for you, they promised. We were on the lookout for snow leopard skins or animal bones, but none were on display that day.

It was time to bid Director Ullah farewell and thank him once again for his hospitality. I hoped then that his ambitions for wildlife tourism in Kashmir would pan out. Indeed, in the early 1980s, before the debacle of war ended access, this kingdom of saffron and snow leopards was one of the most romantic places on earth. But his plan for peaceful development was not to begin anytime soon. A few years after we visited Srinagar, Kashmir became a bloody battleground between Pakistan-backed separatists fighting for independence from India, and the Indian Army troops sent in to restore peace. The next decade was anything but tranquil. Two wars were fought to standoffs. A few foreigners, one a field biologist, were kidnapped. Tourism withered and died. However, as of January 2005, new talks between India and Pakistan offered some hope for a peaceful resolution and a more secure future for snow leopards.

So did new conservation plans for the region. Together with George Schaller, Rod, Joe, Pralad Yonzon, Mingma Norbu Sherpa, Eric Wikramanayake, and many other Asian and non-Asian biologists, I helped develop a vision for conservation of the Himalayas that focused considerable effort on establishing a network of reserves to protect snow leopards and other endangered montane species. One part of our study revealed that, as in North America, the existing national parks and reserves of the Himalayas do a magnificent job of preserving scenic mountain landscapes (or what some cynics refer to as "rock and ice") but are less effective in protecting the more diverse areas that are more valuable to humans for livestock grazing and high-elevation farming of barley and millet. Based on that concern, WWF and its partners developed a plan for the Himalayas that, if implemented, would extend protection for snow leopards and other montane species much farther down the slopes from the existing parks. Then, with the help of scientists who had combed the Himalayas, we designed altitudinal corridors from the lowlands to the alpine and trans-Himalayan areas along the edge of the Tibetan Plateau. These linkage zones are vital to many seasonal altitudinal migrants—species that inhabit different altitudes at different times of the year—and in the event of climate change, could offer refuge for species to reestablish their original ranges.

Helen retired officially from the Woodland Park Zoo in the late 1980s to run the Snow Leopard Trust full-time. During her tenure, captive breeding and snow leopard longevity in zoos had improved greatly, and she now wanted to work full-time, rather than what her job as education curator would allow, to improve conservation of snow leopards in their natural habitat. She later wrote to me that "the inspiration to make this decision came on a camping and hiking trip to Alaska. We were in Denali National Park, sitting at Polychrome Pass. The natural magnificence and vast panorama were so overwhelming, I could almost hear it calling to me, 'Go to the wild, go to the wild.' So I did." Under Helen's direction, the Snow Leopard Trust funded research and conservation efforts across the entire range of this great cat: From the mountains of the Altai-Sayan in Russia, to the high plains of Mongolia; from the Zanskar range in the west to the Bhutan Himalayas in the east, the snow leopard, and snow leopard biologists, had found their patron.

Our trip to Asia had expanded Helen's role as the roving ambassador on behalf of snow leopards and other endangered wildlife that cling precariously to the roof of the world. But from the day we began our Zanskar trek, Helen's health deteriorated, and she never fully recovered. Not until we were back in the United States did we learn that she had contracted pneumonia. Today, she gamely keeps up her effort while relying on a handy oxygen tank and breathing tubes. In 1983, she had no idea she might risk her life to save the species she loved so passionately. The truth is, I don't think knowing that would have dissuaded her from going. Every endangered species needs a Helen Freeman, at least one valiant person determined to turn the tide, at whatever personal cost.

In the years since, I have given talks at a variety of venues about endangered species conservation. Invariably, at the end of the lecture, among others, a cluster of women approaching midlife, often with children in tow, migrate to the stage and inquire, "What can I do? How can I make a difference? I'm just a housewife with two kids." Whenever I hear that question, I think of my intrepid companion being led on horseback through the deep snow into a blinding whiteout, searching for the wild snow leopard. I tell them of what Helen accomplished to conserve this magical cat and its habitat for future generations and what she does to this day, even if somewhat slowed by her respiratory problems. I share with them what she said to me when she slipped off her horse, weak from pneumonia, at the end of our trek to Zanskar. Her blue eyes sparkled with fierce pride, and she said, "Not bad for a former housewife from Bellevue, Washington." Not bad, Helen. Not bad at all.

PART TWO

FURTHER DETOURS

chapter four

LAST VOYAGE OF CAPTAINCOOKIA

BEFORE THE COUP D'ÉTAT OF VIDEO GAMES, CHILDREN PLAYED
with globes. Where is Outer Mongolia? How did Marco Polo
reach China? The caress of small hands back and forth over a large
globe summoned the genie of childhood fantasy. In my own game, I
would close my eyes and spin it like a planetary roulette wheel, then
press my finger against it to brake its rotation and point to my new
destination. More than once I had to pack my imaginary bags for
Yakutia, the stretch of Siberian tundra where temperatures have been
known to reach –60°F. My descent into the tropical latitudes was just
as risky. The forbidding Simian Mountains of Ethiopia and the remote
Amazonian rain forests both had their set of dangers and adventures.
Most often, though, I found myself adrift in the Pacific Ocean. During
the dull summer days of childhood, I must have spun my globe a hundred times or more. But never in all those revolutions had I ventured

where, some forty years later, my plane was now about to touch down: the island of New Caledonia. And should my finger have landed on this tiny speck in the Coral Sea, I would never have imagined my great luck.

The Air Nouvelle Caledonie jet departed from Brisbane, Australia, and flew due east for seven hundred miles over unbroken ocean. The pile of scientific papers, maps, and field guides on the empty seat next to me grew ever higher through the two-hour flight, as I crammed in as much information as possible in advance of our landing. As the plane dipped over the brilliant blue water on our approach, a long barrier reef came into view, encircling the island like a coral necklace. When the jet banked toward land, the color changed to green, as groves of tall, geometric-shaped monkey puzzle trees, the signature species of this ancient island, came into view. When Captain James Cook "discovered" this tiny southwest Pacific outpost in 1774, he named it New Caledonia, using the ancient Roman epithet of his father's native land. Was it merely a sentimental gesture to a faraway homeland or did he notice a resemblance to Scotland? Perhaps it was the monkey puzzles, which I suppose, as distant relatives of pines and firs, summoned up Scotland in the great explorer's mind.

In truth, this island more closely resembles South Africa, bits of the southern cone of South America, Australia, New Guinea, New Zealand, and even Madagascar, which, like New Caledonia, are all former pieces of the southern supercontinent of Gondwanaland. That giant land mass ruptured more than 200 million years ago into fragments separated farther by the earth's shifting plates. When the smaller continents and large islands drifted apart, they carried with them a breakaway colony of Gondwanaland's ancient plants and animals. Its Gondwanaland origin, plus long isolation, has given New Caledonia a flora and fauna so distinct and so ancient that they eclipse those of many of the more celebrated places on earth. Yet nine out of ten biologists can't even find it on a map, and hardly any have ever visited.

The lucky few who have visited return home in rapture about an arkful of bizarre species, such as the only parasitic species of conifer tree and the world's grandest gecko, a foot-long monster that, in the absence of terrestrial mammals, is the island's largest predator. More than 3,200 plant species spill over the islands that make up New Caledonia. Together, those islands are equal in size to New Jersey, yet the so-called Garden State boasts not a single plant restricted to it, while 2,500 species of rare plants can be found on this isolated splinter of Gondwanaland in the southwest Pacific and nowhere else in the wild. The idea of a species restricted to a single place or small geographic area is captured in a single word that conservation biologists value enormously: *endemism*. A founding principle of conservation biology and biogeography holds that endemism is not equally distributed globally; rather, it is concentrated far more in some places than in others. Another fundamental observation is that the threats of habitat loss, fragmentation, and degradation—the tools of an antinature Shiva—are also unevenly at work. Thus, one way of focusing on where to act first to save rare nature is to look for those places that are the most irreplaceable biologically, as measured in part by levels of endemism, and that are most threatened by habitat decline. There is enough plant endemism here that New Caledonia should be considered if not the world's seventh floral kingdom—after the Antarctic, Australasian, Boreal, Neotropic, Paleotropic, and Cape Floral Kingdoms—then at least a floral dukedom. And it is perhaps the most endangered dukedom on earth.

Most biologists and conservationists and even many subscribers to *National Geographic* can locate the Amazon, the Galápagos, or the Serengeti on a map of the world. With such high name recognition and attention, it's no surprise that those areas have been the main focus of global conservation efforts. New Caledonia presents a more difficult challenge. How do you conserve a place that few people in the world have ever heard of and almost no one can find on a map? Even more difficult, how do you promote global concern for a place best known for its weird plants rather than charismatic vertebrates, like elephants, tigers, and polar bears? I had to remind myself that though prehistoric dinosaurs are no longer around, the ancient vegetation of monkey puzzle and kauri trees, cycads, palms, screw palms, tree ferns, and other primitive plants were all still here. For the first time in my life, I would walk through forests that dinosaurs knew well.

That Captain Cook "discovered" New Caledonia in 1774 is a Western indulgence. Melanesians first settled the islands more than 3,500 years ago. They must have been startled when they ventured from their outriggers and stumbled onto the native fauna. They would have encountered giant monitor lizards and terrestrial crocodiles lumbering about like dinosaurs. Towering *Agathis* trees, known as kauris, so large they were thought to be possessed by spirits, formed an imposing backdrop. The toxic soils that underlay this weird forest must have made farming a futile endeavor, however; the Melanesians surely didn't realize that the nickel- and cadmium-rich soils, especially in the mountains of the main island of Grand Terre, held buried treasure that the world would someday covet.

In Nouméa, the capital, I was greeted warmly by Arnaud Greth, a charming, mop-haired man in his mid-thirties. His warm, sleepy eyes belied his boundless energy and passion for nature. He had the build of a French alpinist and was indeed an avid hiker. He had recently assumed the position of director of science and conservation at WWF-France. He recognized the importance of conserving nature in the *Outres-Mers*, the French overseas territories—French Guiana, the islands of Mayotte in the Indian Ocean, and New Caledonia, to name a few. Annexed by France in 1853, New Caledonia became an overseas territory, as it remains today, in 1946. The French settlers, known as Caldoche, still dominate the southern part of Grand Terre, an area called Province Sud, while the Melanesian descendants known as Kanak live semiautonomously in Province Nord and the Loyalté Islands off the coast.

Arnaud had invited me and fellow WWF biologists David Olson and Linda Farley (husband and wife) on a "petite expedition" across New Caledonia. Smart, abundantly cheerful, and ready for adventure, Arnaud might have distinguished himself in the French Foreign Legion, had he lived in a previous era. A veterinarian and wildlife biologist by training, he spent two years working in the Gabon rain forest, in a coastal reserve famous for its surf-loving hippos and elephants that, escaping the humid forests, loll in the Atlantic waves. At the other climatic extreme, he spent four years in the Saudi deserts helping to reestablish oryx and other species of antelope that once flourished there. Nothing could please him more than to strap on a rucksack filled with French bread, some pâté, a bottle of wine and some water and spend all day marching through the wettest rain forests on the island in search of giant geckos or kagus—rare, near-mystical endemic birds.

We would be on the hunt for the record-breaking geckos in a counterclockwise natural history expedition of Grand Terre. We would leave Nouméa and head south and east to the few parks in Province Sud and then drive up through the wettest parts of the island on the east coast. We would drive to the island's north tip and there come about and run with the cool breezes of the Coral Sea behind us as we made our way along the dry western coast. Finally, after a few days of searching for intact examples of the rarest forests on earth, the New Caledonia tropical dry forests, we would have a chance to explore New Caledonia's vast, largely intact coral reef. My joy at the prospect of seeing a new world down under the equator's belt was tempered only by the urgency of our mission.

Before we could immerse ourselves in New Caledonia's natural glory, we had to take care of some official business in Nouméa. Arnaud, together with Marcel Boulet, the head of the park service in Province Sud, had arranged for an afternoon meeting with the territory's top conservation officials and scientists at the Province Sud

Parks Department. For the first time in my professional life, I felt as much cheerleader as biologist. The local scientists and conservationists seemed somewhat surprised that outsiders should be so interested in their backyard. We rolled out maps of the Global 200 ecoregions, the places on earth—terrestrial, freshwater, and marine—that David and I, along with help from many of the world's best scientists, had identified as the top priorities for global biodiversity conservation. We highlighted tiny New Caledonia's global importance to nature conservation and its core role in the Global 200, as represented by four outstanding ecoregions: its dry forests, wet forests, freshwater rivers and streams, and coral reef. Arnaud then explained that we had come to seek their advice and to hear how we could be of help in local conservation efforts.

Instead of a lively discussion about opportunities for conservation, however, we listened while they explained their challenges and frustrations. First and foremost were the devastating effects of mining, which had been visible from my airplane window. New Caledonia supplies more than 40 percent of the world's nickel, and not merely coincidentally it is home to some of the worst soil erosion in the world. To expose the nickel, earth movers push away the tops of the mountains, which are euphemistically called the "overburden," burying the unique and rare vegetation, exposing bare slopes, and silting up the streams. Ultimately, toxic-laden sediments pollute the coral reefs.

Next, the scientists and conservation officials there described the rampant burning and clearing of the tropical dry forests. A plague of dry season fires set by hunters to expose deer and other game had degraded native forests into savannas dominated by *Melaleuca* trees, far beyond their natural occurrence. The tropical dry forests on Grand Terre alone had shrunk dramatically, making that particular habitat one of the most endangered on earth. Furthermore, the spread of invasive species, such as a booming population of rusa deer imported from Indonesia, was destroying the native vegetation. Argentine ants and introduced land snails were pushing out the native species in the last pockets of dry forest. Fifty *million* years of mostly tranquil isolation and evolution had come to an end.

Most serious of all, however, was the general apathy of the local populace, the French government, and conservation donors. Every political decision and new initiative in the territory seemed subservient to King Nickel. Major donors for conservation had shown little interest in lending financial support to this island because it belongs to a rich member nation of the G-7. Yet in 1997, like the ignored stepchild of a wealthy family, New Caledonia received precious few francs from the French government, and hardly much more today in 2005. This was particularly frustrating because even a modest amount of money from the government or a private donor could make a huge difference; the number of rare species protected per dollar invested must be among the highest anywhere. I sat there silently, wondering how I could attract the interest of a U.S. donor to such a faraway place with so many unfamiliar species. The three-hour meeting felt like one long fatalistic shrug. Thanking them for their time and insights, we pledged to encourage our organization and other donors to become more involved in trying to conserve what remained of an island that has rightly been called the Madagascar of the South Pacific.

Had Diane Arbus been a nature photographer, she would have found a wealth of subjects in Madagascar and New Caledonia. Both islands are populated by evolution's freak show, a collection of giants and midgets and odd things in between. When Madagascar split off from Africa perhaps 180 million years ago, it carried with it prehistoric lemurs. Only forty species of that primitive primate remain from the many more that once existed. Some are called mouse lemurs, so tiny they can fit in the palm of your hand. At the other end of the scale were the now extinct mega-lemurs that reached the size of modern-day gorillas. Like the mega-lemurs, the elephant bird, also extinct, which could have looked down on the modern-day ostrich, exhibited the biological phenomenon known as gigantism, a feature typical on islands where there is an absence of competitors. To top it off, Madagascar boasts eight massive species of odd-looking baobabs, the trees that appear to grow with their roots in the air. Compare this to Africa, which has just one representative.

New Caledonia, like its sister island Madagascar, could fill up its own wall calendar of weird animals. When the island left the Australian coast 85 million years ago, it harbored giant tortoises that sported cowlike horns and armorlike plates on the feet and tail. Then there was *Mekosuchus inexpectatus,* a terrestrial, short-snouted crocodile that fed on land snails. That sounds like a hard way for a crocodile to make a living, but some of New Caledonia's land snails were giants in their own right. Today, the largest living species of land snail found on the Isles des Pins and the Loyalté Islands off the coast of Grand Terre measure six inches long and weigh up to a quarter of a pound—a mighty escargot. Grand Terre had no elephant birds, but it did have giant kagus, the extinct relatives of the remaining near-flightless species we were to see in the Province Sud rain forest parks. The giant kagu, in contrast to the extant smaller kagu species, lived in the dry coastal forests until a few centuries ago, when the last individual probably ended up in a fricassee. One giant bird, the world's largest arboreal pigeon, the notou (*Ducula goliath*), has persisted. But it is heavily hunted and considered threatened; like its gigantic compatriots, it may soon disappear completely.

A common feature of many Pacific Islands is the conspicuous lack of one or more major vertebrate groups, which either never made it to the islands in the first place or never became established. In New Caledonia, for example, there are no native amphibians or terrestrial mammals, although there are nine species of bats. In the absence of native terrestrial mammals, lizards went wild: New Caledonia now has sixty-eight species of lizards, sixty of which are endemic, an amazing number for such a small scrap of land. Even with nearly seventy species, however, virtually every terrestrial lizard is either a kind of gecko or a kind of skink, the monitors and crocodiles having disappeared. The best example of supersized island lizards is on the island of Komodo in Indonesia, where the Komodo dragons are the top predators (these "dragons" reach ten feet in length and one hundred pounds in mass). The New Caledonia giant gecko, *Rhacodactylus leachianus,* is the largest gecko in the world and, although a midget compared to a Komodo dragon, is still the apex predator of Grande Terre. The giant gecko might have to share that title with the world's largest skink, although that New Caledonia endemic has not been seen in more than a century. On islands such as Komodo and Grand Terre, lizards are the top predators. Thus, those islands are reminiscent of dinosaur-dominated ecosystems, where the local mammals had to be small and stealthy, because they were not at the top of the food chain.

I was eager to get going the next morning, but sleepy Nouméa was still in its bathrobe. We would not be heading out until after a late breakfast, so with a mixture of glee and disappointment, I headed down to a nearby café for fresh-baked croissants, jam, and café au lait. From up the street came a sound totally unexpected but familiar. Not a birdcall, but the mechanical whir of racing bicycles approaching at great speed. An early morning peloton of bike racers bedecked in vibrantly colored jerseys whizzed past. I waved and shouted, "Alléz!" the encouraging cry of Tour de France fans. For a moment, I wished I could join them—riding with local bike racers is my second greatest passion after natural history. I was now bonding with New Caledonia culturally as well as scientifically.

Arnaud offered a hearty "Bonjour, mes amis" to David, Linda, and me as we grabbed our field gear. He was staying with his sister and brother-in-law, both doctors who had moved from Paris to Nouméa to set up practice in this far-flung French outpost. It turned out not at all to be the "hardship" post they anticipated. New Caledonia may have the most favorable climate in the world. The Pacific trade winds gently bathe the islands in soft, cool breezes, and the thermometer hovers around 70°F year-round. The views of the reefs are superb, and you can snorkel from your front door. The fabulous natural history on land and on the reef, the gracious comfort of French culture, and the chance to hang with the local bike racers made me feel like I had found the perfect place to retire. Geologically, New Caledonia is an offshoot of Australia and Gondwanaland, but in many other aspects, it seems like a piece of the French Riviera cut adrift.

The chauffeur, guide, and self-appointed raconteur for the first part of our visit was Marcel Boulet, head of the parks board. A tall, distinguished man with a shock of white hair, he ushered us into his car, and we headed into another New Caledonia, leaving behind the western overlay of Nouméa and entering an ancient landscape, almost unrecognizable as the same planet. A feeling came over me that I had experienced before only in Papua New Guinea and the upland forests of Hawaii's Big Island. Everything seemed different. Everything *was* different. Once we entered the habitat known as *maquis miniers,* the scrublike vegetation common to areas underlain by the famous toxic soils, I couldn't recognize a single plant. I pride myself on having at least a passing knowledge of the plants I find in any new destination. The New Caledonia flora made me feel like I needed to study botany all over again, or at least the lectures on gymnosperms and other ancient plant groups.

The elongated island of Grand Terre, especially the southern third, has an extremely diverse geology characterized by *ultramafic* soils, meaning substrates rich in heavy metals, Marcel explained. Nickel, cobalt, manganese, magnesium, chromium, and other metals "contaminate" the soils of the maquis miniers, yet the region is full of rare plants. The development of adaptations to such nutrient-poor earth often leads to extensive speciation in flowering plants as well as in insects, land snails, and other invertebrates. The island's varied climate and topography also contribute to the abundant plant life. Grand Terre is essentially a mountain chain that runs down the center of the island, with five peaks that exceed 4,500 feet in height. Many smaller ranges and valleys crisscross the island's northwest-southeast orientation, creating isolated pockets of biological treasures waiting to be discovered by motivated naturalists.

As we traveled through New Caledonia's outback, our group ticked off the island's other botanical virtues. The first is "high taxonomic diversity": New Caledonia has 196 plant families, 5 of which are endemic, both extraordinary numbers for such a small island. On top of that, nearly 14 percent of the plant genera are endemic.

We drove past forests dominated by monkey puzzle trees like those I'd seen from the plane—tall, straight trees with branches covered in sharp, needle-like leaves, a backdrop often used for dinosaur flicks. The name comes from the observation that it would puzzle a monkey to figure a way to climb these spiny trees. Monkey puzzle trees (family, Araucariaceae) have an ancient lineage dating back to the time before flowering plants arrived on the scene. They are also an example of extraordinary endemism, diversity, and now, rarity in nature. There are two dozen species in this genus worldwide, and of those, nineteen are endemic to New Caledonia. As for rarity: Marcel showed us one tall individual along a mining concession road that he said represented 50 percent of the entire known population. The road was soon to be widened, and he refused to speculate on the future of this proud ancient plant. I hoped that someone was collecting its seeds. The Araucarias belong to the group called gymnosperms, the primitive non-flowering plants that include conifers. Gymnosperms are remarkably varied in New Caledonia; there are forty-four species, forty-three of which are endemic. That is arguably the highest diversity of conifers and conifer-related plants in the world, and certainly represents the highest endemism.

We stepped out of the car and into the rain forest of Rivière Bleue National Park. Besides the unusual gymnosperms, there were strange plants that lack internal vessels to transport nutrients. Early-flowering plants lack vessels, and the New Caledonia flora is full of such primitives. One such plant is called *Amborella trichopoda,* the only species in its family (Amborellaceae) and is one of the closest living relatives to the first flowering plants.

As we walked through the forest, it started to rain. Marcel led us down a slippery trail, at the bottom of which was an enormous kauri tree, which is found throughout Queensland and parts of the southwest Pacific and might be compared to the giant sequoias in the Sierra Nevada of California. Kauris are the titans of the forest and were worshipped by some native groups who believed they were possessed by spirits. This particular towering monarch was reported to be over a thousand years old. Tragically, most of the giant kauris have been felled because their wood is so valuable. A few still stand and may continue to do so for another thousand years if the government takes steps to protect these goliaths of the island.

Marcel walked up to a large tree near the kauri and made a deep slash in the bark with his machete. I winced at his act of vandalism. The blade was too large to carve his initials, and I didn't think that was his intention. I walked up to see the gash, and a bright blue latex, of a hue favored by Matisse, oozed out of the cut. The tree we were looking at was a cobalt-loving species in the dogbane family, and up to 20 percent of the tree was full of that toxic element. There were also nickel- and manganese-loving trees in the forest, one a wild species of macadamia. I thought it seemed suicidal for a leaf-eating creature to chew on such plants—then I realized that was the idea.

In the rain and wind, we moved on to the Chutes de la Madeleine, another important park for conserving the assortment of odd plants hidden away in Province Sud. Along the route, Marcel introduced us to the world's only parasitic conifer (*Parasitaxus ustus*), a cone-bearing plant that takes its sustenance by tapping the tissues of other plants. I suppose if there is to be a parasitic cone-bearing plant, New Caledonia is a good place for it. The park was near the Plaine des Lacs, and there were small waterfalls everywhere. Besides stunted gymnosperms, there were insect-eating pitcher plants and sundews, another odd specimen that catches bugs for food. Toxic soils also boast an impressive number of carnivorous flowering plants. If you can't tap nutrients from the soil like a normal plant, you have to improvise. And that's just what the sensuous-looking sundews and bulbous pitcher plants do in the maquis.

Besides the blue latex from the cobalt tree, Matisse would have admired the color we were turning: red. Not from the exertion of keeping up with Arnaud and Marcel or from the tropical sun, but from the maquis miniers soil itself, which coats everything in an ochre-colored dust. Like a true naturalist, Arnaud spent much of his time off the trails, and by the end of the day, he looked ready to do the full Monty in a Nouméa launderette. Eventually, even he had to call it a day, and we headed back to town.

The director of the zoological gardens, Christophe Lambert, who had participated in our Nouméa meeting, insisted we pay him a visit, and the next day we did so. The zoo turned out to be a small park next to the botanical gardens on a rise above Nouméa. We first toured the gardens, which offered an impressive collection of native cycads, screw palms (*Pandanus* trees), true palms, tree ferns, kauris, and monkey puzzles: a celebration of gymnosperms.

Two small exhibits at the zoo were of particular distinction. The first held the attractive Ouvea parakeet, also known as the horned parakeet, which sports a jaunty head crest. The bird is limited to the island of Ouvea, one of the Loyalté Isles off the east coast of Grand Terre. Aside from loss of habitat, the Ouvea parakeet is threatened by capture for the pet trade. For another species in the parrot family, the New Caledonian lorikeet, it may be too late. Many ornithologists consider the species to have gone extinct in the last century. But more optimistic scientists say that the last stronghold for this species is on Mont Panié on the northeast coast, a stop on our itinerary. Of the 350 members of a family that includes parrots, parakeets, parrotlets, macaws, lorikeets, lories, lovebirds, cockatoos, and cockatiels, more than 20 percent are found exclusively on small islands, and many of them are endangered from loss of habitat and the pet trade.

Unlike the ancient plants that dominate the local flora, the birds of New Caledonia are mainly examples of modern, or recently evolved, forms. One ancient family, however, the Rhynochetidae, is endemic to New Caledonia, and it is currently represented by a single species, the famed kagu. The kagu is the national bird of New Caledonia and is listed as endangered by the world body that evaluates the status and protection of species, the Species Survival Commission of the World Conservation Union (IUCN). There are other endangered birds on the islands—a rail and an owlet-nightjar, to name a couple—but none command attention like the kagu. Fanatical ornithologists from around the world make a pilgrimage to this island to get a mere glimpse. No more than a thousand remain in the wild, with the main concentration in Riviére Bleue. The few we were about to see were kept in a special enclosure at the zoo.

A bird lover meeting his or her first kagu is like a Beatles fan gaining an audience with Ringo. The excitement of the encounter leaves you shaking. Both the formerly mop-headed drummer and the kagu have an abundance of a certain *je ne sais quoi,* but you wouldn't call them handsome. Ringo is no Paul, and the kagu is no golden pheasant. Rather, the kagu resembles a ghostly gray, somewhat overweight night heron with a gaudy orange-red bill and feet. As we approached the kagu in the enclosure, we came too close, triggering a threat display. The male erected his long shaggy crest, spread his wings to expose some striking black and white barring, and uttered a series of hissing sounds that reminded me of a point-and-shoot camera rewinding. In truth, the kagu would be considered comical if it weren't so rare and endangered, and if the threat posture weren't its only defense against the feral dogs that hunt them.

Done with our visit to the gardens, we headed for the jeep and the road leading south. Nouméa resembled a city along the Mediterranean coast, yet the scrublands outside the capital, in the maquis miniers, were far less picturesque than the lovely French country-side. The spindly, narrow-leaved branches of the scruffy-looking shrubs couldn't compare with the cypress and citrus of Provence or the interplay of chateaux and forests along the Loire. The French countryside is among the loveliest on earth, as advertised by a generation of impressionist painters. Yet if one were to inventory the species of pastoral northern France, it would seem depauperate, like the rest of northern Europe. A large part of that continent was once covered by glaciers, and when they retreated, generally uninteresting, low-diversity beech forest sprang up. The maquis miniers, for all its scraggly appearance, holds more species of endemic plants than all of chateaux country. What an irony: Low-species-diversity habitats are lovingly painted and revered, and high-diversity zones like rain forests seldom get the attention they deserve from poets and painters, excepting the occasional Henri Rousseau.

If we were to try to change the attitudes of French officials about the wild places on the globe that urgently needed their attention, we would have to understand the perspective with which they approach the natural world. Arnaud explained that the French idea of nature is of nature serene and beautiful, but also carefully manicured to the point it has lost its wildness.

We waited at the gate of Rivière Bleue to rendezvous with Yves Le Tocquart. Yves was not yet there, but in the parking lot to greet us was a once white mongrel dog covered in splotches of ochre. "Regarde, le chien de maquis," joked Arnaud. We all missed our dogs back home and stooped down to pet the friendly mutt. Would this same animal spend his afternoon hunting defenseless kagus? To be a committed dog lover and a biologist often causes much internal conflict on islands where terrestrial mammalian predators never occurred until humans brought them along.

Suddenly, a car pulled up, and a man in what I guessed to be his mid-sixties jumped out to greet us. Yves apologized for arriving late, but he had a good excuse. He had been trying to locate some radio-tagged kagus to show us, and he had found some, so we raced off. At the edge of the forest, we pulled into a picnic area and got out. Yves surprised us by sinking to his hands and knees. He picked up a stick and started making scraping sounds on the leaves carpeting the forest floor. Instantly, two powder-blue rooster-sized birds came charging out of the forest. I thought that this territorial pair of kagus had come to see if a nosy neighbor had strayed too far onto their turf. It turns out that Yves had habituated this pair to come running to him. He could thus check on their breeding status and other aspects of their biology, and he could also more easily please the hordes of "life list" birders who arrive merely to see this rare bird so they can check it off and then quickly head to the next Pacific island.

Perhaps it was my imagination, but the pair of kagus I saw in the wild, even though habituated to the call of their guardian, appeared far lovelier than the birds we saw in the zoo at Nouméa. Their feathers seemed a luxuriant, opalescent bluish white instead of ghostly gray, and their bills and feet shone a more vibrant shade of red. Something flew into a *Vitex* tree near the picnic table. There, in all its glory, was a notou, the world's largest arboreal pigeon. It was not as colorful as some of the vivid fruit pigeons of the South Pacific, but it made up in size what it lacked in show-stopping plumage. We felt torn between the rare kagus and the equally rare king of arboreal pigeons.

We drove around until darkness fell. Yves suggested we go back to his cabin deep in the forest, eat dinner, then venture out on foot to listen for giant geckos. Ravenously hungry, I was looking forward to the food Arnaud had arranged for our week-long trip around Grand Terre. I had imagined that, as a Parisian, he would have gathered a cornucopia of portable delicacies: wonderfully smelly cheeses, rich pâtés, delicate pastries, deep, complex bottles of Bordeaux. Instead, we unpacked loaves of overly spongy French bread, cheap wine in a carton, and processed cheese.

I had forgiven Arnaud and was washing the dishes with him, when a question occurred to me, one that could earn me the guillotine by the French scientific establishment. "Arnaud," I asked, "why is it that except for rare individuals like you and Yves, there are so few French field biologists or amateur naturalists compared to the number in England?" I went on: "I mean, you cross the English Channel and everyone and their cousin can recite the common and Latin names of every British bird. Why is it that the two most famous British scientists were Charles Darwin and Alfred Russel Wallace, the fathers of the theory of evolution and some of the greatest scientists to ever handle a butterfly net? Whereas France's chief scientific luminaries, Louis Pasteur and Marie Curie (who was actually Polish), made their great discoveries in a laboratory?"

Arnaud shrugged. "My friend, the answer is simple: It's the lifestyle." Here is my translation of his somewhat tongue-in-cheek theory. First, French cuisine is among the finest in the world, and British food is widely acknowledged to be a few notches below awe inspiring. Second, the Mediterranean climate of the southern part of France is perhaps the most comfortable on earth. The English countryside is lovely, and it's as manicured as the French *paysage,* but you seldom get to enjoy it in sunshine. So with their bad food and rotten weather, British scientists and naturalists are preadapted to thrive in the wildlands of the world, from the sweltering tropics to the icebound poles, and glad to get away from their confining island of few species. The French, on the other hand, would miss their extraordinary cuisine and their lavender-scented gardens if they ventured afar. Laboratory studies permit the pleasure of scientific curiosity within the comforting bosom of French culture.

We pulled out our headlamps and trooped out the door behind Yves into the night. Despite nearing retirement, he was full of energy and ready for the evening shift of the herpetologist. There was no moon, so it took a few moments to get our bearings. Once we reached a large clearing, Arnaud suggested we turn off our headlamps. As if a larger switch had been flipped, the brilliance of the southern night sky turned on like a million chandeliers. There were new constellations to learn, but they would have to wait. It was time to tune in for the geckos.

I should mention that I am a practiced gecko listener. On too many lonely nights in Nepal when I was a Peace Corps volunteer, it sometimes seemed like the only other vertebrates speaking to me were hungry geckos coming to eat the moths attracted to my kerosene reading lamp. "Geck-o! Geck-o!" they would call, as if touting their arrival. Years later, when traveling across Southeast Asia, I loved to listen to the loud "To-kay!" calls of the giant purple-spotted geckos, known also as the tokay gecko. In a sparsely furnished rest house in Ujung Kulon National Park on the western tip of Java—one of the last two refuges of the Javan rhino—I once spent a night in a room where the only objet d'art was a large portrait of President Suharto. A tokay gecko had taken shelter behind it, and all night I felt like Suharto was trying to keep me awake with his gecko imitations.

Arnaud, Yves, David, Linda, and I kept our ears cocked but heard no geckos in New Caledonia that night. Yves thought that the breeding season might be over. We did hear the calls of a frog, a species introduced from Australia. There are no native amphibians on the island and, thankfully, no introduced cane toads or bullfrogs that might usurp everything else. Yet it's the eeriest sensation to be in a tropical rain forest and not hear a chorus of amphibians. It's like a Manhattanite spending an evening on a fire escape without hearing a single taxi horn, police siren, or car alarm.

We rose early the next morning and, before coffee, went out to listen for kagus and other birds. As we walked down the road from Yves's cabin, we soon heard the kagus' doglike barks in the most singular dawn chorus on this planet. Yves, a world expert on the kagu, explained that they can live as long as fifty years. Their longevity also involves delayed development. Young kagus hang around their parents and help to raise their siblings. A pair occupies a rather large territory, so it takes a lot of land to maintain a large population. Yves coauthored a book on the birds of New Caledonia and knew all the calls of the characteristic birds of the islands: the whistlers, the trillers, and the honeyeaters. Although Yves was a quiet man, his actions spoke volumes and reaffirmed the traits I find in so many field biologists: dedication, modesty, and the ability to shrug off loneliness. As we bade him goodbye, I wondered who would take his place when he retired.

We had finished our brief exploration of the wonders of Province Sud. The plan was now to head north, hugging the eastern coast of Grand Terre. We would look for kagus and visit other rain forest locales and maybe even satisfy the alpinist in Arnaud by going up a few mountains. No sooner had we left Rivière Bleue, however, than it began to rain with a vengeance that seemed out of character for this calm outpost in the Coral Sea. The downpour lasted all day, and the mountain trails became torrents, drowning out any hope of serious wandering. And we continued to head north into the storm. We decided to spend the night in a small oceanside resort near the village of Poindimié.

The rain wouldn't let up. To our chagrin, we were catching the tail end of a typhoon. The palm trees along the road were bent before the force of the gale, and our windshield wipers beat frantically to deflect the stiff rain. Near the village of Hienghène, which we never grew tired of mispronouncing, we had to stop at the banks of a broad river. There was a small car ferry that carried one or two vehicles across at a time, but it was grounded. This was no time for valor. The most common wrecks at the bottom of Southeast Asian and South Pacific seas are not Spanish galleons filled with doubloons and pieces of eight, but the rusting hulks of unseaworthy passenger ferries. We had intended to launch a mini-expedition up the Massif du Panié in search of the possibly extinct New Caledonia lorikeet. The massif lay just on the other side of the swollen current. We would have to wait for a return visit to look for that rarest of New Caledonian birds.

There is nothing less interesting to hear about than an abandoned expedition, or a rerouting of plans. Admiral Peary would never have kept his audience or won his medals if a freak blizzard had stopped him halfway. The Explorer's Club celebrates no Hall of Partial Journeys. I wished that I could reach a giant faucet and shut down the deluge, or use my last adventurer's chit to beg nature's forces for good weather in exchange for a more severe tropical storm at some more convenient interval in the future. But my disappointment only seemed to make it rain and blow harder. There was nothing to do now but head south again and hope the typhoon didn't follow us. We would cut across Grand Terre using the connecting road over the mountains at Houaïlou, past Némeara, and north to Pouembout (more fun with the Kanak names). Arnaud called ahead to arrange for meetings with the conservation officials of Province Nord. We would try our luck on the dry side of the island.

The drop in humidity as we headed west lifted the soggy spirits of me and my companions. The real purpose of our rescue mission was about to begin. David and Arnaud stood up through the sunroof of our rented Renault, while I drove along the coastal dirt roads of northwestern Grand Terre. "Hold it," someone commanded from above. I stopped several hundred yards below a relative speck of woods in the middle of cattle pastures so that our spotters could examine the patch more closely through their binoculars. On this sunny warm morning, I was struck by how the scenery resembled the Pacific coast of Costa Rica. "No, keep going," David said. I could hear the disappointment in his voice. We had spent the last three days scanning the landscape for a rare sighting. This time, we were looking not for kagus, notous, rare parakeets, or any endangered species, but for patches of dark green canopy, the identifying feature of a remnant piece of tropical dry forest. A letter from Dr. Philippe Bouchet, an expert on the ecology of New Caledonia and a top scientist at the Museum of Natural History in Paris, had encouraged Arnaud to organize our dry forest expedition. Under his guidance, we had switched from looking for threatened birds to looking for something whose plight was much more urgent—the rarest type of forest on earth.

Compared with the species-rich tropical rain forests, tropical dry forests are an afterthought, if anybody thinks about them at all. Part of the problem is name recognition. How can a tropical forest be dry? Doesn't it rain all the time in the tropics? There are tropical regions where it rains hard like in rain forests but only for half the year. The other half is essentially a drought period, and during that time most of the trees shed their leaves. The more scientific name for tropical dry forests is *dry sclerophyllous forest*—difficult to pronounce and not exactly an attention grabber, either. Although not as rich in species as rain forests, dry forests contain plants and animals that are highly distinctive and that display clever adaptations for dealing with lengthy dry seasons, hot climates, and fire. The animals that live in dry forests learn to shift their diets from insects or animals to flowers, fruits, and nectar in tune with the seasons. And some plants store water in special organs or develop tough waxy coats on their leaves to avoid water loss.

It's a shame that more people don't know about tropical dry forests, not just because they are so threatened and biologically interesting, but because they are so aesthetically pleasing. The trees native to tropical dry forests—those in the coffee family, the catalpa or trumpet creeper family, and the guava family, for example—produce spectacular springtime blossoms that rival anything on display in a florist's shop. Somewhere in one of those forest scraps, we knew, was the last population of what might be the world's most stunning flowering plant, the flagship species of the dry forest, *Captaincookia margaretae*. Named after the "discoverer" of the island, this member of the coffee family displays an extraordinary bloom of pinkish red tubular flowers in dense clusters along the entire length of its trunk. If only we could find one. *Captaincookia* had met the fate of many dry forest trees. The climate of tropical dry forests is much more pleasant for human settlements than that of humid rain forests, and the soils much more productive for agriculture and ranching. Hence, tropical dry forests are perhaps the most endangered on earth and *Captaincookia* is at extinction's epicenter.

The most diverse tropical dry forests in the world are found in Bolivia and Mexico, but the most unique in terms of rare species occur in Madagascar and New Caledonia. New Caledonia dry forests support 330 native plant species, including 59 species that exist only in dry forest and many more that are unique to other habitats on the island but occur only in New Caledonia. Other dry forest specialists include a variety of geckos, skinks, land snails, beetles, and a type of fruit bat. Their distributions are so localized that many of these species occur at only a few sites.

Published statistics and maps show that tropical dry forests once covered 1,500 square miles along the western coast of Grand Terre. A more recent survey showed the shocking level of loss over the past thirty years. In 1997, reliable estimates suggested that a mere 40 square miles of intact dry forest remained. Our brief survey found a situation even more dire: So far, we hadn't seen any intact forest at all. We had stumbled onto a biodiversity crisis that should be of global concern but that environmental journalists and other watchdogs of the conservation movement had so far failed to detect.

Arnaud contacted the head of the forestry services in Province Nord, Christian Papineau, who gave some direction to our wild goose chase. Papineau was a tall, serious, dark-haired forester who worked hard with the local Kanak and Caldoche farmers to promote forest conservation by fencing off patches of dry forest on their land to protect them from cattle grazing. He had also created public awareness campaigns to explain the harmful effects on native plants and animals when forests are burned too frequently. We told him that every likely patch we had encountered so far had been grazed by cattle, burned by locals to improve conditions for hunting rusa deer, or turned into savannas of *niaouli*, the local name for the native tree species *Melaleuca quinquenervia*. (American conservationists know *Melaleuca* as an invader from abroad and a scourge of the Everglades, choking out the native vegetation wherever it gets a foothold.) Tropical dry forests on Grand Terre are adapted to cool, infrequent fires, but intense, annual fires lead to the conversion of forest to savanna and to the spread of niaouli. Papineau assured us that there was still hope and directed us to two places that could serve as the seedbanks of recovery.

First, he advised us to visit a state park in Province Nord that had a few acres of dry forest. The cattle had been removed several years ago, and the results were striking. What had once been a degraded forest dominated by niaouli had come back to life. Large niaouli were still present, but with protection from fire and with natural processes at work, they were dying back to a level that was more natural in the forest mix. The park official who showed us around pointed out the tree species found here, which showed no overlap in species from the forest on the wet side of the island. When we returned, we encouraged Papineau by telling him of the remarkable recovery of tropical dry forest in Gaunacaste, Costa Rica, one of the great success stories in the tropics. The recovery effort was led by Dan Janzen and assisted by scores of Costa Rican ranchers who saw the economic and social benefits that a restored dry forest ecosystem could provide.

"There is something else you should see," advised Papineau, as he called to arrange for two foresters to escort us. "You must see the last home of our flagship species." We drove out to a hamlet called Tiae, near the village of Pouembout, a place you won't find on a map. At a junction of dirt roads, we met the two tall, husky foresters, Alain and Paul, dressed in khaki green shirts and shorts. They reminded me of descriptions of the early Boers of South Africa, rough and ready to pioneer and take what the land gave them. They greeted us in their strong Caldoche accents. Arnaud told us earlier that the Caldoche speak with strong Marseilles dialects. I couldn't really tell. All I know is that it didn't sound at all like the Parisian intonations taught by Ms. Moutinot in my high school French class. I listened intently as we approached a small remnant of tropical dry forest flanked by cattle pastures.

We entered the patch of forest along the stream, and it was as if a spell had been cast. In the pastures we had walked through to get here, the morning was hot and sunny. But once under the forest canopy, the air was cool and the light dim. There was a beautiful species of *Croton*, whose crinkly, spotted leaves would have been the envy of any horticulturist. At the edge of a dry seasonal stream was a species of wild rice, *Oryza neocaledonica*, found in only a few dry forest patches on Grand Terre. A number of species of wild rice exist in the world, and they hold great value as a potential source of new genes for the cultivated species of rice *Oryza sativa*. The New Caledonia native rice species is remarkable in that it is adapted to withstand long drought periods.

At a bend in the streambed, a rare, endemic New Caledonia fruit bat took wing and flew past us. It must have been disturbed by our conversations. I took it as a good omen. A more ominous ecological sign was the ubiquitous footprints of cattle. Cattle fare poorly in hot climates unless they can escape the sun and drink on a daily basis. These domestic herds were using the Tiae forest as their shelter from the midday sun. But in doing so, they were destroying any recruitment of young trees and causing mortality in adult plants. Alain and Paul pointed out a group of trees that had been particularly abused by the local Holsteins. Then, "*Voilá!*" exclaimed Alain in his guttural French, "*Cap-ten-coo-ki-ya.*" At last, we had found what we were looking for. To our dismay, however, the grove of *Captaincookia* was in sorry shape, and none were in flower. A decidedly nonrobust species, most of the individuals showed signs of abuse from cattle rubbing against the trunks. A few had already keeled over. For the flagship species of the New Caledonia dry forests, the last voyage was at hand if something wasn't done immediately.

A well-known principle of conservation biology is that small isolated patches of habitat islands lose species at a predictable rate. The most recent map of the remaining fragments of dry forest in New Caledonia showed that about fifty isolated patches remained. Alarmingly, the largest piece was about four hundred acres, another was half that size, and the rest fell in the four- to ten-acre range, mere postage stamp remnants. If someone didn't come up with a way to rapidly expand the size of the dry forest fragments, the New Caledonia fruit bat and other rare species of the dry forest might disappear for good.

Besides the small size of the parcels, another major threat was the invasion of exotic species. Since Europeans arrived, about eight hundred non-native plant species, at least four hundred invertebrate species, and thirty-six alien vertebrates have settled in New Caledonia. Fortunately, most have remained near urban areas or farmland, but a hardy few have made it into the dry forest fragments. One of the potentially most serious invaders is an introduced ant known as the electric ant or Argentine ant (*Wasmannia auropunctata*). Electric ants hitched a ride on Caribbean pines imported in 1972 to stock tree plantations, and they have since invaded most dry forest patches. These aggressive ants are believed to be extirpating native lizards, insects, and land snails and could be attacking nestlings of birds. Targeted control of electric ants, a problem being tackled elsewhere around the world where they have shown up unannounced and unwelcome, is an urgent piece of field research. Ironically, one way that some exotics, such as the electric ant, may be spreading is on the boots of the very people who are trying to save the dry forests. Exotics can stow away in the mud lodged between the corrugated soles of boots of biologists moving from one dry forest patch to another during surveys. The rule of wiping your shoes, or in this case disinfecting them before you enter, long enforced by diligent grandmothers is worth heeding.

As we moved from patch to patch, the species composition seemed to change completely. This roster change, where species A, B, and C are replaced by species D, E, and F, is called *beta-diversity*, an awkward-sounding name for a fundamentally important concept in conservation biology that basically gives you a nearly complete replacement of species, one after another, on contiguous land. Often this happens with changes in elevation, but it can also occur on flat land, where the underlying soil type might change from one type of forest or shrubland to another. The critical message for conservationists is that in places where species have extremely narrow ranges, as do the micro-endemics of the New Caledonia flora and fauna, and high turnover from one patch of natural habitat to the next, we may need to create a larger number of reserves to preserve all of the biological diversity present. One or two large reserves won't do the job as they might in a grassland habitat, where there is often lower endemism but species range over wide areas and are good dispersers. This is another illustration of the principle in conservation biology that one size doesn't fit all when it comes to optimum solutions.

With luck, we found another population of *Captaincookia* on a private farm in Province Sud. This cluster had found a safe haven and a protector, Marcel Metzdorf, a third-generation farmer in his seventies. He had erected a deer-proof fence around his own forest patch and kept the fires out. When asked why he did this, he smiled and said that he wanted his grandchildren and other young people to know how beautiful the dry forests were on the island. The forests that had still been widespread in his youth had almost vanished, and he wanted to set an example of how to bring them back. At last, here were the seeds of the regeneration of the dry forest and the individuals concerned enough to bring it about. All we needed now were the funds to begin.

Some scientists, such as Michael Soulé, argue that we have entered the era of the Homogocene, when, because of invasive alien species and the overall mixing of biotas, every place looks like every other place. It's the biological equivalent of randomly picking traffic intersections in the United States and finding the same fast-food, video, coffee, and gasoline franchises at each crossroads, from California to Pennsylvania. But there are still places, such as New Caledonia, where even the seasoned natural historian and traveler can say, "I've never experienced anything like this." We returned from our expedition determined to start a major program to save this remarkable island, starting with the tropical dry forests. We had been given the rare privilege of seeing a live kagu, touching a *Captaincookia*, and walking through dinosaur-era forests. Now it was time to return the favor.

Arnaud, working on his end, gained the support of WWF-France to commit staff to New Caledonia restoration. He hired another Arnaud, Arnaud Collin, to head a program to promote greater financial support in the territory, but funding was still a problem. Arnaud Collin wisely pushed Christian Papineau to lead the dry forests restoration effort from the bottom up. Inspired by David Olson and Arnaud Greth, who together became the ecological conscience at WWF for conserving this forgotten island, I decided to take the New Caledonia dry forests under my wing. There was a standard wager among the vice presidents at WWF about how much time would go by in a meeting before I mentioned the words "New Caledonia." The smart money never gave it more than ten minutes. But funds were tight or already committed, and although we had generated much greater awareness, we were still penniless. Six months after standing under the great kauris listening to the kagus, I had nothing to show for my own efforts to save that ancient land, regardless of what Arnaud was trying to do. I had never felt so frustrated or powerless.

One snowy winter day in Chicago in January 1998, about as far from New Caledonia as one could get on the globe, I found myself in the office of Marshall Field IV, a great philanthropist in conservation and a stalwart supporter of WWF, the Field Museum of Natural History, and a host of other charities. We were sitting with a dear friend of mine, Cynthia McKee, who was a leader in our fund-raising program. Cynthia brought Marshall up to date on the Global 200 work and our new campaign based on its blueprint, while I remained mute, mustering my courage to overcome the shyness I used to feel in the presence of major donors, those, like Marshall, who had given millions of dollars to our cause. Marshall inquired, "So Eric, you look rather tanned. Have you been anywhere interesting recently?" As if the power of the kagu, the notou, the giant geckos, and the rare monkey puzzles were forcing me to speak, I proceeded to tell Marshall about the extraordinary place where I had been a few months before, rather than about Nepal, where I had gained a tan. How I had seen the forest the dinosaurs knew, in the middle of the Coral Sea. And I told him about the plight of *Captaincookia*—the world's most endangered and most beautiful flowering plant, which could go extinct in the next year if someone didn't come to its rescue.

"Well, what will it take to save *Captaincookia*?" Marshall asked. I explained about the need to fence off the populations in the several acres of forest tracts where they still occurred in order to keep out the cattle and the deer, and to build fire breaks. "So how much is this going to cost?" Marshall didn't mess around. I looked over at Cynthia, swallowed hard, and said in a quiet voice, "About $15,000."

Marshall barely hesitated. "I guess $15,000 isn't going to break me. So here's a check. Go do it." I was overwhelmed. Here was someone who had never heard of New Caledonia, let alone *Captaincookia*, an hour earlier, and he wrote a check based on my verbal voucher that this was the right thing to do.

Marshall's gift turned out to be catalytic to the fate of *Captaincookia* and the dry forests. With his grant, we immediately set to work fencing off the Tiae forest containing the first of the two remnant *Captaincookia* populations. The landowner, Alexandre Nicoli, agreed to keep better control of his cattle and to stop burning the forest. Arnaud could point to the immediate success of our trip and activated WWF-France to aggressively seek funds for conservation in New Caledonia dry forests. Based on the proposal that he, David, and Arnaud Collin wrote, the MacArthur Foundation, the Lafarge Corporation, and WWF-International stepped forward with timely donations. The dry forest fenced off by Monsieur Metzdorf was expanded. A new conservation program for New Caledonia was launched with Christian Papineau and another biologist, Jean-Christophe Lefeuvre leading the efforts on the ground. At last, the conservation world and the donor community were paying attention. Soon there would be a vision for conservation of the dry forests adopted by a large number of groups, greatly extending the road paved by Dan Janzen and his pioneering efforts in Costa Rican dry forests. *Captaincookia* and all of the rare dry forest wonders might still be there for Monsieur Metzdorf's grandchildren and everyone else's, as well.

But our work was not done. Arnaud and I rendezvoused in Paris and headed straight for the Museum of Natural History on the Left Bank to meet with Philippe Bouchet, who had first alerted us to search for the imperiled dry forests. We pledged to work together to save these rare centers of endemism; some of Philippe's students would join the WWF New Caledonia program. We went to Versailles, where the WWF-France office was located. I gave a talk on the Global 200 and urged the staff there to really focus their efforts not just in la-belle France, but in their incomparable overseas territories. Financial assistance for conservation in the territories was woefully inadequate. The French had created their own global conservation fund to support nature protection around the world, but I felt they had yet to give New Caledonia enough attention.

One venue we have not yet been invited into is the boardroom at INCO, the multinational mining conglomerate that operates the nickel mines in Grand Terre. The destructive mining techniques it practices result in the loss of endangered species and rare habitats, and do sustained damage to streams and pristine coral reefs. Convincing INCO to upgrade its practices and pay for restoration may require conservationists to apply pressure on INCO headquarters in Canada and its subsidiary in France. INCO in New Caledonia seems ready to contribute and help underwrite a conservation plan. But conservationists in Canada were advising us not to give the company anything it could point to as positive until it cleans up its act at home, too.

New Caledonia needs to be thrust into the world's spotlight, as Madagascar, its sister Gondwanaland island, has been with the recent declaration by the current president of his intention to triple the area under formal protection over the next decade. As of 2005, plans are taking shape to launch a much larger conservation effort in New Caledonia, but everyone must now contribute—the French government, INCO, the major conservation groups, and the multilaterals—and apply the same rescue effort promoted for Madagascar.

I hope they invite a roundtable of top scientists to advise this recovery, those whose work epitomizes what needs to be done, such as the contributions of Yves Le Tocquart. I heard through the grapevine that Yves had relocated to New Zealand and returned only infrequently to New Caledonia to check on his kagus. Every year for several years running, David and I nominated him for both the Getty Prize and the Goldman Prize, the two most prestigious awards bestowed upon those splendid people who have made a difference in conservation. Perhaps, like the Nobel Committee, which often recognizes the accomplishments of recipients long after they retire, the jurors of these awards committees will eventually give Yves the recognition he is due. Until then, words of praise are all we can offer. Whenever I think of Yves, I think of his quiet passion, a humility for our place in the grandeur of the natural world and our mission to preserve and restore it. I think of the last lines of Emily Dickinson's "Not in Vain," which I suppose could stand as the coda for all of our conservation efforts, in New Caledonia, the South Pacific, and on our own doorstep:

> I shall not live in vain:
> If I can ease one life the aching,
> Or cool one pain,
> Or help one fainting robin
> Unto his nest again,
> I shall not live in vain.

chapter five

RETURN TO THE LOST WORLD

WHEN I WAS A CHILD GROWING UP ON THE NEW JERSEY shore, the first bird to catch my attention was the osprey, with its impressive five-foot wing span and fearsome gaze. I delighted in its hunting maneuver, the daring hover, the feet-first plunge into the ocean foam, and I took a slightly sadistic satisfaction in watching it fly off with a fish impaled in its talons. But, oddly, what intrigued me most of all was the osprey's gravity-defying nest, an enormous clutter of sticks and branches balanced on a spindly utility pole. Osprey nests, like the nearby homes of the new upper-middle class, put square footage before style. Osprey parents constructed such shelters to deflect the feather-ruffling gales of coastal winters. Or so I assumed at age ten. Not until September of my thirteenth year did I learn that ospreys were, just like northerners who travel to sunny climes in winter, snowbirds. I asked an Island Beach State Park naturalist to what land they had vanished. "To the tropics," he replied, "to Venezuela."

Venezuela? Why should the osprey fly all the way to South America? If in search of warmth and exotic-sounding destinations, why not winter in Florida, like my grandparents? An osprey could surely settle comfortably in the Okeefenokee Swamp or along the Appalachicola River. There an aerial predator would rule above the underworld of alligators, water moccasins, and snapping turtles submerged in the peat-stained waters of the Deep South. But before I could discover what triggered their attraction to Venezuela, my interest in osprey biology flickered out, and instead the allure of beach life and the promise of the Woodstock Nation carried me through the rest of adolescence. Thirty-six years later, I had a chance to revisit the childhood riddle of the missing osprey when I joined an expedition to Venezuela to find one of the rarest of mammals, the giant river otter.

The nation's capital was gripped in a winter campaign of snow and ice that grounded even the most relentless lobbyists. I was chatting with David Olson, a good friend and colleague at work, about our mutual love for creatures of the tropical rain forest and our desire to escape the coldest week in February. Our recent trip to New Caledonia was still fresh in my mind, as if we had just returned the week before. I always enjoyed traveling with David because of his vast knowledge of natural history. I imagine the first object he picked up as an infant was neither a baseball bat nor a hockey stick but a butterfly net. From conversations about our youth, I formed images of David digging for mastodon bones in Montana, catching salamanders in the Blue Ridge Mountains, and studying cichlid fish in the desert pools of Cuatro Ciénegas, Mexico. My hobbies and favorite books overlapped little with David's. While I wrestled with Dostoyevsky and dueled with Robert Louis Stevenson, David absorbed the complete works of Roger Tory Peterson. (Only as curious adolescents did our reading lists merge, with *Lady Chatterley's Lover*.) By his late teens, David had devoted himself to memorizing the Latin names of insects, birds, mammals, marine shells, reptiles, amphibians, and plants. He sketched what he saw like an amateur John James Audubon. In graduate school, he pursued his long-standing passion for ants and studied their biology along the slopes of Panama's mountains. Above his desk hung an autographed picture of one of the great naturalists of our time, Edward O. Wilson, whose lifelong devotion to ants and nature conservation inspired David in his career.

That wintry Washington day there was something brewing in David's mind besides a conversation about rain forests. His real purpose was to invite me to accompany him and his naturalist wife, Linda Farley, to the outback of Venezuela. They were escorting the CEO of a New York investment banking firm, Wendy Lee, to giant river otter country. A committed conservation philanthropist, Wendy was determined to help save giant river otters from extinction and had helped WWF to finance the Ya'Kwana Indians and local biologists to survey their populations on remote stretches of the Orinoco and Amazon tributaries.

Most tropical forest aficionados pick locales more hospitable than the rain forest we were about to visit, areas without the poisonous snakes and deadly illnesses of the Orinoco rain forest, with lodgings that are comfortable for even the most discriminating tourists. I wondered what compelled Wendy to take such a bold journey in the company of virtual strangers. And how would she hold up spending several days in a motorized dugout canoe, heading up rapids, getting drenched by rainstorms, and sleeping in a hammock? Even if she didn't wade into a river full of piranha, stingrays, and electric eels, or succumb to the region's deadly strain of malaria, how well would a New York investment banker cope with the discomfort that lay ahead?

"You know, some say the Caura's even wilder than Manu. Do you still want to come?" His words had the invigorating effect on me of a double espresso. The Caura River, a tributary of the mighty Orinoco and one of the last strongholds for this highly threatened otter, flowed through what many considered a nearly pristine tract of rain forest. To tout the Caura landscape as "wilder than Manu" seemed close to blasphemy, though. Manu National Park in southeastern Peru is possibly the most famous protected area in South America, celebrated in the writings and research of the conservation biologist John Terborgh and his students. To biologists, the name *Manu* is synonymous with *diverse*. Two decades ago, ornithologists Scott Robinson and the late Ted Parker counted 332 species in a single day of birding near the Manu Research Station, still a world record. Manu researchers have found 13 species of primates living in the same forest, a record for the continent. Even amateur naturalists have wandered within yards of unperturbed jaguars. I accepted David and Linda's invitation without hesitation. "Wilder than Manu" had to be seen to be believed.

The Caura and Manu pass the litmus test for tropical wilderness with flying colors. They contain healthy populations of species that typically disappear when market hunters arrive to collect the pelts, feathers, and flesh of wild game, or to capture tropical animals for the illegal pet trade. The most prized quarry are spotted cats, tapir, monkeys, parrots, large fruit-eating birds, and, of course, otters. Few mammals are more sensitive to hunting pressure than the giant river otter (*Pteronura brasiliensis*), a species once common across the lowlands of north and central South America and now restricted to the more remote tributaries of the Amazon, the Orinoco, and the Guianas. The *nya-nyu-ri*, as the otter is known to the Ya'Kwana Indians of the Caura region, is revered as an incarnation of the goddess of the dry season that protects their crops. In turn, the respectful Ya'Kwana shelter the otters and other threatened wildlife in their indigenous territory.

Our farthest point of exploration would be a remote field station, two days upriver from where we would meet our guides. We would spend two days there while we searched the Caura for otters. However, it was possible to reach the camp only if the river was navigable—neither in flood and full of dangerous uprooted trees nor too low, forcing us to portage around exposed boulders and rapids. The field station was the home base of Venezuelan biologist Tibisay Escalona, known locally as Tiby (pronounced TB). To monitor wildlife populations that "fluctuate naturally," that is, without the confounding effects of human exploitation on population size, reproduction, mortality, and even basic behavior, usually requires biologists to live in remote locations, and Tiby was here to study the ecology of one of the Orinoco's massive river turtles.

Nearly one hundred years ago, perhaps tiring of the eccentricities of Sherlock Holmes, Sir Arthur Conan Doyle wrote his classic adventure story, *Lost World*. His tale describes Professor Challenger's discoveries in a place that had escaped the march of time, where dinosaurs and other prehistoric biota flourished in a hidden kingdom in the remote Venezuelan highlands. Guarding this lost world from intruders were steep, forbidding flat-topped mountains of sandstone and granite, and the Caura flowed right through them.

Some biologists claim that those mountains, known as tepuis, contained plants that were the ancient precursors to the plants of the Amazon rain forest. Maybe in Professor Challenger's day giant river otters were as common as squirrels across the Orinoco basin and in the headwaters, but today they have been wiped out from many parts of their original range. The Caura is a refuge not only for river otters but also for South America's largest vertebrates. Linda knew the upper Caura as well as any naturalist and could lead us to where we might have a chance to see otters, as well as jaguars and tapirs. She had also volunteered to be our scout, arriving several days earlier to ensure that our Ya'Kwana guides would indeed meet us on the Caura to lead us into the lost world.

After meeting up in Caracas, David, Wendy, and I flew early the next morning south to Ciudad Bolivar, the major town along the banks of the Orinoco. It was only 9 a.m. when we met Linda at the hostel where she had spent the night, but the blast furnace of the tropical sun was already at the red line. We would first travel several hours west along a well-paved highway through the Llanos, the seasonally

flooded savanna of the Venezuelan interior, Linda explained. We hur-
tled along past endless landscapes of horse and cattle pastures dotted
with wild calabash trees. Finally, we veered off the tarmac onto a dirt
road that snaked south to the Caura. Five hours of bouncing on a
bumpy track through the midday heat is enough to irritate even the
most intrepid of biologists, let alone investment bankers prone to impatience. I offered Wendy what I hoped would be an encouraging
perspective: To find true wildlands these days requires at least a five-
hour jeep ride on a dreadful dirt road or a day's walk from the last village. Only then do you finally outrun the human footprint.

At last, we arrived at the banks of the Caura, where we pulled into a
tourist lodge to spend the night. We would wait here for our guides to
steer the motorized dugout up the river and collect us. I sat with
Wendy under the shade of a massive fig tree and looked out at the
sprawling river winding a hundred feet below us. The intense humidity
and heat turned my shirt into an envelope of sweat. Wendy, looking remarkably at ease in her new setting, patiently accepted my unsolicited
advice: "You know, it takes three days for your thermostat to adjust to
the tropical heat. Think of it as your initiation rite. You sweat profusely
for seventy-two hours, and then you'll walk through the forest like a
Ya'Kwana." "Regardless," I continued, "the trick is to suppress your
sense of physical discomfort and focus instead on the fascination of
life in the rain forest." "Look!" Wendy cried, interrupting my ser-
mon. Shooting around the boulder-strewn pools below us was a brown
torpedo-shaped creature: a river otter. Not the king of river otters we
were seeking, but the giant's smaller cousin, *Lutra longicaudis*, the
more common species that ranges over a wide swath of Latin America.
Wendy beamed at the river as it swirled and shifted around an asteroid
belt of giant boulders. Then she stretched out on the wooden bench,
under the umbrella-like crown of the strangler fig, and perhaps for the
first time in her life, turned her back on the Western world.

Julio, our Ya'Kwana guide, and his first mate, Pablo, arrived several
hours late the next morning. The boulder-strewn Caura carves a route

through the green chenille of rain forest and between the tepuis. Could a motorized dugout make it through this rough wilderness? Were these guides capable of showing us giant river otters? Julio, it turned out, was a veteran of the otter surveys Wendy had funded, so at least we were with someone who had seen them.

The dugout slipped into the current, the hollowed-out tree trunk whispering against the rolling stream. Julio coaxed the outboard motor to life. At last, we were under way. Wendy took a position at the bow of the twenty-five-foot-long dugout, gazing intently at the water, twisting here and there to see behind boulders and along the riverbank for any sign of otter. Suddenly, something broke the surface near us and then once again in another calm stretch. We had come upon a group of *tucuxi*, or river dolphins. The Amazon and the Orinoco are famous for their pink river dolphins, endemic to South America. Ahead of us was the less flamboyant gray-colored species, *Sotalia fluviatilis*. Still, it's a marvel to behold any dolphin, in a freshwater river or in the ocean. Their presence indicated that the fishing was good here; perhaps a family of nya-nyu-ri lay just around the corner.

Taking in the sheer size and flamboyant behavior of giant river otters is like seeing a fleet of heavyweight wrestlers sashaying through an airport. They create natural drama wherever they go. The California sea otter is more robust, but none of the eighteen other species of freshwater otters comes close in length or girth to *Pteronura*. Males reach six feet long and after a catfish banquet can tip the scales at seventy pounds. Females are only slightly smaller (about five feet long and weighing between forty-five and fifty pounds). Most Neotropical mammals are silent, small, nocturnal creatures like bats. Giant otters by contrast are strictly diurnal and keep an active schedule of feeding, horsing around, and squabbling with neighbors, all while maintaining an incessant banter of squeals, screeches, and high-pitched hums.

Each otter sports a distinctive pattern of white spots on a brown throat, making individual identification relatively easy. Giant river otters live in family groups of five to ten individuals, consisting of the parents or a male and his harem, one to four juveniles, and one to four pups. Otters do everything together, from cooperative hunting to social grooming. They even sleep heaped together in a riverbank burrow, the entrance to which sits above a steep mud embankment, allowing them to slip into the water at the first sign of danger. Older otters fiercely defend their young and reportedly have driven off jaguars in group attacks, using displays of impressive canines and a chorus of threatening snorts.

Otters are also messy campers. They denude patches of underbrush at strategic locations, such as bends in the river, where they perch alertly or lounge with their extended families. Even if we couldn't see otters outright, the signs of a recently used campsite, scattered with scales and fish bones and smelling like the back alley of a seafood restaurant, would indicate their proximity. Nicole Duplaix, the world's authority on giant river otters and the doyenne of the dozen or so other researchers who study them, says that finding otters is possible only during the dry season. Giant river otters often occupy flooded forests like those along the Caura, where water levels can shift as much as sixty feet between the dry season and the rainy season. At flood stage, otters move into the small channels and streams to find spawning fish, which makes them virtually invisible to observers. During low-water periods, they stay near the shallow pools of the big rivers, putting down roots and defending a nice string of fishing holes from other otter clans. Family groups mark off territories that in some parts of their range, such as Manu, can be as small as 250 acres. Adults eat eight pounds of fish a day, a remarkable percentage of their body weight, so finding a good fishing area near an active otter campsite would enhance our chances of locating these busy creatures.

My naturalist companions were nearly as impressive as the wildlife. Linda began naming the birds flying overhead before David or I could take a breath. "White-throated toucan," she announced seconds before I turned to see it, a big-tuxedoed comedian flying by, as if pushing a plantain attached to its head. The readiness with which Linda, a small-boned woman as fit as an Olympian, felt at home in the tropical wilderness was something I envied. She once spent two weeks in the deepest stretches of the Caura and quickly developed a love for and unrivalled understanding of its ecology. She hailed from that noble school of biologists who feel more at home in the woods than in the lecture hall.

Then there was David. Drop him off anywhere in the world, and he will be on a first-name basis with much of the local biota. It is not surprising that by his mid-twenties, he had won a field naturalist's ultimate prize: a species named after him. It matters little that in David's case it happened to be a kind of flea.

Along the riverbanks of the Caura, we saw pockets of *Cecropia*, a fast-growing tree that had quickly filled in sites where the forest had been disturbed and allowed to recover. A member of the fig family, *Cecropia* is easily recognized by its tall narrow trunk and umbrella-like leaves. Linda scanned its supple branches for a gray-green lump: the silhouette of a three-toed sloth. Unlike the playful, sleep-in-a-heap, warrior otters, sloths are pretty Zen. They are typically silent and motionless, taking long periods to digest leaf material in their multichambered stomach and, apparently, to contemplate nothingness. This also has the great effect of making them less noticeable to sharp-eyed harpy eagles and jaguars, their major predators. In her field guide to neotropical mammals, Louise Emmons reports that sloths have another technique to avoid becoming dinner: Their hair contains minute pits and grooves that provide a substrate for greenish algae to grow. The algae eventually coat their fur, creating natural camouflage.

Sloths are the subject of numerous just-so stories: an oral tradition of fictitious accounts and half-truths handed down by tropical biologists and rural hunters. Sloths may never set the world on fire, but the tediousness of their lives is greatly exaggerated. Take the claim that they spend their entire existence living in a single tree eating only *Cecropia* leaves. An excellent natural history study conducted by Gene Montgomery and Mel Sunquist, the first biologists to use radiotelemetry to monitor sloths, debunked that claim. On Barro Colorado Island, Panama, they found sloths using nearly a hundred different species of trees for feeding and roosting, moving from tree to tree every thirty-six hours or so. Not a record-setting pace among arboreal mammals, but enough activity, I believe, to refute the sloth's Spanish name, *perezoso*, or lazy. Perhaps the most peculiar sloth behavior is that they descend to the base of a tree to dig a hole with their tails, deposit their feces, urinate over it, and then cover their handiwork with leaves, using their hind legs to spruce things up. What might cause doctors to worry is that that behavior happens but once a week. It's not constipation but natural selection to reduce their exposure on the ground; sloths are nearly helpless on the forest floor and highly vulnerable to patrolling jaguars.

The other notable occupants of the *Cecropia* are the *Azteca* ants. Along the trunk of a *Cecropia* are structures known as nodes, which are hollow and filled with exceedingly aggressive ants. In one of the great examples of ant-plant mutualisms in the tropics, *Cecropia* provide the ants with free housing, and the stinging ants protect the trees from herbivores, excepting sloths (somehow, the sloths tolerate the ants).

People don't tolerate some ants so well, however, including *Azteca* and some of their even larger cousins. Mel Sunquist once went up a tree to catch a sloth with a dog catcher's pole and was greeted by a *Paraponera* ant—the largest ant in the New World, called *bala* in Spanish, or bullet—a giant black monster with a paralyzing sting even nastier than *Azteca*. Poor Mel couldn't move his swollen arm for twenty-four hours.

In the calm stretches of the river, an abundance of fish leapt everywhere. And breaking that calm with splendid maneuvers flapped the mystery raptor of my youth: osprey! Around nearly every bend in the river was a pair or a threesome—back from a vacation in New Jersey—putting on an air show. They searched for fish from the air, swooped down with talons extended, and pulled up sharply with a meal squirming in their grasp. Osprey feet have incredibly rough scales that can pop up, like the headlight lids on certain sports cars, creating a sandpaper effect. When osprey grab fish, the scales on their feet lock onto the scales of the fish to give them extra gripping power.

Osprey, along with barn owls, peregrine falcons, black-crowned night herons, and mallard ducks, are found on every continent and on the bird lists of virtually all of the countries on earth. The implication is that the migratory aspect of osprey behavior has maintained a strong genetic connection among populations over time, preventing isolation and the evolution of several species. There is only one species of osprey, which migrates from north to south in the New World, from Africa to Asia, and from Australasia to East Asia. Sea eagles in the Northern Hemisphere, including our own bald eagle, are ecologically similar in the way they hunt and in the habitats they select, but they don't migrate like osprey. They've also diversified into four species.

So, thinking back to my childhood riddle: Why do ospreys migrate so far? The rigors of the annual migration from the northeastern United States undoubtedly stress the birds, but the costs are more than offset by the shooting-fish-in-a-barrel ease of foraging in tropical rivers where humans have yet to harvest the bounty. In the grand evolutionary struggle, migratory osprey must have produced more healthy chicks that survived to breed than those ancestral birds that stayed put in prehistoric New Jersey. The really interesting question about osprey is why they bother to come back to New Jersey at all. My guess is that they return north when the South American rivers rise and turn muddy in the rainy season, making the fish harder to catch.

David calls South America the bird continent, because there are more species here than on any other large land mass. But it just as appropriately could be declared the fish continent. In the Amazon River alone, estimates claim more than three thousand species of fish, an order of magnitude greater than every other river except the Orinoco. Taken together, the fish faunas of those two neotropical rivers are unparalleled.

The surprising array of freshwater species in those two rivers includes the famous electric eels, which produce electromagnetic currents to aid in navigating and finding food in turbid waters. It was recently discovered that many types of fish, often unrelated taxonomically, have independently evolved the capacity to produce such currents, presumably to help them to "see" through the murk. Water is an excellent conductor, and the fields emitted by these fish convey essential information about the underwater traffic all around them.

There are also the gorgeous tetras that attract mates with their bright neon stripes. Some of these species live and breed locally, but others, such as the *dourada* catfish, undergo continental-scale migrations from the river deltas to their spawning areas in the headwaters of the great rivers. The *dourada* is big, often reaching three feet, but the *arapaima* (or *paiche* or *pirarucú*, depending on where you are) is even bigger. This primitive fish regularly grows to six or seven feet in length and can reach as much as thirteen feet and 440 pounds. A member of the bonytongue family, the *arapaima* resembles species known from fossils dated over 100 million years ago. This monster is a top aquatic predator of the Amazon and Orinoco, counting among its prey everything from the large *dourada* down to small insects and aquatic plants.

As impressive as the *arapaima* may be, the most notorious predator of these river systems is the comparatively diminutive piranha. A member of the Characidae family, the piranha is about the size of a small perch but with greater attention to the dental area. The Orinoco, the Amazon, and several other river basins together hold upward of fifty kinds of flesh-eating piranhas. The piranhas' penchant for human flesh is just Hollywood lore, but there is a perverse guild of

Characids, the *Serrasalmus* group, that covet and consume their neighbors' scales and fins.

Perhaps most interesting among the characids is the *tambaqui*, the largest member of the family. It reaches three feet in length and can weigh sixty-five pounds. Like gauchos who have switched from beef jerky to sunflower seeds, the *tambaqui* has made a remarkable transition. Instead of jaws full of sharp teeth designed for tearing off chunks of flesh, this heavyweight ingests fruits by crushing some of the seeds between its molar-like teeth. Many tropical trees depend on the unorthodox diet of this species. In the *igapó*, as the flooded forest is known in South America, some trees rely on fish as seed dispersers, a phenomenon found nowhere else in the world. Fish swim and feed in the lower canopy of the rain forest for half the year and in the normal river channels for half. A portion of the seeds ingested pass through unharmed. At one of our stops, I grabbed a ripe fig and tossed it into the river like a pebble, only to watch a small frenzy erupt over my offering. Dinner for the fish, dispersal for the trees.

Figs are the manna of the forest dwellers. Some of the massive fig trees along the riverbanks were bursting with fruit for those species agile enough to climb up or fly in to pluck them. As thunderheads began to build like a stack of dark pillows on the horizon, we talked with Wendy about the concept of the keystone species. Ecologists call species like the figs keystone, using the analogy of the Roman arch. Like the strategically located brick in a Roman arch, you pull out the keystone and the structure collapses. The loss of keystone species, like figs, from an area has a cascading effect on the survival of fruit-eating birds, mammals, fish, and insects. Biologist John Terborgh identified tropical figs as keystones because they fruit year-round and so many species of vertebrates and invertebrates rely on the abundant, sugar-rich fruits to see them through periods when other fruits are scarce. It's also an axiom in tropical ornithology that if you want to see a large variety of birds quickly, stake out a fruiting fig and ready your checklist. Toucans, barbets, tityras, flycatchers, tanagers, and many other frugivorous birds seek out what the monkeys left during the day and the fruit-eating bats passed over the night before. Keystones are not restricted to the tropics, though. Close to home, we can think of the explosion of deer populations in suburban areas with the removal of top predators and keystones like wolves and mountain lions from the eastern deciduous forests.

The first rain squall of the trip interrupted our discourse on figs. One drop, a thousand, then the whole sky fell down. I threw Wendy a poncho from her daypack, and we secured the rest of the gear. It always pours back home at the end of winter, but the pattern in this forest is quite different. Scientists recently discovered that the rain that falls at the mouth of the Amazon, caused by the moisture-laden trade winds moving over the ocean to land, evaporates back into the air. The evaporated moisture then collects over the rain forest and rains again and again, the cycle repeating itself perhaps five to ten times before the clouds move onto the upper slopes of the high Andes to the west. A similar recycling of rain probably occurs in the Orinoco system, though that is still conjecture.

Recently, a number of atmospheric scientists, including Duke University's Roni Avissar, have come to suspect that most of the rainfall for Brazil's breadbasket and heavily populated southeastern coast comes from rain generated in the southwestern Amazon, which is deflected off the Andes and rerouted on a southeastern air current to São Paolo. Deforestation in the Amazon is starting to cause regional climate effects, such as local droughts, that the atmospheric modelers are only now beginning to comprehend. Most of Brazil's power comes from hydroelectric projects, so if Amazonian deforestation results in a decline in rainfall, power generation would suffer, as would agriculture and the overall economy. Fortunately, the Amazon is still 85 percent forested, and the Orinoco basin is even more intact. But what would happen if all of the planned roads and the development forecast for this great swath of rain forest were to occur? What if forest cover were reduced to 70 percent or only 50 percent of what it is today because of

logging and fires to clear the land to make way for more cattle ranching and soybean production? Where is the tipping point at which the
normal precipitation of a tropical rain forest becomes like that of a
seasonal moist forest or, worse, a tropical dry savanna? The deforestation of the Amazon, scientists agree, is the land-use change experiment we don't want to make.

The Amazon's hydrology has global implications as well. Atmospheric scientists have discovered that some of the moist air currents
deflected by the Andes move back across the south Atlantic Ocean
and dump their remaining moisture in southern Africa. In fact, agricultural forecasters believe that rainfall patterns in Amazonia may influence the bounty of next year's corn crop a continent away from
where the rain first fell. Even the few wet winds that slip westward
over the Andes influence the extent of the snowpack in the Himalayas.
Three decades ago, when Edward N. Lorenz, the noted MIT meteor-
ologist, posed his whimsical question, "Does the flap of a butterfly's
wings in Brazil set off a tornado in Texas?" many may have viewed him
as daft. Now his musing seems prescient. The interconnectness of the
world is no longer a cliché, biologically or in a cell phone advertisement. I started to wonder how hydropower development along the
Orinoco could affect the ecology of its seasonal osprey population and
the snowbirds that go back to New Jersey.

Having received our prescribed daily dose of rain, we were coming
to the end of our first day on the river. We were running out of daylight and only about halfway to the field station. At 6 p.m. near the
equator, the sun plummets like a hot coal. We had just come upon an
Indian village, where I assumed we would make camp for the night.
But Julio got permission from the headman to camp on a narrow shelf
along the edge of the river a half mile upstream of the settlement. I
wondered why we didn't just stay with the Ya'Kwana. The village,
though full of tick-covered dogs and naked children, was clean and
pleasant, but Julio wished to avoid the malaria that centers around human settlements. This section of the Caura has suffered horribly from

periodic outbreaks of cerebral malaria. With no access to medicine, several people had died of the disease in just the past year. Even with the spread of HIV-AIDS, malaria is still the number one cause of mortality in the tropics. The mosquitoes that carry the disease are most active at dusk, and in a few minutes the entire village would climb under its mosquito nets to reduce exposure. We quickly donned long-sleeved shirts and liberally applied insect repellent.

To set up camp expeditiously, we all pitched in. Julio and Pablo made a quick rain fly of leaves and palm fronds, while David and Linda set up hammocks underneath. I started preparing dinner, a simple penne putanesca à la Caura, which prompted Wendy and me to reminisce about great Manhattan restaurants and cafés. After a quick dinner, all that remained was to slip into our hammocks and drift off to the whispers of the river.

There is no sleep as rewarding as that which follows a first day's journey into wilderness. No generator sounds, no laugh track from a sitcom rerun, not even the crackle of a short-wave radio. Only cicadas, night monkeys, and kinkajous called out in the dark. Nine hours of slumber later, a mutiny of scarlet macaws let out earsplitting shrieks. I lingered in mock sleep, trying to focus on the more melodic-sounding birds of the dawn chorus, but it was hopeless. Kraaaagh! Kraaaagh! It was like being roused at boot camp.

Between spoonfuls of oatmeal, we watched and listened to the chatter of parrots. At the time, Linda was working for the ornithologist Mike Parr, who cowrote *the* book on this group, *Parrots*, along with Mike Juniper. According to Mike Parr, parrot diversity is highest in Peru's Tambopada Field Station, where one can see six macaw species visiting a clay lick, and in northeast Australia's Queensland, where, with a bit of effort, one can find twenty-six species. Last but not least, there is the parrot wildlife refuge known as South Florida, where all the released and escaped pet parrots, parrotlets, parakeets, and macaws compose the most diverse parrot menagerie on earth.

Parrot talk brought to mind my favorite parrot story. A friend of a friend in New York had rescued a very expensive African species left abandoned in an alleyway, an adult male with quite an impressive vocabulary. In a city where pedestrians blurt out their deepest secrets to total strangers, this bird fit right in, revealing to one and all, "Help! I'm trapped inside a parrot's body!"

We broke camp and headed upriver once again. If we didn't stop too often we might be able to reach the field station by late afternoon. I began to wonder why we hadn't seen any giant otters yet. We had seen the other orthodox fish eaters—dolphins and large numbers of osprey, terns, and kingfishers—and judging from the number of fish jumping, there seemed to be enough to feed an entire army of otters. But unlike other fish-eaters that are adapted to active hunting, giant river otters prefer prey they do not have to chase, and there may not have been the right species at the right depths for them. The otters' prime fishing grounds are shallow pools less than ten feet deep, where they easily capture species of *Hoplias*, their staple. Though we were in the Ya'Kwana Indigenous territory, where the otters are protected, perhaps the first day's leg was also still too close to human settlements for the otters to feel at home.

The carefree life of otters portrayed in Disney films is far from reality. Their life span is relatively short for such a big mammal—on average about five to eight years in the wild—and females typically have fewer than two litters in their lifetime. If group size drops below a certain critical number, clans fail to maintain their territories or reproduce. Humans pursue them for their valuable pelts, and in some parts of their range, gold mining has polluted streams, or miners have scared them off from their preferred fishing grounds. Danger is part of everyday life, with large caiman and jaguars lying in wait to feed on otter pups. Even within their own society, otter clans fight over space and fishing areas, and in the rainy season, they disperse into the forest and clash with other territorial otters.

David, Linda, and I started to wonder if we would find any otters at all. Friends of mine, I knew, had searched during the wrong season and been skunked. Would Wendy's patience hold out? Was she silently thinking, "I came all the way to Venezuela for this?" But we need not have worried. Wendy was having the trip of her life. The farther we moved upriver, the more time began to slow down for all of us. We had settled into a peaceful cruising speed, with the water curling past the prow. I joined Wendy in the bow of the dugout to share that particular reverie, found only in wilderness, the feeling that you could die tomorrow thankful for having experienced the tranquility of an earthly Eden.

Once again, Wendy was the first to spot them. Six appeared right in front of us, bobbing and diving like a family of chocolate Labs out for a swim, rising out of the water to get a better view of us and, as they did so, revealing their unique patterns of white throat spots. I knew scientifically that the otter is related to the weasel and to all members of the mustelid family that includes skunks, wolverines, and badgers. But these otters looked enormous! For once, the common name seemed more taxonomically accurate: *perros de agua*, water dogs.

Before we could get closer for Wendy to photograph them, they sped off. We decided to employ a maneuver I had used frequently to capture rhinos and tigers in Nepal. We would drop off Wendy and Linda on an island of gravel and small boulders where they could hide from the otters. The rest of us in the dugout would circle back downriver and gently herd the family of otters toward them. In Nepal, instead of a waiting camera, there would be a tracker with a tranquilizing gun, and we used a dozen or more trained elephants to herd the rhinos and tigers. Julio gunned the outboard. With only a single dugout, his skill as a boatman would be put to the test.

Once we had moved far downstream from the otter family, Julio swung the dugout around and began moving up the river in alternating wide arcs. The otters reappeared, snorted and chattered something in otterspeak, and headed upriver. Julio swung the boat again, in a flanking tactic to move them closer to Wendy and Linda, who were now crouched in position. What appeared to be the adult male of the group looked back at us again and moved upriver to keep a safe distance between his clan and our dugout. When we had the otters within fifty feet of our companions, Wendy and Linda sprung into action. As if on cue, the otters rose halfway out of the water, posing as if for a family portrait, their throat patterns on full display.

I recalled Nicole Duplaix telling me that she had conducted a population survey of otters by photographing and sketching the individualized markings on the throat. Similarly, I had censused rhinos in Nepal by using their distinct skin folds and other features as identification. Individual tigers can be identified by their stripes in pictures taken by infrared camera traps. Biologists are able to recognize unique individuals in many large animal groups, from humpback whales to zebras to spotted cats, this way.

An otter snorted, signaling the end of the photo session. Nicole had learned to answer the otters' throaty snorts, but she refused to disturb or antagonize her study animals by doing so, and we weren't capable of it, even if we had wanted to. After admiring the otters for a few more minutes, we picked up Wendy and Linda and went looking for more. The look on Wendy's face needed no interpretation. Even if her photographs turned out as blurs of brown heads that her friends would liken to miniature Loch Ness monsters, she had had a moment of contact with these extraordinary creatures that would never fade from memory.

After another delightful encounter with giant river otters in the afternoon, we veered off the Caura into a white sand–lined stream. Caiman lay sprawled on the banks in the afternoon sun, like alligators back in Florida. On a fallen tree in the river, I spotted a day roost of delicate sac-winged bats. We drifted quite near to the male and his harem before they flew away, looking like silk purses taking flight. Around the next bend, we came upon a landing with several motorized dugouts braced against the embankment. It was Tiby's camp, at last. We scaled the steps to the station high on the bluff overlooking the river, eager to meet Tiby face-to-face. But the camp's only occupants were some young Ya'Kwana girls preparing food in a makeshift cookhouse. Tiby was in the field and wouldn't be back until dark.

The station's circle of thatch-roofed huts seemed more like an abandoned guerrilla hideout than an active research camp. At one time, the center had been supported by the Wildlife Conservation Society (WCS) of New York, but the last researcher to use it had fled years ago. Too remote and too many diseases to worry about. Besides the malaria, there was fear of Chagas' disease, a disorder spread by the bite of an assassin bug, which hid by day in the thatch and landed on its victims at night, inserting its needle-like proboscis into the flesh and unleashing an army of protozoans that could kill its host many years later. After the last WCS researcher left, the camp had remained unoccupied until Tiby arrived, undaunted by doing her research in a place where basic survival would be a major first accomplishment. As a naturalist from North America, I loved visiting here, but I must admit that if I were South American, I would have studied anolis lizards on a rum-soaked island off the Caribbean coast, a much less stressful way to earn a Ph.D. than monitoring turtles in this Timbuktu.

I was not prepared for Tiby in person. I was expecting an unkempt, nervous loner, curt and unwelcoming, acting as if her world had been invaded by frivolous emissaries from Caracas and beyond. I couldn't have been more wrong. Before us was a woman in her late twenties, attractive and well groomed even in field vest, faded khakis, and gum boots, the uniform of the tropical field biologist. She had a confidence and charisma unusual in people under thirty, and a warmth that made her all the more charming. She helped us to get settled and inquired about our interest in the Caura and the otters. Over coffee in the cookhouse, we learned that in addition to studying the basic biology of river turtles, her goal was to help ensure that the Ya'Kwana, who relied on the eggs of the turtles for protein, harvested them in a way that was sustainable both for the tribe and for the future of the turtles. As

Tiby began talking with Wendy in greater length about life in the Caura, I went to string my hammock and to look for a place to erect some mist nets to catch bats that night. I also poked the thatch above my mosquito net to test for the presence of assassin bugs. By the time I returned, Wendy and Tiby had already headed down the bluff for a bath in the river.

Dinner was an unintentional "blackened" piranha and rice. Everyone laughed at the charred fish served up by the young Ya'Kwana girls, even the local fishermen. I liked the flavor of the piranha, but the bones were large and numerous for such a small fish. By kerosene lamplight, we plotted out the next day. Before going to bed, I unfurled two mist nets I had set up earlier and within minutes captured a juvenile short-tailed fruit bat. I quickly disentangled the young male, so Wendy could handle her first bat. She stroked the soft fur, her nervous fear quickly turning to awe. The bat's modified hand, a sensitive leather wing stretched between the fingers, responded to her touch. When we released him, he flew into the trees, bragging to the others, no doubt, of how he had been captured and held prisoner by gringos but had heroically escaped.

Over breakfast the next morning, I asked Wendy what had inspired her interest in conservation. One day, she said, as a young girl growing up on the windswept Saskatchewan prairie, she had been out in the garden with her mother and stood by in horror as an innocent prairie dog was brained with a shovel. Ever since then, she felt a passion for wild animals of all kinds. Perhaps the soul of that prairie dog, joining the great mandala, had been reborn as a giant river otter, offering her a chance to right that long-ago injustice.

We spent the next few hours exploring small tributaries, stopping now and then to listen to the howler monkeys, the lions of the rain forest, roaring to each other across the treetops. Our goal was to look for signs of tapir and jaguar and possibly to track them. Although comical looking with its long prehensile snout, a tapir can fling off a pouncing jaguar and escape through the forest with a burst of uncharacteristic speed. Not only scarce in most forests, they are also secretive. I know of no biologist who has seen more than a single wild tapir. We didn't have even that luck, but we did see a few unmistakable tracks; no other animal leaves such a prehistoric three-toed print.

Tapir are related to rhinos and, like them, shape the composition and structure of the forest by chewing on the seedlings and saplings and dispersing fruits and seeds in their dung. First encounters with tapir in a zoo prompt most visitors to categorize the animal as one of nature's truly weird creatures, but 14,000 years ago, the tapir look was *in*; most South American ungulates of that time had extended snouts and protruding lips. The tapir is the only remaining example of the lineage of long-nosed creatures' former glory.

We found some jaguar tracks, too, but nothing fresh. Tiby told us that a week before, a jaguar had passed right by her camp. With such large territories to patrol, often as big as twenty square miles, it might be a while before one would pass this way again. In the late afternoon, we came upon a small clearing that looked like it had been sprayed with Agent Orange. Nearly all the leaves had been clipped from the branches and stems of the understory plants. "Leaf-cutters!" exclaimed David and had us stand back to avoid stepping on the most industrious ants of the tropics, *Atta cephalotes*. The sweeping drama of leaf-cutters at work is a biological spectacle. At our feet, trails of busy ants carried dime-sized sections of leaves several times their body size to a burrow. There, other caste members were cultivating vast underground gardens of fungi grown on vegetable matter deposited from their forays in the forest.

It was a banner day for observing ants. We had just detected a swarm of army ants when, at another clearing, Linda heard the calls of a group of ant-following birds. Such guilds of unrelated bird species, she explained, follow army ant swarms, feasting on arthropods—grasshoppers, beetles, and bugs—flushed out by the oncoming Huns, which are known to attack whatever stands between them and their bivouac, including other ant species unlucky enough to cross their path. Sure enough, we saw a local variety of ant-bird perched above legions of ants, waiting for the dinner bell.

Over dinner that evening and under a rising full moon, we talked with Tiby and her companions about the future of the Caura and what could be done to preserve the region. We all agreed that the giant otters, tapir, jaguars, and macaws needed increased protection from conversion of forests to cattle ranches, flooding by hydro schemes, and the ubiquitous market hunters. But how? John Terborgh and Carlos Peres, a Brazilian expert on the effects of hunting on wildlife, have argued strongly for a strict protectionist approach—even limited hunting has a decimating effect when the targets are the top predators that hold the herbivore populations in check. Their solution is a network of nature reserves, occupied only by indigenous peoples, where access is controlled effectively and cheaply by establishing guard posts at the confluences of the major rivers. In the Amazon and Orinoco systems, the rivers and streams are the thoroughfares of human traffic, as roads are still fairly rare. Thus, market hunters and poachers could easily be interdicted by a system of strategically placed checkpoints.

The Ya'Kwana reserve offers a different solution, the creation of a large indigenous territory where the locals—not the government—set the rules of conservation practice, an arrangement that seems to be working well. In Venezuela, Ecuador, Brazil, Bolivia, and parts of the Guianas, indigenous reserves are the largest potential conservation areas for wildlife. Twenty-three percent of the Brazilian Amazon is currently allotted to indigenous reserves, far more territory than is protected in the country's national and state parks. Dan Nepstad of the Woods Hole Institute has mapped the distribution of those reserves and compared them with satellite data on the extent of wildfires in the region and the advance of the agricultural frontier in the eastern Amazon. The pattern he found was remarkable: Indigenous reserves serve as natural firebreaks. His overlay map revealed a green dike formed by a network of closely situated native territories holding back the deforestation, the spread of agriculture, and illegal incursions into the heart

of Amazonia. More than any government edict or the efforts of any international conservation organization, native homelands may be maintaining the integrity of the Amazon forest cover in the battleground on
the eastern edge of the basin.

If indigenous reserves are to be the most common form of land use,
we need to ask how effective they are at biodiversity conservation,
particularly compared with strict nature reserves where human occupation is prohibited. This is one of the most controversial questions in
conservation biology. It is also the overriding reason Tiby is here. In a
sense, her project is a microcosm of the great debate. Her role is to
provide enough scientific information about the population structure
and reproductive biology of the Orinoco river turtles to ensure sound
management by the Ya'Kwana. If they follow the clear harvesting
guidelines established for collecting the turtle eggs, they will have a
protein source as long as the sun rises over the forest. But do native
peoples, any more than non-native peoples, always have the best interests of nature in mind? Once Tiby left the Caura, what was to keep
a few Ya'Kwana from gathering up all the eggs and selling them for
hard cash to buy television sets? One side contends that the Indians
were here first and know better than outsiders about how to conserve
their resources. And if they want to buy TV sets, who are we to tell
them they can't? Some conservationists take a more cynical view
about people of any kind living inside parks. They suggest that, left to
their own devices, Indians are just as likely as people elsewhere to
wipe out the macaws, jaguars, otters, and the fish the otters eat, and
even to slice up the forest in which they live if offered enough cash by
predatory loggers. Because both sides of the debate provide data to
support their firmly held positions, the controversy continues.

Against this cultural backdrop is a nation in political turmoil about
the future of its democracy. Of most concern is the ambitious plan of
President Hugo Chavez to develop the near-pristine Venezuelan interior through large hydroelectric projects, heavy industries, and mech-
anized agriculture. The expectation is that poor Venezuelans from the

overcrowded coastal cities will resettle along the Orinoco and its tributaries. But will anyone want to leave the seductive salsa bars and lively *calles* of Caracas for the isolation and malaria of the interior? Similarly, during the Soviet era, Russians were enticed with incentives to move to cities too far north or too remote for year-round human habitation. Now the incentives are gone, and most people stranded in Norilsk and Magadan want desperately to escape to Moscow and St. Petersburg.

There is no consensus on what will save the Caura and other great rain forests, if anything will. Some believe that malaria, ebola, sleeping sickness, Chagas', and other diseases will continue to make vast areas of the tropics inhospitable to large human populations, and some rain forest regions may thereby survive. More science-based solutions are in the offing. Science is now discovering the role that the tropical canopy plays in maintaining the hydrological cycle in South America and even the climate on other continents. This *should* prompt politicians and international lending agencies to create financial mechanisms to protect the rain forest, as are now being discussed in the wake of the recently ratified Kyoto Protocol. To aid this effort, an important experiment is now under way, the largest of its kind in the history of our planet, to save the integrity of the Amazon. The Amazon Regional Protected Areas Program (ARPA) was designed and funded by the Brazilian government, in partnership with the World Wildlife Fund, the World Bank, and the Gordon and Betty Moore Foundation, to set aside and upgrade a network of Amazon reserves the size of France, essentially 10 percent of the Amazon. Assistance is also going to extractive reserves, where locals would sustainably manage tropical forests while engaging in rubber tapping, brazil nut collection, and best-practice logging—in which only individual trees and not whole swaths of forest are cleared. The ultimate goal is to keep the Brazilian Amazon under continuous forest cover by helping to create more indigenous reserves, more federal reserves, and forest reserves where best-practice logging will yield the timber essential for Brazil's domestic market but exact minimal damage to the integrity of the greater Amazon. Other programs are now actively doing the same for parts of the Amazon basin that fall within the boundaries of Peru, Ecuador, and Bolivia: For example, in February 2005, the government of Peru, with strong support from WWF, announced the creation of Alto Purus National Park, a huge tract of forest that includes an indigenous area of uncontacted tribes. Together with Manu National Park in Peru and Chandless National Park in Brazil, an area the size of the state of Massachusetts would be protected, large enough for a good number of tapirs, jaguars, and, of course, giant river otters. A Venezuelan version of ARPA may be the next experiment to undertake.

There will also be the pressing need for people like Tiby to work with locals in the indigenous and extractive reserves to harmonize, as well as possible, poverty reduction and nature conservation. If giant river otters are to roam wild across the Amazon and Orinoco, they will need local guardians, motivated by defenders like Tiby, who see that sound river resource management and otter conservation are inseparable.

After goodbyes to Tiby and her colleagues, we began the journey back downriver. We stopped several hours along the way to meet some of Julio's relatives. The villagers displayed mats and vibrantly colored baskets woven from grass, all with distinct animal designs. David had already accumulated enough artifacts from previous trips to establish a small museum, but that didn't stop him from collecting more. "The Ya'Kwana are the best basket makers in South America," he told us. The baskets were beautiful, and Wendy and I joined the buying spree. As we moved farther downriver, I began to wonder if the only way locals can earn hard currency is to sell their finest artwork for virtually nothing—as in parts of the Sepik River of New Guinea, in remote Tibet, and for the waves of tourists in the Serengeti—how their lot will ever improve. Why does anyone expect the Ya'Kwana to remain as they are now? What if the desire to develop their land and sell off its resources comes partly from within the group and is not simply implanted by a smooth-talking charlatan from a timber company?

Osprey patrolled the riverbanks, escorting our loaded dugout back to the lodge. Maybe it was an illusion, but the population seemed larger now than on the way upriver. Or perhaps more had arrived over the past few days to feast along a river churning with fish. An osprey flew over the boat and landed in a tree draped in lianas. I imagine that osprey experience an emotional transformation in their migration. After a spring and summer of sharing mid-Atlantic beaches with throngs of oiled humans and their blaring radios, with the best fishing grounds invaded by jet-skiers, they perhaps need the balance offered by a place where osprey and giant river otters outnumber people. I thought about my osprey from New Jersey, banking south off the Orinoco breezes to lead their descendants to the vast untouched Caura. And I realized that we had adopted their ways, too, that, however briefly, our souls needed to migrate to a place wilder than Manu, to seek the restored perspective that only a tropical rain forest can provide. For Wendy, it was relief from the pressures of the financial jungles of New York investment banking, and for biologists like David, Linda, and myself, it was the kind of restorative fix needed from time to time to reassure the conservationist in each of us that the world still contains untrammeled wilderness and to remember vividly what we are fighting to preserve.

Humans will have reached a pinnacle in the evolution of our species when our actions match our sentiments to save wild nature. Certainly in our culture there are expressions of the desire to do so in poetry, prose, and other forms of art. Words that carry the emotion of Wallace Stegner, who inspired armies of North American conservationists when he wrote, "Something will have gone out of us as a people if we ever let the remaining wilderness be destroyed. . . . We simply need that wild country available to us, even if we never do more than drive to its edge and look in. For it can be a means of reassuring ourselves of our sanity as creatures, a part of the geography of hope."

Until that day when such words count as much as the promise of petrodollars, much of our effort to save the last of the wild will be like pushing a boulder from the Caura up the steep slopes of the tepuis. The challenge, it seems to me, whether in the Caura, the jungles of Nepal, or the tropical forests of Costa Rica and New Caledonia, is to mainstream the goals of nature conservation, so that they are "built in" from the start to regional development plans, rather than viewed as nuisance "add-ons" by nongovernmental organizations badgering governments and world financial institutions. Only then will tapirs and jaguars be able to walk safely through a big stretch of rain forest set aside for them.

We made one more natural history stop on our return downriver. On previous visits, Linda had observed the most spectacular bird of the New World, the Guianan cock-of-the-rock (*Rupicola rupicola*). Decked out in bright orange plumage with a bizarre rakish crest on the forehead, male cock-of-the-rock swivel and shake on the dance floor of the rain forest to attract females. Each *lek*, the term used to describe where the males compete to impress females, is populated by a dominant male who gets to breed, as well as a host of impersonators. To see one, we had to climb straight up a small densely forested mountain. Linda ran through the forest, heading straight for the base of the mountain where the path started to switch back. One of the best women Ultimate frisbee players in the United States and certainly one of the fastest, she was far ahead of us by the time we reached the steep terrain. I labored along with Wendy, while David and Julio brought up the rear.

A pelting rain started to fall. This would be a wet ascent, and if the rain kept up, the river could rise quickly, making our return perilous. I wondered whether we should abandon the side trip and continue down the river. Linda had promised a great view at the top, even if Elvis-of-the-rock was shut up in his dressing room and refusing to take the stage in the downpour. In the end, we didn't find the display leks, but we did hear the loudest call I have ever heard by a bird in the rain forest, the metallic whipping song of the screaming piha, whose voice is the hallmark of the region. As we climbed higher, the rocky summit of the mountain appeared. The rain was halting and wisps of clouds clung to the canopy of trees below us. The wind picked up, but the sun was about to emerge, signaling the drenched, near-hypothermic sloths to leave their concealed roosts and spread their limbs in the treetops to dry out and catch the welcoming rays.

The cloud cover receded like a lid pulled off the sky. Suddenly, we stood before an unending panorama of tropical rain forest. From the southern Venezuelan highlands to the northern Amazonian city of Manaus on the Rio Negro in Brazil, this place on earth was virtually empty of human settlements. Below us was a world where we were not equipped to survive for long, but where other species remain perfectly suited to thrive in our absence. Maybe there were no more Conan Doyle dinosaurs, or the giant ground sloths and their relatives that disappeared in the Pleistocene, but the smaller ark that spilled its neotropical passengers—night monkeys and anteaters, white-lipped peccaries, capybaras, pink and gray river dolphins, scarlet macaws, white-throated toucans, screaming pihas, cock-of-the-rock, caiman, Orinoco river turtles, and giant river otters—had landed in a safe haven where they could pass their whole lives and perhaps never see a human being. I had no illusions of a peaceful kingdom below us; it is a harsh eat-or-be-eaten land: relentless jaguars stalking tapirs, giant river otters defending their turf like street gangs, entire civilizations of leaf-cutter ants stripping the green lining from the forest floor, the mayhem stirred up by raiding parties of army ants, harpy eagles terrorizing defenseless sloths, and howler monkeys roaring at the intruding dawn. Perhaps not a peaceful kingdom, but at least a free state where humans claimed no dominion. After five days of searching, we had reached the edge of the map. We had crossed into the Lost World.

chapter six

MIOMBO WARRIORS

WHAT BEGAN AS A TRICKLE OF SNORTING WILDEBEEST swelled into a small river of antelope surging across the Serengeti plains. Within seconds, the herd streamed past our caravan of white Land Rovers gleaming in the hot African sunshine. This advance guard was part of the 1.5 million animals that moves every year in a great circle from the Serengeti National Park in Tanzania to the Masai Mara Game Reserve in Kenya and back again. We could empathize with the restlessness of the herd. We were on the final leg of our own migratory circuit, a round-the-world trip to eleven of the planet's most ecologically fabled destinations in a whirlwind twenty-five days. Our plane had just arrived from the Seychelles that morning, and after a quick shuttle flight from the airport at Arusha to the park headquarters, we were whisked off on safari for a postcard glimpse of East Africa: two days among its high society of graceful giraffes gliding by flat-topped groves of acacias, and below them, the nimble choreography of gazelles, zebras, and impala stirring up the dun-colored landscape.

Africa is the kingdom of antelopes. More than seventy species are found on the continent, and they fall into distinct social classes. The size, grace, and beautiful facial markings of the roan and sable antelopes make them monarchs. Next come the noble eland and princely greater kudu, the latter a chic blend of classic spiraled horns and contemporary white pin stripes on a tawny brown coat. In the drier regions, the regal gemsbok commands a desert fiefdom with its bold stripes and saber-like horns. The wildebeest, the hartebeest, and a few other dull-colored hoofed mammals—the commoners of the kingdom—trudge across East Africa's grasslands, ignored by the wildlife paparazzi dangling out of 4x4s to capture shots of the royal family, unless, of course, a wildebeest should enter into a life-or-death drama with a hungry cheetah.

The name *wildebeest* sounds far more poetic than *gnu*, the other common name for this species, used in children's rhymes and crossword puzzles. I pointed out to my fellow travelers how the wildebeest looks like it was assembled from body parts left over from an evolutionary yard sale for ungulates. Even the local tribes make light of its appearance. Fortunately for the wildebeest and other homely mammals, evolution is not a beauty pageant. Wildebeest may lack physical allure, but they are blessed with keen instincts. They survive in a dry landscape by chasing the rains, navigating by the dark clouds on the horizon toward the promise of tender grass. And they are nimble from birth, quick to flee from the loping gait of the hyena or the orchestrated attack of lions.

Because wildebeest are so sure-footed, I was astonished to see one topple to the ground near our vehicle. It immediately jumped to its feet, but before it could rejoin the herd, the hidden instigator of its tumble, an enormous male lion, rose up and swatted it once again to the turf. Using its massive forepaw to prevent a second escape, the king of the plains seized its prey by the throat. The wildebeest flailed helplessly with its hooves and cast a final glance up at the intensely blue sky. Within moments, the lion had dragged its kill into a strip of bushes. Another male, likely his brother, had observed the takedown without lifting a paw but was now ready to join in on dinner.

The inside of our Land Rover fell stone silent. The sudden attack rendered speechless even the chattier travelers. As naturalist for this trip, I did my best to come up with an Attenborough-like observation. "Not to be too disparaging of lions, but they have a clear advantage over the ungulates this year." I was referring to the rains, which had been much heavier than usual in the Serengeti, so its normally stubble-like grassland had grown tall enough to hide a crouching big cat. The wildebeest never had a chance. Though predation is a powerful structuring force in animal evolution, it's rare to see it in action. "You don't get a chance to be killed more than once," I said, uncertain whether my commentary sounded insightful or profoundly stupid, "so the social behavior of plant-eating animals is largely driven by concern for avoiding the kind of incident we just witnessed." I mentioned the notion that lions and other flesh-eaters cull only the weak and aged from the herd. In this case, the lion had ambushed an animal in its prime. Why was this particular individual singled out from the hundreds of wildebeest that must have filed past the concealed hunter? For those who seek life's lessons from observing nature, the obvious message here is that when the lion of death pounces, save your last breath for contemplating the blue African sky.

I'm not usually so philosophical about mortality when watching wildlife. But this trip was partly a nostalgic, and sometimes painful, reminder of the passing of a dear friend and colleague, Henri Nsanjama. I owe my introduction to the continent's wildlife just six years earlier to Henri, one of the leading conservationists in the region. Unlike many other biologists, I had explored Latin America and Asia first, saving this wondrous land for last.

"Eric, when are you going to come to Africa? Nepal must be great, but we have elephants and rhinos, too." Henri's teasing continued until he came to me with two special requests. First, he asked if I would bring a group of scientists from my program to Tanzania to teach African biologists the principles and tools of conservation biology, including the latest computer mapping programs used to design parks and map animal locations. I jumped at the chance to help advance one of his missions: to create an exceptional class of African wildlife professionals. Second, he wanted me to visit and evaluate a key project on rhino conservation he had been supporting in the Selous Game Reserve in southern Tanzania. Henri knew of my particular fondness for rhinos, and so he'd put together a trip he knew I couldn't refuse.

Henri's life had been devoted to preserving Africa's biodiversity. Born near the center of the miombo region near the town of Malosa, Malawi, he grew up surrounded by nature. Inspired by his grandfather's stories, his passion for wildlife emerged at a young age. By the time he was a teenager, he had already chosen the career path of wildlife ranger, turning down a college scholarship to study business administration to volunteer with the Malawi Department of Wildlife. His competence and dedication earned him a grant to attend the College of African Wildlife Management in Mweka, Tanzania, the premier training institute in Africa. He then worked as a warden at Kasungu National Park in central Malawi until 1978, when he was awarded a scholarship to study at the University of Massachusetts, where he earned a bachelor's degree in wildlife biology. With the help of another scholarship he earned a master's degree in environmental management at the University of Sterling, Scotland, before returning to Malawi, where, in 1988, he became director of national parks and wildlife. In 1990, he was named the vice president of WWF's Africa and Madagascar Program, the first African to be appointed to such a high-level position in any international conservation organization. Henri passionately believed that the way to promote and sustain African conservation was to focus on its charismatic large mammals. But with that came a need to set aside large tracts of wilderness for them to continue to survive on a continent where wild places were, at least in some areas, shrinking and being hemmed in from all sides by human settlements. There was good science to support what he was proposing, as many of Africa's big mammals are what biologists call *area sensitive*, that is, they need large areas to maintain healthy populations.

Henri was the Pelé of African conservation and the most popular man I have ever met. He could charm even the crustiest scientists, the most cynical donors, and the sternest bureaucrats. There was something about his broad smile and upbeat attitude that made people want to hug him, even if they saw him every day at work. His devotion to the species of the African plains was unwavering, but he had an even stronger passion. "Go, enjoy the parks around the Serengeti. Learn your natural history," he encouraged me. "But then you must head south to see the miombo. That is the real Africa."

Spanning the largest block of natural habitat in sub-Saharan Africa, the miombo is a broad cummerbund of woodlands, forests, and glades just below the expanse of dense rain forests in the Congo basin and the Serengeti grasslands. The miombo covers 1.4 million square miles, a vast swathe straddling part or all of eleven African countries, and supports over three thousand animal species and about eighty-five hundred plant species, over half of which are restricted to the region. In contrast, the postcard version of East Africa—the grasslands of northern Tanzania and Kenya in the shadow of Mount Kilimanjaro—covers a mere 14,000 square miles, roughly one-tenth the size of the miombo, and is much less diverse biologically. Yet few tourists have ever heard of the miombo, and even fewer have been there. My own knowledge of the region was limited, as well, which only heightened my anticipation, particularly to see the Selous Game Reserve, the most intact remaining example of eastern miombo. Henri could not travel with us because of other commitments, but he promised us an exceptional guide.

Our training program took place in Arusha, Tanzania. My colleagues and traveling companions from WWF, David Olson and George Powell, cotaught the course with me, and by the end, promising young African biologists had learned the theory of reserve design, techniques for displaying their data on wildlife populations, and ways to produce compelling maps of their work to help persuade decision makers.

After four days of staring at computer screens and digitizing tablets, I jumped at the chance to travel to some of the northern Tanzania nature reserves that we had mapped during the course. But there was a more emotional reason to make the trip. For a natural historian over forty, to experience a new wildlife-rich region for the first time is tantamount to reliving the unfiltered joy of childhood wonder—a precious opportunity to utter over and over again, "Wow, look at that!" a phrase that often drops from adult conversations after years of mortgage payments and car pooling. And when that new region is an entire continent—and when that continent is Africa—well, the thrill is indescribable.

I once heard an English teacher say that if you want to interest indifferent students in classic literature, don't hand them a novel by Marcel Proust or Thomas Mann. Hand them a book by Robert Louis Stevenson or Dickens, something full of color and action. To entice a budding naturalist, similar advice holds. Avoid tropical rain forests as the first destination. All the trees look the same to a novice and the animals are often frustratingly hard to see. The place to baptize a young naturalist is Africa; and for mammologists, dunk them in Tanzania, with its wide diversity of habitats and rich list of ungulates, predators, and abundant small mammals. For ornithologists, many enthusiasts would recommend Kenya, specifically a birding route running from the forests along the coast up to the scree slopes of the high mountains. And for botanists, Cape Town, South Africa has the highest concentration of spectacular flowering plant species on earth.

We began by visiting four world-renowned reserves that lie to the north of the miombo. The Ngorongoro Crater, our first stop, is famous among biologists as the site of a long-term study of lions. Over the past few decades, Craig Packer and his colleagues have worked out the genealogy of the local lion population and the process by which a feline ascends to be the Lion King of the Ngorongoro. A somewhat chilling aspect of the study was the documentation of rampant infanticide that occurs when a male lion overtakes a rival's pride. All the lions we saw when we visited, though, were sleeping, except for a few playful cubs, unaware of the danger posed to them by ambitious suitors with amorous designs on their mother and aunts.

Seeing my first lions in the wild was exciting, of course, but I was even more anxious to see a black rhino. Had I been in East Africa around 1900, that would have been easy. With a population estimated at one million, the black rhino was one of the most numerous large mammals on the continent at the turn of the last century. When compared with the thirty-six hundred black rhinos remaining in the wild today, the stark difference in zeros conveys a tragic loss. The great poaching episodes of the 1960s and 1970s nearly exterminated the species, making it hard to find black rhinos anywhere in Africa. Where they still range freely, they are often secretive and mostly nocturnal. To increase their numbers, some of the animals have been taken from the bush to private game ranches, where they can breed unmolested. These relatively small facilities serve as a kind of maximum-security fortress, patrolled by well-armed guards to deter relentless poachers. As sad as that seems, such a confined setting is essential for the protection of these great beasts, which once roamed freely and in great numbers across the African bush.

It took all day to find a single black rhino in the wild. Early in the morning, we had met the head of a rhino monitoring project who was

171

studying the remaining twenty-five or so individuals left in the crater.
Because they are so difficult to spot during the day, he suggested a few
places to look. Even with our insider's map, hours went by without a
sighting. Then, in the fading light of the late afternoon, we spotted a
huge rock in the middle of the grassland. As we approached, the rock
abruptly shifted, and the phrase "like a gray boulder come to life"
leapt to mind from the pages of Beryl Markham's memoir, *West with
the Night*—it was the perfect description for the massive rhino we saw
rising quickly to his feet. The silhouette of his huge head and horns
was something to venerate: a rare sighting made possible through the
dedication of the Tanzanian Park Service.

This solitary male was the only black rhino we encountered in the
four parks we visited over four days: Ngorongoro, Tarangiri, Lake
Manyara, and Arusha. The valiant effort to save these ancient creatures from extinction is ongoing. Guards patrol the parks to defend
the rhinos from the well-armed poachers and to search for and remove leg snares set by poachers bent on stealing the animal's valued
horn. Risking their lives every day for an animal that would just as
soon trample them as a poacher, the park guards are the unrecognized
heroes of this dramatic rescue effort.

That there are any rhinos alive anywhere today is a miracle. During
the Pleistocene and before, scores of rhino species once rumbled
across our planet. Only five species are still with us: the black rhino
and white rhino of Africa, and the greater one-horned, Javan, and
Sumatran rhinos of Asia. Today, the southern variety of the white
rhino is by far the most numerous. In 1900, however, its numbers
dipped below one hundred, all of which were confined to one reserve
in South Africa, the Umfolozi Game Reserve. A phenomenal recovery
effort was launched to save the largest of the five species, and today
there are more than eleven thousand southern whites, which have
been reintroduced to their former strongholds across southern Africa.
That populations of other species besides the southern white are increasing, such as the black rhino in Namibia and the greater one-

horned rhinos in Nepal and India, is an even greater marvel. Unfortunately, not all rhino species are doing as well. The rarest large mammal on earth, the phantom-like Javan rhinoceros, nears extinction. Fewer than sixty live in the wild, zero in captivity. But the success of rhino recovery programs offers some real hope: Large slow-breeding mammals will rebound quickly if we just do just two things: protect them from poachers and preserve their habitats from human encroachment.

The highlight of the next stop on our tour of northern Tanzania nature reserves, Tarangiri National Park, was its stunning display of East Africa's birds. Red and yellow bishops, sunbirds and bee-eaters, lilac-breasted rollers and starlings, orioles and kingfishers, weavers and lovebirds, waxbills and firetails—the list goes on. Most species are so richly colored that even the most reluctant bird watcher quickly becomes entranced, especially because the tree canopy is low enough to make the birds easy to spot, and their vivid plumage stands out in such poetic contrast to the dull browns of the dry-season grasslands. It felt like being in the audience of nature's Broadway, from the Baryshnikov leaps of the secretary birds to the shimmying of the ostrich's natural feather boa. Even the diversity and feeding habits of the local vultures are captivating. In Tarangiri, as elsewhere in eastern and southern Africa, six species of vultures are visible at most locales, probably more species than any place else in the world. The pecking order around fresh carcasses is strict, even if it's accompanied by a lot of posturing and squabbling. There's even a mostly vegetarian vulture called the palm-nut, who prefers the cuisine offered at the lower end of the food chain—fleshy fruits such as palm nuts rather than the animal flesh preferred by its more gruesome brethren.

Driving through Tarangiri takes you through some of the densest stands of baobab trees in Africa. Sausage trees, an odd member of the catalpa family that bears fruits shaped like a huge salami, are also in evidence. African bush lore warns tenderfoots never to camp under a sausage tree for fear of a falling fruit crushing their skull. Now I had another species to add to my list of homicidal trees, joining the cannonball and monkey pot of Latin America and the durian of Southeast Asia, each with bomb-sized, woody, seed-holding structures that spell doom for whatever lies below. I wondered if an elephant's cranium could withstand the force of a falling sausage fruit if caught daydreaming under a grove of trees.

We wanted to linger longer among the baobabs and elephants of Tarangiri, but we were on a tight schedule to return to Arusha for the night. So our time at Lake Manyara National Park was limited to the midday hours, in heat that would leave even the most diehard nature lover longing for a chaise lounge, anything on ice, and a swimming pool. We didn't find such a resort in the park, but we did come across some impressive pools populated by an unruly male hippo and his harem of females and their young. The male watched carefully over his domain, pausing briefly to note our curious stares. What an odd turn evolution took in designing this animal. Who would think such a comical appearance could belie such ferocity? Hippos may resemble oversized rubber squeaky toys, but each year they cause the death of more Africans than lions, elephants, crocodiles, and black mambas combined.

We watched as the male used his tail as a propeller to spread dung around the pool. Hippo pools attract scores of birds because the waters are rich in hippo excrement, the source of a complex food web. We saw rafts of ducks and Egyptian geese, ibis, several kinds of sandpipers, and jacanas, odd-looking birds that resemble coots on stilts. In the midst of those hangers-on at the hippo party lurked black herons, with their remarkable foraging technique. The heron stands still and folds its wings forward over its head, creating a small canopy of shade under the intense African sun. Small fish, amphibians, and invertebrates flock to the cover provided by this temporary umbrella, only to be speared by the ravenous trickster.

We escaped the withering heat of Manyara and headed back to Arusha. The next morning, we visited our last stop in the cluster of game reserves, Arusha National Park, a mountain gem. Perched on the slope of Mount Meru, an extinct volcano, and surrounded by a sea of coffee plantations, Arusha is one natural wonder after another. Never had I seen so many stunning species crowded into such a small park. We were treated to an acrobatic display of dashing black and white colobus monkeys, leaping through the trees in tuxedo-like fur coats and tails. For the second act, we turned our attention to a group of turacos, or louries. With their blue, green, and red feathers, louries are regarded by many as the most attractive family of birds endemic to Africa. Next came a feeding party of helmet shrikes, settling into a nearby tree. Helmet shrikes are cooperative breeders, so the family gathering consisted of the parents and their offspring, with each generation helping to raise the next.

When the science of conservation biology was born in the early 1980s, one of its founders, Michael Soulé, suggested that East African parks, such as Arusha, and the greater scientific community were in for a rude awakening. A fundamental theorem of this new science—based on the theory of island biogeography formulated by Robert MacArthur and E. O. Wilson in the late 1960s—predicted that if the smaller parks became increasingly isolated as land use changed around them, large species requiring significant areas of habitat would start going locally extinct. The phenomenon Soulé described, dubbed "faunal collapse," thus had three forces at work: the size of the reserve, the quality of the habitat surrounding it, and the distance between it and other reserves, where a dwindling species might possibly reestablish itself. Unfortunately, few biologists took notice of the warnings, instead remaining focused on their personal research interests.

During the 1960s and 1970s, wildlife research in East Africa was dominated by ethologists interested in how animal societies functioned. Those researchers sat in their Land Rovers; named the individuals of the baboon or vervet monkey troop, the hyena clan, or the elephant herd they were studying; and then kept detailed notes on the soap opera playing out before them. How long did it take Brutus to usurp Caesar and become the alpha male of the baboon troop? How many pups did Mandy the hyena raise successfully? Among the vervet monkeys, did Harry get to copulate with Sally after he showed off his bright blue testicles in a ritualistic display? In fairness, few scientists at that time paid attention to the science or effectiveness of reserve design or protected area networks—hallmarks of current-day conservation biology—because most of the parks were still surrounded by large areas of similar habitat, and, even better, most parks were still connected to one another by natural corridors.

Thus, in addition to poaching, the absence of large intact habitat is putting the wildlife in much of East Africa in peril. Our itinerary brought this reality into sharp focus as each wildlife habitat we visited decreased exponentially in size: Ngorongoro Conservation Area is tiny but is connected to the vast Serengeti National Park, so together they comprise 8,900 square miles, roughly three times the size of Yellowstone. Tarangiri drops to 1,000 square miles, a small fraction of the Serengeti, followed by the pocket-size Lake Manyara and Arusha National Parks, both under 80 square miles.

By the late 1980s, faunal collapse had begun, driven by dramatic changes in land use across East Africa. Bill Newmark, one of Soulé's students working in the Tanzanian parks I visited, demonstrated that the loss of large mammal species is related to park size. David Western, an outstanding African-born ecologist and later director of the Kenya Wildlife Service (KWS), published similar findings and suggested that relying strictly on Kenya's parks and reserves to halt loss of its biological diversity was a nonstarter. At that time, parks covered only 8 percent of Kenya's territory, and much of the wildlife and some unique habitats fell outside the reserve borders. If conservation of biodiversity in East Africa was to have a future, entire landscapes would have to be designed and zoned by working in concert with local people who controlled or had access to lands essential for conserving rare species or habitats.

Western's vision, and similar concepts put forward by others, is now generally referred to as "community-based conservation." The flames of controversy over this new paradigm still smolder in lonely camp-fires tended by a dispersed group of African conservationists. Both sides have legitimate points to make. The fence-it-or-lose-it camp headed by Richard Leakey, former head of the KWS, advocates the tactic of essentially sealing off parks from locals when the endangered wildlife they were established to save comes under intense threat by armies of poachers. But that is clearly a holding action, and his successor, David Western, sought more sustainable solutions by enlisting the support of local people and ensuring that the benefits of conservation flow directly to them rather than to the Ministry of Finance. The latter solution is an essential strategy for lasting conservation but one that takes patience and major policy changes to enact. Western and his supporters argued that local peoples coexisted with native wildlife for eons, and that we could rediscover how to make that coexistence work again in the new millennium. In the meantime, responded the critics, without urgent and strict protection measures, all could be lost quickly in the smaller parks.

The problem of small, isolated wildlife parks has become a global conservation priority. But studies in other parts of the world bear out the finding that large mammals disappear relatively quickly when their habitats become too small and isolated. The single, most powerful treatment for avoiding faunal collapse does not require field note-books full of data or years of observation: Simply double or triple the size of individual reserves, or, better yet, secure networks of mega-reserves linked by functional wildlife corridors, and the extinction threat will disappear. There is an interesting analogy here with the human body. Some holistic doctors claim that half of all the symptoms people see a physician about are a result of dehydration. If patients would rehydrate a few days prior to their office visit, many ailments (sore throats, headaches, dizziness, skin rashes) would disappear. Similarly, identifying and protecting large blocks of natural habitat maintain the health of natural ecosystems and avoid expensive management interventions, especially if we can secure them before they become too degraded.

A living demonstration of this concept is Africa's largest sanctuary, the Selous Game Reserve, which is 21,000 square miles, roughly the size of Switzerland. Faunal collapse there is far from imminent. About fifty years ago, the Selous had more of every species of note than any other reserve in Eastern Africa: more elephants, more black rhino, more lions, more buffalo, more kudu, and more crocodiles. Beyond its great size, one reason for its success is its relative obscurity; it lies far from the most popular game park itineraries such as the one I took earlier. Because of the abundance of large animals, one of the Selous's legendary wardens, Brian Nicholson, devised a scheme to permit carefully controlled hunting in restricted areas. Western hunters, attracted by the certainty of a trophy and the secrecy of the Selous, drop small fortunes to bring home a record-busting kudu, elephant, lion, or buffalo. That money maintains the Selous, making it an anchor in a regionwide endeavor to protect the extraordinary large mammal assemblages of the miombo woodlands.

As promised, Henri had arranged for my colleague David Olson and me to travel to the Selous with an astute guide and a recent hire of WWF in Africa, Max Morgan-Davies. Max had spent the past few years monitoring black rhinos and working toward their recovery in the Masai Mara Game Reserve in Kenya. The idea was strategic yet simple: Black rhino numbers were increasing rapidly on small, private game ranches where they had been moved to escape poachers' bullets and gauntlets of leg snares. But the sanctuaries were too small to support more than a handful of rhinos, because the animals need a lot of space to maintain their large territories. Max, along with WWF and other groups, was promoting the establishment of intensive protection zones (IPZs) within large reserves—safe havens of eighty to one hundred twenty square miles. The IPZs would be large enough to allow for rhino populations to stretch out within their native habitat but small enough to be effectively monitored by dedicated teams of top guards and trackers. The Selous was a perfect candidate for replicating the IPZ method of protection. Black rhinos were once abundant across the Selous, but years of poaching had seriously reduced the population, and they clearly needed additional protection.

Max picked us up in a spanking-new green Land Rover, complete with WWF's familiar giant panda stickers on the doors. Leaving from Dar es Salaam, on the coast, we would drive southwest across the fabled Rufigi River and then east into the heart of the Selous. Our first stop—nearly eight hours' drive—was Kingupira, where we would meet park officials and guards. Our base camp would be another two hours' drive to a small outpost that served as a research station for biologists studying elephants. At the remarkably spry age of sixty-eight, Max was a bundle of energy, as ready to get started as we were.

Max drove at one speed: a notch below terrifyingly fast. For the first few hours, we went south, passing through a series of villages. Groups of women, clad in vividly colored print dresses, carried baskets of food and water jugs—the basic possessions of Africa—on their heads. Their chatter turned to laughter as Max smiled and waved as he drove by. Then we turned sharply inland onto a track of red clay roads, roller-coastering over the low hills of south central Tanzania. The heat of the day was intense, but the new Land Rover had excellent AC, and we roared along in comfort through the African heartland. As he drove, Max described his efforts to census black rhinos in the Mara Reserve by maintaining photographic records of individuals. I listened with empathetic interest, as I had done the same thing in Nepal with greater one-horned rhinoceros—but I had been thirty-five years younger than Max when I embarked on such an exhausting project.

Our Land Rover was now hurtling down the rough roads of the Tanzanian bush, rocks and gravel spraying the underside of the chassis like a reverse hailstorm. The appearance of flat-topped trees and giant termite mounds indicated that we had crossed into miombo country. Another unifying feature of miombo woodland is the presence of three types of trees, all in the legume family and all with impossible-to-remember Latin names: *Brachystegia*, *Julberdnardia*, and *Isoberlinia*, a helpful contribution made by early botanists to keep the miombo a secret. Suddenly, Max swerved the Rover into a long hedgerow of shrubs armed with stout, woody thorns that shrieked with delight as they raked the unblemished flanks of the 4x4. "Have to break it in sometime," muttered Max, throwing us a look with his dancing blue eyes.

Max was humble, so only with some difficulty did we manage to pry out of him the rich saga of his years in Africa. He was born in Sri Lanka, into a family of expatriate British tea planters. At nineteen, desperate for adventure and seeking to escape from the seemingly inevitable career in tea planting, he answered an advertisement for the position of game warden in Tanzania, then known as Tanganyika. And just like that, Max became the first warden of Lake Manyara. He went on to become warden of Tarangiri and over the past four decades has worked or spent time in virtually all the significant parks of East Africa. One of the most memorable stories he told us was of his vehicle breaking down in the middle of the Serengeti. With no other options, he had to walk for days to reach help, spending the nights in trees to avoid becoming a lion's midnight snack.

I had been exposed to transplanted white African wildlife experts from my research stints in Asia in the mid-1970s. With few exceptions, those individuals were ex-pats who liked to grumble about how African conservation had deteriorated in their absence. Max was nothing like that. For one, he had a dogged commitment to remain in the field. Second, he clearly understood the African yearning for *uhuru*, freedom from colonial rule. Unlike others, who left when African nations started nationalizing their wildlife programs, Max stayed put, rapidly adapting to the changing political winds, during which his position would change from park warden to consultant, allowing him to politely provide sage advice when invited.

The habitat shifted from forest to woodlands as we moved closer to Kingupira. Chanting goshawks stood watch in the low trees along the road, while go-away birds—so named for their call, a nasal "ka-way"—crisscrossed in front of the vehicle. Also known as the gray lourie, the go-aways are from the same family as the dazzling turacos we had seen in Arusha National Park, but creation's closet was clearly cleaned out of vibrant plumage by the time the go-away arrived. Only an unflattering gray costume was left, but the bird compensated by developing a Don King–looking crest, allowing it to boast the most distinctive hairpiece in Africa.

I rolled down the front window for a moment to smell the air, and my nostrils nearly filled with tsetse flies. A cloud of them flew in and started beating themselves against the inside of the windshield. Max expertly flattened them with his hand, and I followed suit. Within a minute or so, they were all dead and our hands were stained with blood. I had heard that tsetse flies were once considered the guardians of wilderness. The sleeping sickness they spread among domestic cattle, and in some areas to humans, made it all but impossible to settle in vast areas of the miombo, thus keeping it wild. "There's some truth to that," Max said. "You can't raise cattle here because of the tsetse infestation, but you can't grow crops easily either. The sun and the rains have been leaching the miombo of minerals for eons."

As we drove to the research outpost, I asked Max about his relationship with Henri. Max told me of the first time they met, in Malawi, and how impressed he had been with Henri's commitment. They stayed in touch over the years, and when the opportunity came up, Henri had entrusted Max to help the Selous team move quickly to develop the IPZs.

On the way to our base camp, we stopped at some water holes where the guards and Max had seen black rhinos drinking only a few weeks before. It was near the end of the dry season, so all we saw was the cracked mud lining and some old footprints. The rhino's characteristic three-toed track was as large as a dinner plate, an unmistakeable sign that at least a few of these noble mammals still roamed the Selous.

The next day, we drove to several spots that rhinos were known to frequent. Max was indefatigable. In the intense heat of the Selous morning, he was bending down in the *Croton* thickets, looking for fresh signs of rhino. Rhinos like to hide in the thickets, he informed us, probably because it is hard for poachers to approach closely without being detected. I was trying to keep up with Max in the heat. I reckoned that when I hit sixty-eight, I would be growing heirloom tomatoes and working on the *New York Times* crossword puzzle, not wilting under the blazing sun, on foot, tracking dangerous rhinos. Still, it felt wonderful to be out in the bush on my own two legs. One drawback to studying wildlife in Africa is that all those fantastically large dangerous mammals limited one to recording observations from inside the protective cage of a 4x4. After a couple of days, you grow impatient for a stroll. After a week, you'll find nearly any excuse to get out of the car.

We had seen only a few fresh signs of black rhino so far. Poaching has affected their numbers drastically. The horns of Asian rhinos are valued at $15,000 per pound, those of African rhinos a bit less. Many people in the West believe the medicinal use of rhino horn is to enhance male sex drive. One of my favorite *New Yorker* cartoons is a rhino with a huge horn confiding to a sympathetic tiger, "They say it's an aphrodisiac, but it hasn't done jack for me." In truth, the horn's main value in Oriental medicine is as an emergency drug to reduce life-threatening fevers. The jury is out on the effectiveness of the remedy. To help alleviate the threat to rhinos, WWF and other groups have worked diligently to persuade practitioners of traditional Chinese medicine to replace rhino horn with products that are equally effective but not harvested from endangered species.

Unfortunately, Oriental medicine isn't the only use for rhino horn. A dagger handle made from rhino horn is worth a small fortune and is a symbol of wealth and stature in the country of Yemen. It sounds like a small pocket of demand, but in the 1980s, the majority of smuggled horn was brought into Yemen. Because Islam prohibits the driving of species to extinction, conservationists have worked with religious leaders to issue bans on using rhino horn for dagger handles. So far, though, the pressure for rhino horn handles remains intense.

We arrived late at the research station, which was composed of two low buildings in a small clearing. Max cooked us dinner, a rough bush stew made of beans and tinned meat. After dinner we traded stories of life both in the field and in the city. Max had settled back into living in Dar es Salaam when he wasn't out in the Selous. One night, he recounted, when he was home listening to music, three intruders, one brandishing a lead pipe, broke into his house to rob him. Even at sixty-eight, he managed to fight them off and chase them out, suffering only a knock on the head but no major loss of property. Perhaps the assailants had heard Mimi's sorrowful aria from *La Bohème* floating out the open window and thought they had found an easy pigeon. Boy, did they choose the wrong opera buff. I began to wonder if a black rhino might even think twice about charging Mad Max.

Our talk turned back to rhinos. I wanted Max's opinion about a controversial tactic to deter rhino poaching: dehorning. Poaching had become so rampant in the early 1990s that park resources were inadequate to protect wild black rhinoceros in large remote reserves. In response, dedicated wildlife vets and park staff in several southern African countries began taking the drastic measure of sawing off the horns of sedated rhinos to reduce the incentive to poach. The main advantage of dehorning is that the animals remain alive and in their native habitats and established territories. Moreover, in theory, only a portion of the population needs to be dehorned, because poachers would have to search longer and harder to find a horned rhino. The idea is that soon word would spread among poaching rings, and eventually the threat would disappear.

Every wildlife management decision in Africa seems to attract twice the controversy it would draw elsewhere, and the policy of dehorning was no exception. A close colleague of mine, Joel Berger, who studied black rhinos in Damaraland, Namibia, suggested that the dehorning of female black rhinos exposed their calves to high predation risks by hyenas and lions. His hypothesis was hotly contested by the government authorities.

In Max's opinion, dehorning was merely a well-meaning stop-gap measure. "It will never work," he proclaimed. And, of course, he was right. The cost to dehorn a rhino turns out to be quite high, as much as $1,500 per individual, and rhinos regenerate their horns at the rate of several inches per year. When vets saw off the horn, which is actually highly keratinized hair, like a fingernail, they must leave some tissue remaining. Even a sliver of horn is considered valuable enough by poachers to risk going after dehorned animals. The well-meaning conservationists in Namibia and Zimbabwe who proposed this measure had assumed rational behavior on the part of the poachers. That was a miscalculation. The poachers killed rhinos indiscriminately, even the dehorned ones.

The next day, we continued to drive around the reserve to visit various potential IPZs. Alongside our Land Rover, bands of Nyasa tessebees, plains wildebeest that have undergone a stylish makeover, trotted by. Unlike the dull gray overcoat of its relative in the Serengeti, this species sports a ruddy brown outfit with a sharp-looking white blaze across its forehead. Everywhere we went, there were small herds of truculent Cape buffalo and the handsome greater kudu sporting spiraled horns like giant corkscrews. Wild game was everywhere, behind every clump of trees—not in the large herds of the Serengeti, but in small groups, watchful and frequently moving.

We passed the remains of a number of makeshift camps established to service the field needs of the big game hunters. The Selous is a huge foreign currency earner for the Tanzanian government. Most of the reserve was divided into blocks that hunters had access to, while the northern section was a no-hunting area set aside for ecotourism and foot safaris. It was obvious which zone we were in—the one governed by the principle of wildlife management popular in southern Africa: "Use it or lose it." We stopped at a guard post where open-bed trucks were being loaded with the horns of kudu and buffalo, the tusks and skulls of elephants, and skins of all sorts. Max seemed indifferent to the body parts that would end up in hunting lodges and in multi-million-dollar homes in Montana, Texas, or Germany. David and I couldn't ignore it. Neither of us hunted, so it looked more like carnage than proof of manliness. Some hunters even shoot their prey from the safety of vehicles, which is illegal in the Selous. At least the rains would be coming soon, making roads impassable and ending the season. Was the kill from the whole season? "No," Max replied, as we all waved to the workers hanging off the backs of the trophy-laden trucks. "That's just from the past week."

After dinner that night, David walked out into the bush to set up his field microphone and recorder. He and his wife, Linda, had become connoisseurs of nature's orchestra, taping the early morning and evening sounds from the wildest places they visited. This way, when they were stalled in city traffic back home, idling in their dented Mazda pickup, they could switch to the soothing sounds of WILD-FM by slipping their homemade tape into the car stereo, and listen to the nocturnal groove of the nightjars, the muffled roars of a distant lion, and the morning chatter of wood hoopoes.

It was too hot to sleep. David joined Max and me for a nightcap, while an unrelenting swarm of mosquitoes dined on whatever exposed flesh we offered them. We did our best to prevent malaria with therapeutic rounds of gin and tonics (with quinine, the nineteenth century's antimalarial treatment) while listening to Max's campfire stories, punctuated by the "Here, here" of a territorial owl in the leafless tree above us. With the pinprick of each bite and the remoteness of our campfire from the network of northern game parks, I began to understand why Alan Rodgers, the foremost ecologist of the Selous, called it "the sleeping wilderness" and why tourists flocked to the more accessible, mile-high parks in northern Tanzania, which offered wildlife viewing in relatively mosquito-free comfort.

As the night wore on, we became inured to our uncomfortable metal folding chairs and the cumulus cloud of mosquitoes about our heads, as our talk turned to one of the most challenging issues in wildlife conservation: what to do about Africa's expanding elephant populations. All in all, this is a great problem to have, though the controversy is far from over. Numbers of African elephants, once super-abundant, had plummeted dramatically in the previous few decades as a direct result of poaching for ivory and a breakdown in enforcement of protection programs. Conservationists responded in several ways. Richard Leakey and his colleagues in the Kenyan government at the time set fire to stockpiles of ivory in a symbolic display that attracted world attention to the severe poaching of wild elephants and their rapid decline. Strong political pressure from Western nations culminated when the treaty on trade in endangered species, known as CITES, enacted an international ban on trade in elephant ivory. Contrary to the predictions of skeptics, the ban has been wildly successful, and elephant populations have rebounded dramatically in parts of their range, thanks in large measure to good protection by the governments in several African countries.

Despite the ban, elephant ivory is still a luxury item and a valuable commodity that if sold in a carefully regulated market could financially support conservation programs that benefit elephant populations and allow cash-strapped wildlife departments to protect other rare species and habitats. Thus, southern African officials ask: Why shouldn't wildlife programs in southern Africa be financially rewarded for restoring their elephant populations by being allowed to generate needed funds?

The controversy has made enemies of many who share the same overall goals of wildlife conservation, and the arguments still rage back and forth. Henri had the capacity to see the elephant ivory issue and the elephant management problem from both sides and tried to find some common ground, to allow utilization as a short-term solution, but to craft a grander strategy under which elephant populations could be allowed to grow in unoccupied areas. His efforts in this regard were heroic, given how polarized the two camps have become.

Max held the same opinion that David and I held: There was plenty of unoccupied elephant habitat left in southern Africa and room for elephant herds to grow still larger. Here in the Selous, elephant numbers were now way down from historical highs. And opportunities existed in a number of transfrontier reserves in southern Africa where vast new parks could accommodate the spillover from reserves now at full capacity. Small reserves, like Manyara and Amboseli, as Max pointed out, had become increasingly isolated, putting elephants at cross purposes with the surrounding agriculturalists. The traditional doctrine of wildlife management in Africa called for culling the herds, and Max had spent part of his early years in the park service engaged in such activities. I believe he had deep feelings of remorse about having taken part in such operations. I now understood what propelled him to continue to charge around like Lawrence of the Selous. It was to pay back the elephants, and rhinos, and the other creatures what had been taken from them. Even if he had played a small role in the culling, he had silently dedicated the rest of his days to preserving, if only in a few wild places, the Africa he had experienced as a recently arrived tea planter from Sri Lanka.

Tragically, the elephant ivory fracas has entered the same tense arena as the battle over abortion rights. Both debates shift quickly from science to ethical values. Perhaps soon, ingenious lab scientists will come up with an effective morning-after injection for female elephants that can be fired from a helicopter or Land Rover. Until then, conservationists from the wealthy nations must help underwrite the translocation of expanding herds from overcrowded reserves to the more remote corners of Africa. This is the most logical and ethical measure until a better solution is found.

The next day, David rose early and was already recording and watching for the movements of big predators when I joined him. "Look out there," he pointed. Moving across the open glade was a raiding party of giant ground hornbills. These turkey-sized black birds are fierce creatures, gobbling up whatever is in their path with their formidable, decurved bills. Their bright red face and throat patches contribute to their ferocious demeanor. A newborn antelope left briefly by its mother would be at risk from these stalkers of the Selous. Frightening as they appear, though, they are extremely sensitive to human intrusion and habitat loss, requiring vast areas of wilderness to survive.

David interrupted my contemplations. "Oh, listen to this," he said, rewinding the tape to play back the recording from the night before. The sounds were of a large male elephant, performing what sounded like deep-breathing exercises. He had been lingering near the bunkhouse, the volume suggested, and sure enough we found fresh tracks and dung. Perhaps with his excellent hearing, he had eavesdropped on our elephant ivory conversation. I hoped he figured out that we were on his side.

The next afternoon, David and I went exploring with some of the guards. When Henri asked me to go to the Selous, he mentioned that it was one the last places left to conserve African hunting dogs, also known as Cape hunting dogs, or African wild dogs. They used to be common in the Selous, running the abundant impala to exhaustion before moving in for the kill. A pack of forty or more animals, each with distinctive bold patches of color, functioned as an efficient killing machine. Having subdued its prey, the pack made short work of the victim, not out of innate savagery, but to quickly ferry bits of meat back to the den to feed the others before poorly mannered hyenas drove the dogs off their kill.

Few species of Africa have undergone a more catastrophic decline than African hunting dogs. Henri had personally raised considerable sums from private donors to study the ranging behavior of wild dogs in order to promote their conservation. Before Europeans arrived, hunting dogs were as common in Africa as wolves were in North America. But the spread of European colonization spelled the end for the wide-roaming dogs. Considered pests, they were mercilessly eradicated from much of their range. Researchers believe that their numbers have plummeted from some 500,000 to 3,000, and rampant poaching has caused the numbers to decline even further. Tanzania has about 800 left, Zimbabwe only 600, Botswana down to 500, and South Africa a mere 200. Radiotelemetry studies show that each pack needs about 300 square miles to prosper; maintaining multiple packs requires areas an order of magnitude larger than most African parks. Perhaps in the Selous and a few large transfrontier parks, African wild dogs still have a future. But that will require a change in attitude about them similar to the shift in attitudes about wolves that is slowly occurring in the U.S. lower forty-eight.

Unfortunately, hunting dogs were nowhere to be found, so we drove on to look at a hippo-filled stream sheltered from the blistering sun by a dense canopy of raffia palms. We had been out for hours, and David and I both neglected to take along water. The guards didn't have any canteens either, but they seemed unfazed by the sweltering 100°F temperature in the shade and 100 percent humidity. I asked David if he knew the location of the hottest place on earth. "Somewhere in Egypt, I think. Or maybe the Sudan." I had never been hotter than I felt at three in the afternoon that day in the Selous. We pressed on. Determined to spot a rhino or to see hippos up close, we left the Land Rover and followed the guards over a grassland that had been mowed to a golf course–like lawn by grazing hippos.

Aside from the mind-addling heat, I thought we were safe from hippos at this time of day because they do their grazing at night, leaving their comfortable pools only when the heat of the day, and the threat of a bad sunburn, has passed. Hippos are thin skinned and will quickly dehydrate and die in the sun. But under the cover of darkness they move about freely. Like rhinos, hippos are surprisingly quick if you find yourself trying to outrun them.

We moved in single file behind the guards, though their ancient rifles offered little sense of security. An active herd of hippos was frolicking in the water on the other side of the trail from the palm curtain. Suddenly, apparently in defiance of the conventional wisdom that hippos stay submerged until sundown, the entire herd was climbing the bank toward us.

We barely had time to scamper up some low trees to avoid a head-on encounter. The hippos knew where we were and circled the trees snorting vigorously. I felt a strong sense of déjà vu. Twenty years earlier, I had been treed by a greater one-horned rhinoceros in Royal Chitwan National Park, Nepal, in the company of three other Peace Corps volunteers. The desire for a close-up photograph and the idiocy of youth propelled us too close to a wallowing male rhino that time. He spent a few minutes encouraging us to appreciate the benefits of our arboreal niche while he thrashed about below us. Only that time, we had water bottles with us. Now we were not only up a tree, but we were up a tree without water. David and I were flirting with heat stroke. Fortunately, the hippos got bored, or hungry, and headed off to graze. We carefully circled around the herd and high-tailed it to the Land Rover. I took back whatever I had said to Max about the artificiality of doing field research from the safety of a 4x4.

We left the Selous for the long drive back to Dar es Salaam, Max lamenting the lack of rhinos we saw compared with how it used to be. He wanted to learn the computer mapping and database program we had taught the biologists at our workshop in Arusha, so he could record his rhino sightings, map the IPZs, and overlay the patrolling routines for the park guards. Henri had indeed found a gem to help start up the program. Such mapping is important, but what Africa seems to need most, I finally concluded—what every wildland needs most, for that matter—is the least glamorous, most maligned aspect of conservation: effective patrolling of reserves and strict enforcement of the laws already on the books. On this subject, modern wildlife conservation, with its emphasis on harmonizing conservation and sustainable development, is in a state of partial denial. No action instigates such a rapid recovery in wildlife numbers as the traditional effort spent on protection of key breeding populations.

There were clusters of enormous old mango trees in the center of the villages we passed on our way back to the coast. Max quizzed us: "Why do you think those mangos grow in such dense groves in the middle of the village and are spaced at equal distances from one another?" I thought that it might be symbolic of some religious association with the mango tree. The answer was more depressing. In the previous century, slave traders marched their captives from the inland miombo to the coast, feeding the shackled warriors and their families on mangos. The mango groves were planted at planned intervals to keep the slaves alive until they could be sold at the ports.

Back in Dar es Salaam, David and I paid a visit to Alan Rodgers, the most knowledgeable scientist to have worked in the Selous. Alan was among the smartest ecologists to set foot in East Africa. After serving as the chief scientist in the Selous from 1966 to 1976, he went on to teach at the university in Dar es Salaam and served as an adviser to the Wildlife Institute of India, helping to design a visionary network of parks for that country. I had read about his exploits in a popular book about East African wildlife and wildlife biologists. In the book, he was portrayed as the Falstaff of local biologists, with his substantial girth, earthy vocabulary, and impressive beard. He was opinionated, quick to challenge the ideas and sacred cows of current thinking in ecology and conservation, and a fount of knowledge. "Come over for dinner," he said when I phoned. "I have an old friend of yours staying with me."

We took a taxi to Alan's house and were happily surprised to meet his house guest, Andrew Laurie. Andrew seemed to precede me wherever I went: Nepal, the Galápagos, the panda reserves of China, and now here. It was his study, supported by the Frankfurt Zoological Society, that led to the design of the IPZ concept that Max was now trying to implement. Andrew had put in a good ten months in the Selous trying to map out the last strongholds of the black rhino. He had completed his Ph.D. on greater one-horned rhinos in Nepal and was the first person to study the species in detail. As a protégé of George Schaller, he had assisted the world's most famous wildlife researcher during his legendary study of Serengeti lions.

When I was in Chitwan during my Peace Corps training program, I spent a few days in Andrew's company. After only a few hours, I understood Schaller's willingness to mentor this young Brit. Andrew was a superb naturalist, good at languages (he was fluent in Nepali and Tharu, and later mastered Chinese), and incredibly brave. He ventured everywhere barefoot just like a native, sometimes even at night, carrying nothing more than his flashlight, binoculars, a satchel for his notebook and night vision scope, and a walking stick in case he encountered a sloth bear. He wore field shorts and no shirt. My fellow Peace Corps volunteers and I quickly adopted his attire and customs in that country. Yet there was another, more compelling, reason to mimic his approach to life in Nepal: He attracted all the beautiful women. We had found our role model, the James Bond of field biologists.

Now, years later in Africa, government red tape was keeping Andrew from starting a series of field projects, and Alan was trying to help him work through the difficulties. As I listened to the conversations that night, I saw emerging a genealogy of the guardians of this enchanting wilderness: Frederick Courtenay Selous, the great naturalist and explorer after whom the reserve was named in 1922; C. J. P.

Ionides, the game ranger who for over two decades earned his reputation as the father of the reserve; the leather-tough Brian Nicholson, warden for many years and a disciple of Ionides; Alan Rodgers, who picked up where Nicholson left off; Henri Nsanjama, who became one of the leading native black Africans to champion the reserve; Andrew Laurie; and Max.

The next day, we bid farewell to Max and began the journey back to the States. I was looking forward to sharing my impressions with Henri and telling him in person what an inspiration his work to save the miombo was.

Unfortunately, I returned to some disturbing news: Henri had been diagnosed with type II diabetes. His father, Peter, had died a few years before from the same illness. Luckily, Henri's condition gradually improved, and he was able to return to work, but his days of bouncing around the miombo were over. The medication and his more restrictive regimen did little to dampen the joy he brought to conservation and his burning desire to help fellow Africans follow in his footsteps. Then, suddenly, on July 18, 2000, Henri died in a car crash on one of the busiest thoroughfares in the Washington, D.C., area. He was only forty-nine.

During my drive to his memorial service, I slipped into the tape deck a copy of the recording David had made from our trip to the Selous two years earlier. The first sounds I recognized were the deep "ooomph, ooomph" calls made by the feeding party of giant ground hornbills and the "hoo-hoo" of coucals, like a concerto for bassoon and tuba. The sweet liquid whistle of orioles made me long for the Selous and a time when Henri was still with us.

The service was held at the cavernous National Presbyterian Church in northwest Washington. The crowd in the church was at overflow. There were easily a thousand people in the audience, from African ambassadors to colleagues at WWF and other conservation groups, to scores of members of his church. Toward the end of the service, a chorus of Malawian women stood and began singing and swaying, their brightly colored dresses reminding me of the plumage of Africa's most vibrant birds. The beautiful lilting hymns in their native Chichewa lifted everyone's spirits. How can a continent that has known a century of misery offer the world some of its most joyful music?

The hymns and African rhythms swirled in my head on the drive home. The number of people at Henri's funeral was a testament to how many he had touched. Perhaps that was one measure of a life well spent, I thought. "We don't have to lead great lives," the fiction writer and essayist Andre Dubus has written. "We just need to understand and survive the ones we've got." In darker moments, I embrace that philosophy, but I find it lacking in inspiration—one emotion that keeps life moving forward in the face of unspeakable tragedy. I thought of how Henri lived his life. Honor those who have gone before you, he might have said; embrace those in your grasp with love and kindness; encourage your contemporaries; and through your actions try to leave the world a better place than you found it. In that regard, he accomplished more in his forty-nine years than many of us do in twice that span.

Several days later, at his funeral back in Malosa, Malawi, where his casket was laid to rest, almost three thousand people gathered to pay lasting tribute to his life and ideals. Henri had flung open the doors for training the young people who care about saving Africa's grand natural heritage. In particular, he had encouraged the advancement of women, who have had little opportunity to crack the entrenched sexism of African conservation. Perhaps some of the young African girls at the National Presbyterian Church service, or those at the funeral in Malosa, would be inspired by his example and grow up to be great conservationists. Nelson Mandela's great gift to Africa has been to show how blacks and whites could live in harmony. Henri Nsanjama's legacy was the profound belief that wildlife and people can share the wealth of the earth, even in the poorest regions. Every region needs its Selous, a place where the wild heart of a continent still beats strongly. Every continent needs its Henri Nsanjama, one who reveres that wild heart of a continent and becomes its champion.

On July 28, 2000, when Henri's casket was finally interred under the gathering dusk of a Malawi winter day, I imagined another requiem beginning for a fallen son of Africa. As if sensing a solar eclipse or the flash of lightning signaling the start of the summer rains, the animals of the Selous and across the miombo ceased their activities in quiet expectation. The ground hornbills, the secretary birds, the ostriches, the kudu, and elephant herds at the water holes looked up at the pink-tinged sky. Along the roadsides, the chanting goshawks held their tongues, and the go-away birds sat erect on their branches. The lions rose abruptly from a day-long slumber. In the soda lakes, vast flocks of flamingos stood at one-legged attention. Even the frenetic jackals and hunting dogs stopped in their tracks. If only for a few moments, the residents of the bush fell silent and still to honor the passing of their defender, Henri Kapyepye Nsanjama, a Miombo warrior.

chapter seven

TRESPASSERS IN EDEN

A MALE GREAT FRIGATE BIRD INFLATED HIS CRIMSON THROAT sac like a valentine balloon and began to vigorously flap his long, pointed wings. He then threw back his head and released a whooping declaration of love at a nearby female. A squadron of challenging males was perched in the adjacent low bushes, their blooming throat pouches also tinged with the color of lust. These suitors were so focused on their biological pursuits that I could have reached over like a Hollywood stylist and smoothed their iridescent greenish black feathers. It was late March, mating season on Genovesa Island for the frigate birds, as well as for hundreds of thousands of boobies, petrels, and other ocean goers that converge on this speck of land in the Galápagos Archipelago. Along the high rim of Darwin Bay, I walked past a breeding colony of red-footed and masked boobies engaged in ritualized foreplay. Hiking on this island, I felt like a trespassing voyeur.

One can closely observe the private lives of wildlife in the Galápagos because this is one of the last sanctuaries on earth where animals live without fear of humans. These remote islands, six hundred miles off the coast of Ecuador, remained unknown to people until the early 1500s. Though the Polynesians, the Pacific's most skilled sailors, discovered Hawaii and other remote islands, the prevailing winds and currents steered them off course of the Galápagos. A few explorers arrived from the South American coast in the 1500s, but the lack of fresh water limited permanent settlement. In the absence of people, native wildlife thrived in what can only be described—cliché or not— as a veritable Eden. To protect it, the Ecuadorian government declared this remarkable archipelago a national park in 1959. Since then, it has become a powerful draw for nature lovers and students of evolution. After all, it was here that in 1835 a young (and slightly queasy) Charles Darwin disembarked from HMS *Beagle*, collected specimens, and, years later, formulated a theory that forever changed our understanding of the natural world.

I arrived as an accidental tourist in March 1999. Roger Sant, the chairman of the board of World Wildlife Fund, and his wife, Vicki, had invited a group of sixteen close friends on a week-long natural history cruise to these enchanted isles, to be led by Craig McFarland, the long-time director of the Charles Darwin Research Station there. Craig is a noted authority on the archipelago's giant tortoises and practically everything else that lives there, from the endemic marine iguanas to the heralded Galápagos finches. Unfortunately, a few weeks before the planned departure, Craig suffered a stroke (he has thankfully recovered). Scrambling for a last-minute replacement, Roger tapped me. I felt like a rookie pitcher unexpectedly called up from double-A ball to sub for a future Hall-of-Famer. I knew little about the Galápagos—I had studied Darwin's theory of evolution by natural selection in college, and I knew that his vessel was named after a hunting dog. And so I crammed over the next three days, absorbing every book, scientific article, and field guide I could find. Fortunately for our guests, there would be other experienced naturalists on board.

Only to Roger and Vicki did I reveal my secret: I had never before visited this biological shrine. When we stepped ashore to greet Genovesa's cavorting boobies on the first day of the cruise, I turned to Vicki and said, "You know, a biologist who has never been to the Galápagos is like an art history major who has never been to Florence." She nodded. Vicki was a well-traveled naturalist and art lover who knew first-hand the power of both destinations to draw you back. Ironically, I had already walked through the Uffizi and stared at Michelangelo's *David* on three separate visits to Tuscany before I corrected my professional imbalance. I have made a number of trips to the Galápagos since, returning each time from a different perspective. Each one has increasingly convinced me, that as naturalists and as citizens of this species-rich planet, we must elevate a few places on earth as sacrosanct, destinations that serve as benchmarks for our species, where we will do whatever it takes to defend and restore the handiwork of evolution, even if that means limiting our own access to those places.

En route to the Galápagos, we spent a few days in Quito, the high-elevation capital of Ecuador. There we were joined by Miguel Pellerano, the head of WWF's Galápagos program. Miguel was well schooled in natural history and possessed a rare combination of qualities—a burning passion for conservation and the diplomacy to actually achieve it. He had the demeanor of a Tibetan monk; I have never met a gentler conservationist. His good nature aside, few individuals had worked harder to achieve a fundamental breakthrough in the protection of the Islands—the Special Law of the Galápagos, signed only a few months earlier, in November 1998. That landmark legislation formally established the 20,000 square miles of ocean surrounding the entire archipelago—roughly the size of the state of Florida—as the second largest marine reserve in the world.

The atmosphere in the islands was still a bit tense following a confrontation between fishermen and park officials the year before, Miguel told us. Incensed by new, more restrictive regulations, local sea cucumber harvesters, known as *pepineros*, had occupied the Charles Darwin Research Station. They held scientists and workers hostage and threatened to firebomb the station with Molotov cocktails and kill the rare tortoises protected there in a captive breeding center unless fishing restrictions were relaxed even more. The standoff was resolved peacefully, but conservationists realized that more comprehensive solutions were needed to protect the islands' wildlife. Yolanda Kakabadse, the minister of the environment; Roque Sevilla, the mayor of Quito, a long-time conservationist of the Galápagos, and a WWF board member; and Miguel joined forces with other groups to draft new policies. The Ecuadorian government began to waver under pressure from local politicians and fishing interests, but a late-night call from the White House by then vice president Al Gore, urging action, helped counter the pressure, and the Special Law came into effect—although illegal fishing continues across the marine reserve, as do periodic sieges of the station by irate fishermen.

Our trip proved timely. Roger had arranged a meeting with Jamil Mahuad Witt, Ecuador's president, and Yolanda Kakabadse to convey worldwide support from conservationists for implementing the Special Law. This support was critical, as almost immediately after the law's passage, it came under attack. Beyond the specific complaints of the local pepineros, influential commercial fishing interests viewed the decree as a ban on their intense exploitation of the marine resources of the islands, an activity hidden from the average tourist's view. At stake were species even more profitable than sea cucumbers: shark fins to sell to Asian markets and tuna and other valuable fish to export globally. Besides the powerful fishing industry, there was the related economy of some sixteen thousand people living in the Galápagos, most of them confined to two islands, Santa Cruz and San Cristóbal. The majority of these residents had arrived from mainland

Ecuador within the last two decades as economic immigrants, looking for a higher standard of living through fishing or jobs in the booming tourism industry. One of the most controversial directives of the Special Law was to cap further immigration of people from the mainland.

We were shown into the Cabinet Meeting Room in the Carondelet Presidential Palace, where President Mahuad greeted us warmly. Over tea and coffee, he stated his commitment to conservation and the future of the Galápagos. He mentioned the obvious threat of over-harvesting of commercial fisheries and the need to carefully regulate the tourism industry. We were impressed, but he faced a far less supportive constituency outside. The windows were open, allowing the cool Andean breezes to circulate through the stately cabinet room. The multilingual, Lebanese-born Mahuad ignored the chorus of women chanting from the streets below, "*Mahuad, fuera! Mahuad, fuera!*" The demonstrators had their wish, for six months later the president was out.

After a quick tour of Quito, we embarked on the two-hour flight to San Cristóbal, one of the two islands reachable by air. There, we boarded the *Flamingo*, a more intimate vessel than HMS *Beagle* but without the permeating aromas of sweaty sailors and cheap rum. Some of the passengers accompanying the Sants on this cruise had been early investors in Roger's corporation, American Energy Services. Some were avid conservationists; others were to experience their first nature-based excursion. For these high-powered executives it would be seven days away from telephone, e-mail, and fax machine. The Dow Jones was going to rise or sink without them. The job of Miguel, the senior Galápagos naturalists assigned to the boat, and me was to help educate our guests about the wonders of a world that could never be enhanced by technology.

Genovesa Island, a comma-shaped scrap of land, was the ideal introduction to the natural drama of the Galápagos. The red-throated frigate birds, when they weren't busy displaying to females, engaged in acts of aerial piracy, stealing food caught by other seabirds.

Scientists call such devious foraging kleptoparasitism. Poor hard-working boobies and tropic birds are so bullied by the kleptoparasites, usually males, that they regurgitate their catch of fish or squid, which the ruffians then snatch in midair. With long pointed wings and a forked tail, which make them sensational fliers, frigate birds are perfectly adapted to their marauding lifestyle. A seriously menacing bill and black plumage cause them to be easily typecast as aerial villains among the harmless boobies. Adding to their dark reputation is their habit of feasting on their neighbors' chicks, when young are left unattended. In fairness, the great frigate birds capture most of their food offshore, but their spectacular heists have made them infamous.

Beyond the daily strife of nest raids and food piracy, Genovesa's nesting colonies periodically confront a harsher phenomenon, El Niño, the purveyor of doom for many Galápagos residents. El Niño is a naturally occurring event that causes periodic changes in global weather, leading to a warming of the normally chilly waters of the eastern Pacific. The trigger for this warming is the unpredictable calming of the trade winds. One might assume that a slight warming of the sea surface temperature during the Galápaganian spring might spawn an exuberance of marine life. After all, warmer waters lead to much heavier rain, a boon for some terrestrial species. But for marine feeders, El Niño brings disaster, as the higher sea temperatures scatter fish and diminish the supply of algae on which marine iguanas depend. For a few months, animals face starvation. Seabirds abandon breeding altogether or allow chicks already hatched to waste away.

On this 1999 visit, we witnessed the grisly legacy of a recent El Niño. The boughs that now supported pairs of nesting frigate birds and their newborn chicks also held the mummified offspring born during a temporary famine. As no large vertebrate scavengers inhabit the islands, those that perish under the hot tropical sun linger as bleached corpses for the next generation of chicks to trample. High on the beach and covered under bushes were dead sea lion pups and booby chicks. The marine iguana population also crashed, just as it had during the last major El Niño event in the islands in 1983–84.

Luckily, eight months had now passed since El Niño subsided, and water temperatures had returned to normal. The enthusiasm of the nesting birds was palpable, as if in one bout of breeding frenzy they could recoup their losses from the previous year. Scientists believe that seabird numbers are closely linked to the capacity of the neighboring ocean to provide fish and other marine creatures to feed the hungry adults and their young, so seabirds are severely affected by abrupt dips in the food supply. I observed an uplifting natural history lesson on Genovesa: Wildlife populations can rebound quickly from natural catastrophe in places that are still unspoiled.

That night in the *Flamingo's* cozy lounge, I gave a lecture on the places my colleagues and I had identified as the most important on earth for nature conservation, our Global 200 ecoregions analysis. The Galápagos terrestrial and marine ecoregions figured prominently as irreplaceable jewels in that treasury. Like many tropical archipelagos, the Galápagos were born from the seismic fury of underwater volcanoes. Those volcanoes eventually surfaced above the sea, and, over the course of time, a hot spot of magma created a complex of islands, the oldest being about 5,000,000 years old and the youngest, the large islands of Isabela and Fernandina, emerging as recently as 600,000 years ago. Few species were able to colonize these remote, bare, lava-covered islands or persist in the presence of hot, dry weather and the scarcity of fresh water. A few pioneer species did manage to arrive, some by flying, others by being transported on the feet of birds. Many also came by "rafting," whereby great masses of vegetation, sometimes as large as several acres, separated from the South American coast during severe storms or floods and floated out to sea, carrying with them species as big as iguanas.

One clever biologist calculated that based on the speed of currents from the Ecuadorian coast, it would take about two weeks for a "raft" to reach the Galápagos. Of course, some organisms, like plants, produce seeds that float, and about 10 percent of the native flora is thought to have arrived by that type of dispersal. There are now estimated to be between seven thousand and nine thousand species in total in the archipelago, and they have evolved, in relative isolation, to be among the most distinct groups of species on earth. About 80 percent of all land birds, 97 percent of land mammals, and more than 30 percent of terrestrial plants are endemic to the Galápagos. A related distinctive feature of the region is the high level of species endemism in underwater habitats—exceeding 20 percent—an unusually high level for marine systems, which are subjected to greater mixing than the more isolated terrestrial habitats.

The visual diversity of these rare species, as well as their abundance and tame behavior, thrills biologist and tourist alike. There are fourteen varieties (subspecies) of the Galápagos giant tortoise on different islands. Giant tortoises were once a common feature of desert, or dry, islands, such as Australia, New Caledonia, Socotra, the Seychelles, and Madagascar. Today, because of human exploitation, they persist only on the remote island of Aldabra in the Indian Ocean and here in the Galápagos. The unique menagerie surrounding the dome-shelled monarchs in the Galápagos include the only marine iguana (out of thirty-six species in the family), sprightly lava lizards, flightless cormorants, and perhaps most special of all, the sole penguin species to occur in the Northern Hemisphere or to breed in the tropics.

We were steaming south from Genovesa to Santa Cruz Island. I mentioned to some passengers that they might want to go flush their toilets now and then again about an hour from now. It was a rare chance to witness the Coriolis effect in action. In theory, when you pull the chain north of the equator, water should drain in a clockwise manner; when you flush south of 0° latitude, the water spins counterclockwise. We were going to cross the equator several times during our journey, and this would be the first opportunity to test the theory. The guests bolted to their cabins.

"My toilet flushed counterclockwise both times," reported one disappointed observer after we crossed the equator. Others witnessed the reverse. Where was the fabled Coriolis effect? I only learned later from a veteran of nature cruises that if you are within 1° north or south of the equator, the Coriolis effect is negligible. Local ocean currents, winds, and even the movement of the ship under power is enough to override the subtle forces determining how water spins down into the underworld.

In between flushings, Miguel Pellerano described WWF's program in the Galápagos beginning with our first grants in 1962 up to the present. The goal, as he explained it, was to take the concerns of the human residents into account while trying to retain the wildness of what we had seen earlier in the day on Genovesa. Local fishermen have done more than simply harvest the abundant sharks, tuna, and sea cucumbers in the waters off the islands, unfortunately. They have introduced exotic terrestrial herbivores that destroy the habitat for native species such as giant tortoises and land iguanas. So that they could enjoy fresh meat while they were out fishing, the fisherman brought goats to a number of locations and set them free to graze. Within several decades, there were 200,000 goats on the largest island, Isabela, and large herds on several other islands, as well. The goat overpopulation necessitated a control program, but the voracious grazers have yet to be eradicated. The introduced goats are not alone. Cats, burros, dogs, rats, and fire ants also have settled on the main islands, facilitated by human transport.

One of the many sharp thinkers on board leaned over and posed a shrewd question to me after Miguel's talk. "You said that there are over one hundred islands in the Galápagos and four of them have human populations and lots of alien species. Why not forget about the islands that already have people and goats on them and just concentrate on those still untouched?" I could see the modern business model being applied to nature conservation: Cut your losses on the products (i.e., islands) no longer in pristine condition and invest only in those still profitable (unspoiled islands) for a better return on your money. "Very strategic thinking," I replied. "The only problem is that not all of the islands are equal in their biological distinctiveness. The islands with people on them are the largest, and they have the greatest number of irreplaceable endemic species. We need to repel a hostile takeover of these islands by goats, rats, introduced guava trees, and anything else not native. I wish there were a simpler way."

The next morning, we slid into the water like the marine iguanas, some of us with fins and snorkel and others in scuba gear, to explore the depths off the island of Santa Cruz. I was with a group led by Greg Estes, one of the top Galápagos naturalists on our trip. He pointed out the most dazzlingly colorful fish I had ever seen—yellow-tailed surgeonfish, blue parrotfish, harlequin wrasse. The bizarre shapes of other fish seized my attention—flattened red-lipped batfish; long clarinet-shaped pipefish and trumpetfish; and, most striking of all, the dramatic white-and-yellow Moorish idol, sporting vertical dark bands and a long white streamer extending from its dorsal fin.

Greg abruptly dove beneath the surface as a large torpedo-shaped creature passed under us. Remembering that there had never been a shark attack reported in the Galápagos, I followed in time to see a group of white-tipped reef sharks. Large, aloof fellows, they wouldn't let us approach too close. With a powerful thrust of their tail fins they disappeared. A few moments later, I saw a cluster of perhaps the strangest looking of all sharks: the scalloped hammerhead. I dove to get a closer look at these ten-foot-long relics of the dinosaur era as they wheeled in large circles.

By the time our two-hour snorkel was over, I had observed four species of shark: white-tipped, Galápagos, hammerhead, and the lovely, diminutive horn shark, with a distinct polka-dot pattern on its body. I pondered the adaptive significance of its markings, which seemed much more like an appliqué of pop art than a simple explanation of increased camouflage. Horn sharks also contradict the belief that sharks must constantly keep swimming and forcing water over their gills to breathe: Horn sharks sit on the bottom and feed on crustaceans. If something larger tries to grab them, poisonous spurs on their dorsal fins encourage predators to hunt elsewhere. This undersea world seemed as full of strange characters, evolved for their own purposes, as anywhere on land. From the sleek moray eels to the clownlike faces of triggerfish, we witnessed a marvelous marine counterpoint to the iguanas and giant tortoises that waited above the surface.

After lunch on the *Flamingo*, we headed in a small craft to the island of Rabida. Our plan was to visit the red sand beaches strewn with basking sea lions and then look for flamingos and other wading birds in the salty lagoons near the shore. But the presence of dark shadows over the water and then wide fins slicing the waves demanded a momentary detour. Ahead was a flotilla of spotted eagle rays. These massive relatives of sharks and stingrays appeared to have risen to the surface from some primeval ocean. Five feet across, their graceful flat bodies and giant flanges extended the boundaries of vertebrate design. Had Keats visited the Galápagos, he surely would have written "Ode to an Eagle Ray," immortalizing this undulating giant membrane of skin stretched over sharkbone. How ordinary is the nightingale in comparison! I began to worry that the puny Galápagos finches and noisy gray mockingbirds, the flagship species underpinning Darwin's theory of evolution by natural selection, wouldn't receive a passing glance among our guests after they'd seen scalloped hammerheads, spotted eagle rays, and moray eels.

Eventually, the driver of our *panga*, or dinghy, swung us back toward Rabida. The diversion was over. A rule in the Galápagos, or in any first-rate location for observing nature, is that chance for awe trumps any kind of plan or schedule. You can't be certain what will cross your path next, and a plan to watch sea lions or flamingos may be derailed when a creature even more spectacular crosses the bow or the trail. The spontaneity of natural history is an endless joy when one sheds the mild tyranny of "must see" species and life lists.

Strewn along the beach were what looked like sandy brown logs—Galápagos sea lions hauled out after an early morning swim. We would have ample time to observe them later, so we headed to the lagoons while the birds were still active. A male sea lion started vocalizing, cueing others, and what followed sounded to me like retching teenagers. The calls provided a discordant soundtrack to the movement of the elegant greater flamingos feeding in the nearby saline shallows. Like every other resident, the flamingos seemed at greater peace in these islands than elsewhere. They stepped with purpose, straining the water with their highly evolved bills, more like baleen whales sifting plankton than the stalk-and-spear feeding technique of most large waders. One wonders what brought them this far from the mainland—a legitimate immigration question that could be put to any of a number of creatures that rafted or flew six hundred miles to arrive here. The absence of many nest predators is probably a big selling point for the wary flamingos. They are also quite sensitive to disturbance during the nesting season, and human visitors here respectfully keep their distance.

Farther up the trail was a rookery of brown pelicans. Grotesque-looking chicks stood by their parents, waiting impatiently for their next meal. The chicks would grow rapidly and soon be out foraging with the adults. Learning how to catch fish on their own is a tough life lesson for pelicans. A common assumption is that immature animals are a lot less efficient in catching food than adults. Yet, surprisingly, it's one of those assumptions that is rarely quantified by biologists. A former professor of mine, Gordon Orians, was on vacation with his family at one of Costa Rica's Pacific beaches, Playas del Coco. While sipping long drinks by the ocean, he observed brown pelicans fishing for their dinner. He had the clever idea of recording the number of successful captures by age class. It's easy to age pelicans by their plumage, as immatures remain distinct from adults until about fifteen months old. It's even easier to assess if a pelican has scored fish, because they swallow their meal only when they are sitting upright in the water. Orians observed that juvenile pelicans were successful in only about half their dives, a frustrating ratio; whereas adults performed significantly better, at a nearly 70 percent success rate. The results were published in a scientific journal, winning laurels for Orians's paper, "Age and Hunting Success in the Brown Pelican (*Pelecanus occidentalis*)" as the first ecological field study conceived and conducted during a Happy Hour.

That evening, we gathered to hear Greg Estes lecture on the life of Darwin and the history of his discoveries. Then in his mid-thirties, Greg had come to the Galápagos a decade earlier to lead nature tours and then volunteered to work on the epic study of the evolutionary biology of Darwin's finches, conducted by Peter and Rosemary Grant of Princeton University and celebrated in Jonathan Weiner's book *The Beak of the Finch*.

In the first few minutes of his talk, it became clear that Greg was much more than a naturalist. He was also a Darwin scholar. Darwin spent only nineteen days in the Galápagos and explored only five islands himself. To have gathered the seeds for his theory of evolution by natural selection from such a short stint is astonishing, even if the strands of his theory were knitted together much later.

That he waited twenty years before publishing his findings was even more remarkable. Being from the upper class, a landowner, and a man of means, Darwin was under no publish-or-perish pressure. Another contemporary, however, Alfred Russel Wallace, a brilliant naturalist of a much more humble background than Darwin, postulated a similar theory of evolution based on his travels in the Malay Archipelago. In a magnanimous gesture, Darwin welcomed Wallace to join him in reading their papers back to back at a session of the Linnaean Society of London on July 1, 1858. The next year, Darwin published his classic *Origin of Species*. That book, along with those of other biologists at the time and the geologist Sir Charles Lyell, disputed the biblical interpretation of creation. One explanation Greg offered as to why Darwin waited so long to release his theory was that he understood the challenges it would pose to his beloved wife, who accepted verbatim the traditional view of creation.

At times it's hard to fathom that observations on the beaks and feeding styles of some rather plain seed-cracking birds, or even the silhouettes of giant tortoises, could lead to a theory that turned the world upside down. But they did. In one of the most famous paragraphs in the annals of science, Darwin wrote in *The Origin of Species* about the natural variation in organisms that he had observed. And then the thunderbolt: "If variations useful to any organic being do occur, assuredly individuals thus characterized will have the best chance of being preserved in the struggle for life; and from the strong principle of inheritance, they will tend to produce offspring similarly characterized. The principle of preservation, I have called, for the sake of brevity, Natural Selection."

The phrasing may be a bit outmoded, but the vocabulary is visionary. Variation, struggle for life, inheritance, natural selection. *The Origin of Species* provided the framework for understanding how a single species of finch arrived in the Galápagos and became many. As the founder birds scattered to various islands, they found different food resources on each. Those with beak shapes best suited for the available food on a given island were assumedly the ones most likely to breed and pass on such traits. The populations on other islands became naturally isolated and eventually evolved to become different enough to be unable to mate with the original group; they are therefore considered separate species. That is the process called *adaptive radiation*, and it has been observed here not only in Galápagos finches and tortoises, but also in mockingbirds, lava lizards, a giant dandelion known as *Scalesia*, and even prickly pear cacti. It's a phenomenon that I saw on an even grander scale in New Caledonia among its skinks and geckos and monkey puzzle trees; and it has been seen in Hawaii among a group of birds called honeycreepers. Adaptive radiation in different groups of species inhabiting a number of tropical islands seems to come with the territory.

Those who attack Darwin's theories often argue that it is impossible to show the principle of evolution by natural selection in action. Darwin himself believed that the evolutionary process required long time periods for the gradual accumulation of variation and shifts in traits to make a visible difference in what we see before us. Contemporary scientists can offer as demonstration of the theory the rapid emergence of antibiotic-resistant strains of bacteria. From streptococcus to staph, medical researchers have shown how quickly the bacteria that cause serious infections can mutate and develop immunities to our current arsenal of drugs, evolution in action. But studies demonstrating evolution in wild creatures with backbones, as opposed to residents of laboratory petri dishes, were for many years lacking.

The work of Peter and Rosemary Grant and their students revealed that even in vertebrates evolution can occur over time frames that biologists can actually see and measure. The Grants started catching finches and measuring bill size and other physical traits with their calipers. Their long-term studies spanned what are termed *selection events*, such as powerful El Niño episodes that resulted in dramatic food scarcity and massive die-offs in parts of the finch population. They were able to demonstrate that traits that allowed individuals to handle seeds of a certain size more efficiently than others became more widespread in the population within just a few generations, offering compelling new evidence of the speed at which selection could occur.

The next morning our panga dropped us into a Jurassic landscape. A single volcano, rising to almost five thousand feet, cast a long shadow over Fernandina and the vast skirt of lava fields along the coasts. The cone is still active; it most recently erupted in 1991. If landing amid the bird colonies of Genovesa made us feel like trespassers or even voyeurs, the welcoming committees of marine iguanas on Fernandina permitted the fantasy of being a seventeenth-century explorer. Punta Espinoza, on the northeastern corner of Fernandina, has the largest concentration of these creatures in the world. The rocks along the spit were crawling with marine iguanas up to four feet long, hundreds of them draped all over each other. From a distance, they blended into the darkened lava surface, their spiny backs forming a skyline of jagged rocks. Only the odd shift or slither betrayed their presence. We had entered the dominion of what Darwin, who had no real fondness for these creatures, called the "imps of darkness."

Following a trail through the rocks, we stepped over and around gangs of lounging iguanas. The big males were waiting for the tropical sun to warm them, prior to their dives into the chilly upwelling of the Cromwell Current. Only the males are true underwater feeders, staying below for up to an hour while grazing on algae. The females and juveniles, both considerably smaller, waited for low tide to expose a marine garden of red and green algae. Despite their frightening reptilian stare, marine iguanas stick to a macrobiotic diet.

The marine iguanas seemed to us to have allergies. But in fact, their frequent sneezes are merely their way of coping with a high salt diet. They have the most efficient salt removal glands among reptiles. Located above the eye, the glands are connected to the nostrils by a small canal. The salt passes down the canal and is then eliminated by sneezing. The iguanas broke into a chorus of "Sssnit! Sssnit!" wherever we stopped to watch them, demonstrating just one of their many marvelous adaptations as submariners.

Fernandina is actually the youngest of the big islands, yet it exudes a sense of timelessness. Perhaps it's the absence of goats and rats; it's advertised as the most pristine of the large islands in the archipelago. It is also home to another primitive endemic: the only species of flightless cormorant in the world. How unusual for a seabird to lose the gift of flight! The other twenty-eight species of cormorants stick with the original blueprint, but this bird has lost its flight muscles and now boasts a more streamlined body for swimming and catching fish. Its vestigial wings are just a poignant reminder of its former life. One can only assume that Darwin's agent of change—natural selection—determined that where terrestrial predators were absent and local fish abundant, flightlessness seemed the simplest body plan.

By the time we bade farewell to the marine iguanas, they had repositioned themselves and were all aligned facing the sun, a bit like baskers on a reptilian Riviera. Because the sun had reached its zenith, however, they were more interested now in staying cool than in sun worship. The cold-blooded iguanas raise the upper half of their bodies to reduce exposure in a posture commonly referred to by animal physiologists as "elevated basking." The iguanas seemed so dignified in this position, I wanted to tell my yoga instructor about this dramatic pose. The "upward iguana" could find itself next to the downward dog and cobra positions in the sequence of yoga maneuvers, named after flexible animals in harmony with the natural world.

In the afternoon, the dinghy dropped us off for the snorkeling event of a lifetime. I tried my best to appear if not blasé, at least not like a chirpy tour guide. My cool persona evaporated after slipping into the water off Isabela Island. Floating before us in the shelter of Tagus Cove was a group of the delightful Galápagos penguins that looked more like cartoon characters than live seabirds. The Disney-like experience was completed by sea lion pups swimming right up to my mask and adult females hurtling toward me only to swerve and twirl around me, as if I were their clumsy underwater dance partner. My snorkeling buddy motioned to me to surface. She was overcome and nearly incoherent. It doesn't matter if you are a newcomer to the Galápagos or Jacques Cousteau: The simple pleasure of swimming with penguins and sea lions transforms even the most unflappable scientist into an awestruck six-year-old.

Penguins in an equatorial setting seem as out of place as musk oxen or polar bears would in the Amazon. Aside from the Galápagos

penguin, the other seventeen species of penguins are cold-water enthusiasts. King and emperor penguins typically grace wildlife calen-
dars as they incubate their eggs or stand next to their chicks in an
Antarctic snowstorm. But on these islands, the air temperature on the
beach was already close to 90°F, enough to melt most penguins. Luckily for the species here, the Bolivar Channel between Isabela and Fernandina is fed by cold upwellings at a temperature that penguins like
and that also provide habitat for the food to sustain the birds. It's why
you find penguins here, descendants from the Humboldt penguins of
Peru that perhaps wandered off course in numbers, found a cool spot,
and never returned to the coast of South America.

There may be as few as five thousand pairs of Galápagos penguins,
and they are found nowhere else in the world. So far, they have been
able to ride out the sea surface warming caused by El Niño, as well as
periodic declines in their food supply. But they live on the edge of the
Northern Hemisphere and on the edge of existence. Dee Boersma, a
world authority on this species and in many ways their guardian, told
me that her greatest fear for their survival is that commercial fishermen might start using nets, illegally, of course, in the Bolivar Channel,
the penguin's stronghold in the islands. Fishing nets spell penguin
deaths.

Our hikes on Isabela exposed the first cracks in Eden we'd seen so
far. Droppings littered the trail, and soon we came upon a herd of
goats eating vegetation that in previous centuries would have been the
exclusive forage of the native herbivores—giant tortoises and land
iguanas. Overpopulation of goats poses a dire threat to the ecology of
Isabela and the other islands; besides eating plants meant to support
giant tortoise populations, they remove and trample vegetation that
serves as nesting habitat or feeding areas for a wide variety of herbivores, from insects to birds to native rice rats. The park guards used
the "Judas" approach, developed by crafty New Zealand biologists, to
eradicate them. New Zealand is plagued by non-native large herbivores, and wildlife biologists there have been successful in removing

the herd-forming exotics by putting a bell and radiotelemetry collar around the neck of one member of the herd, a designated Judas. Then bounty hunters go in and shoot all of the unmarked ungulates. They allow the Judas to live to unite with a new herd and repeat the process over and over. That technique helps to control the goat population here, but to truly save Isabela, every goat must be eradicated. A seemingly huge reduction of 200,000 to 10,000 will be meaningless because if control is relaxed, the population will grow back to its original number a decade later.

A member of our group, the owner of an electronics outlet chain, offered a novel solution. "Why don't you offer a financial incentive to Ecuadorian hunters? A penny each for the tails of the first 100,000 goats. A nickel each for the next 50,000. A dime for the next 40,000. A dollar for the next 9,000, and then ten dollars each for the last 1,000 goat tails." The plan sounded intriguing. "Except why wouldn't there be an incentive to let the goats come back so the hunters could be employed again?" responded one fund manager. The only answer, it seemed to me, was some kind of yet-to-be-developed biological agent that would spread infertility in goats in the region. Until then, we would have to rely on bounty hunters.

As we headed back to the boat, we passed male lava lizards doing push-ups, a behavioral undertaking not unlike that of their primate descendant counterparts on Venice Beach, to determine hierarchy in the social milieu. The seven species of lava lizards in the Galápagos are scattered among most larger islands in the chain, and, like a number of vertebrates in the archipelago, they display a variety of colors, shapes, and behaviors unique to each island.

Unfortunately, cats have been brought to a number of islands, and they are fond of lava lizards. Their predatory habits are causing an evolutionary shift of the lizards in what biologists term their *life history strategies*—an expression that covers how an organism goes about its affairs, from birth to dying breath and everything in between. Some creatures opt for what I call the James Dean life history strategy, shorthand for what one population geneticist described as "Live fast, die young, and leave a good-looking corpse." The hamster, a common childhood pet, fits this mode. Hamsters reach adulthood a few months after birth and produce as many young as they can in a relatively short life. They die in their cages without a gray hair, looking as sleek as when they were purchased from the pet shop. At the other extreme are rhinoceros, whales, and elephants, all of which take a long time to mature, grow very large, and by the time they die bear the scars of decades of skirmishes with other suitors and challengers and the wear and tear of age. Lava lizards live up to 10 years, not bad for a small lizard but short by giant tortoise standards, some of whom may live to 150. However, predation of adult lava lizards by cats has led to selection for individuals who breed at a much younger age than their counterparts on cat-free islands. The inference here is that predation by cats is selecting for shorter generation times and a shift in the life history of lava lizards. Those able to breed early in life leave more offspring than those that delay and wind up as feral cat chow.

It was Happy Hour on the *Flamingo*, and we sat on the deck, lifting *cervezas* to the beauty of the islands and the impressive Alcedo Volcano of Isabela. The discussion turned to books. "Name the most important book of the past two centuries," demanded one passenger. *"The Catcher in the Rye,"* I offered sotto voce. The consensus among the newly formed Galápagos Book Club chose three other classics: *Das Kapital* by Karl Marx, *Interpretation of Dreams* by Sigmund Freud, and *The Origin of Species*. Among the three contenders, one sat on a shelf by itself: Darwin's opus won out as the most influential book of our time. We raised a toast to the greatest of all naturalists just as a group of pilot whales, or false killer whales, were spotted off the port bow. The other guests went below to observe the small cetaceans breaking the waves of the Bolivar Channel. I remained on the deck and leaned into a stiffening wind. This strait is where big whales are often sighted and is home to the roughest water in the archipelago. Before the night was over, some of our more sensitive guests would be flushing their toilets with no intention of checking on the Coriolis effect.

I find it remarkable that Darwin never returned to these islands that he made so famous, even though travel to and from the islands from Great Britain was a bit more inconvenient in his day. Nevertheless, nineteen days of field notes and hundreds of specimens kept him occupied for decades. I knew I would be back. From the iguana-covered rocks of Punta Espinoza to the water ballet with penguins and playful sea lions, I had experienced a perfect day. I waved goodbye to the high volcanoes of Isabela—Alcedo, Darwin, Sierra Negra—passing on the left. To the right, I gestured to the great cone of Fernandina. The shifting and pitch of the *Flamingo* simulated a wooden ship from three centuries ago. How remarkable it would have been to be the first naturalist on these shores during a volcanic eruption. To see armies of giant tortoises and land iguanas, sensing the trembling earth, head en masse toward a safe refuge ahead of rivers of fast-flowing lava. To see birds swirling up from the cataclysm and flying to safety. I could pass the remainder of my life here, I felt, each day devoted to pursuing the natural history of a new species or each year a different island, filling notebooks with sketches, descriptions, and perhaps a poem or two to a spotted eagle ray. I lingered in that moment of quiet celebration. Even if I couldn't remain, I felt the urge to come back every year, if only for a week or ten days, to relive this picture—a horizon of dark volcanoes, whales surfacing before me, and seabirds rising and falling in the building wind. Not a single human being in my viewfinder, only the creatures that came before us. I felt another purpose for these enchanted islands: not just as a living laboratory to study evolution, but as a natural sanatorium, where they send you to recover when the rigging of your life is ripped from the sails, a safe harbor to undertake repairs of the soul. Maroon me.

As impossible as it might seem to eclipse the beauty of the Bolivar Channel, at sunrise we found ourselves on top of the island of Bartolomé, an extinct lava cone in the midst of the most breathtaking vista the islands have to offer. The panorama of this elemental volcanic landscape—lava fields flanked by golden beaches and turquoise waters and the dramatic finger of Pinnacle Rock—earned this site the award as the tourists' most photographed scene in the Galápagos. Just ahead of our party, a long-time park naturalist was delivering a short lecture about the establishment of native plants in the barren lava fields. He was long-haired, bearded, deeply tanned, and barefoot. This last feature, along with a sleeveless field vest, seemed to be a sign of tenure among the nature guides: to walk barefoot, oblivious to the spines of cacti or the other ubiquitous thorn plants. I felt mild envy toward this castaway who had been here for decades and shed everything English except his accent. He became engaged in a discussion with another nature guide about whether lava cactus has the ability to make its own soil. He supported the widely held belief that these spiny pioneers secreted acids from their roots that dissolve lava, thereby releasing nutrients for the colonizing plant to absorb and increase its toehold in a sea of rock. The other guide expressed his doubts about that claim.

Normally, I would be transfixed by such a conversation. But I found myself focusing less on the nature guides in the foreground and more on a desire to burnish into memory the palette of colors in this vibrant, primeval landscape. It is times like these that I wish I could paint, draw with crayon, or compose a decent photograph in case I never come back. As the naturalists carried on, I thought of the artist whose sense of color and form best suited these islands, the great American contemporary painter Milton Avery. His paintings of seabirds, rocks, and waves seem at some times whimsical and at other times deeply spiritual and reverential. Avery's own description of his work could easily be the aesthetic coda for the Galápagos: "I do not use linear perspective but achieve depth by color. I strip the design to essentials; the facts do not interest me as much as the essence of nature." The naturalists carried on debating facts, while, as Avery's lost student, I applied broad horizontal strokes of taupe against gold to a canvas dotted with the vertical green pencils of cacti.

We dropped anchor at nearby Santiago Island and landed at Puerto Egas to explore moonscape-like lava formations and the microcosm of intertidal pools. Dancing around us, crimson Sally Lightfoot crabs performed pliés, while lava herons, short stocky birds whose dark plumage blends into the outcrops, escorted them over the rocks. The entertaining dance performed by the near-camouflaged heron and the brightly colored Sally Lightfoots can be seen on all the islands, often with a deadly climax, as herons are quite fond of snacking on young crabs.

Images of dancing crabs, herons, and Santiago's fur seals evaporated once the *Flamingo* entered Academy Bay in the town of Puerto Ayora on Santa Cruz Island. One of two large settlements in the Galápagos, Puerto Ayora is home to the Charles Darwin Research Station, the Galápagos National Park headquarters, and much of the human population, about fourteen thousand inhabitants, minus the seasonal tourists. Motoring past scores of fishing boats in the harbor awakened me to a different perspective of the Galápagos—an alluring place where adventurous Ecuadorians might escape the grinding poverty of the mainland and, for the more entrepreneurial, a place to get rich quick. The distinctive tackiness endemic to beach towns was evident everywhere. Souvenir shops, cheap restaurants, loud music. It had been only five days since we landed on Genovesa, yet we had totally lost track of the days and date. The Galápagos wall calendar had come to life, and we had stepped into it. I was unprepared for this jolt of commercial human reality.

While the other members of our group enjoyed a tour of the captive breeding center for endangered giant tortoises, Roger and I headed for a meeting with Robert Bensted-Smith, the director of the station. Before we entered his office, I mentioned to Roger my idea about buying up the boats in the harbor, offering the artisanal fishermen a generous settlement package, and finding them jobs in the tourism sector or as part of a marine patrol for the Galápagos Marine Reserve. At least for the next twenty years, that would give the islands a chance to recover ecologically from being stripped of sea cucumbers and slipper lobsters, and from having their sharks massacred. "Why stop with the boats?" Roger asked, echoing a thought I'd had, too. "Why not buy the islands, or at the very least, lease them for conservation from Ecuador?"

Roger had been my benefactor at WWF. When he first became chairman, he heard me give a talk at an organization-wide gathering about a new way to set priorities for WWF conservation investments in Latin America that could be applied to any other continent, or for that matter, the entire globe. My point was simple: If we can integrate two sets of data—biological distinctiveness (including levels of endemism, species richness, rare habitats, and ecological phenomena) with conservation status (as determined by measurable features such as amount of intact habitat, levels of fragmentation, protection, and overarching threats)—we can sort the world's ecoregions in a strategic new way. By sorting out ecoregions in this manner, an ad hoc approach to conservation planning could be replaced with something more transparent, rigorous, and objective. Roger was the first to raise his hand. "This is what we do all the time in the business world," he said. "Set priorities with the best data available." Afterward, he came up to me and said, "So you've done this for Latin America. How long would it take and what would it cost to extend this work to the rest of the world?" I was momentarily speechless, unprepared to answer a question I had hoped for but never expected. I quickly grasped the visionary insight of successful CEOs: Seize new ideas that offer powerful solutions to fundamental problems. Roger has changed forever the way WWF, and much of the rest of the conservation community, goes about its work. He also helped finance that transformation. Just before our trip departed, it was announced that Roger and Vicki had made an extraordinary gift of $10 million to finance conservation in the MesoAmerican Reef, the Atlantic Forest of Brazil, and other priceless areas within WWF's list of Global 200 ecoregions.

The Charles Darwin Research Station was one of WWF's first grant recipients in 1962. Widely heralded as a research station of unparalleled productivity, it has been a rallying point for conservation. Robert, the polite director, who had led the station through the tumultuous past year, welcomed us into his office. We immediately began discussing the upcoming workshop to develop a fifty-year vision for the islands, an effort he and I would cofacilitate. Before we left, I couldn't resist asking him, "So Robert, how much would it cost to buy the Galápagos and put it under management of an international conservation agency?" He looked at us half-incredulous, half-smiling. "That's an interesting question, but it probably wouldn't get very far," he responded, attempting to deflect further discussion on the subject.

Not only private citizens were inquiring about the price tag. The U.S. and British governments each made several (unsuccessful) attempts to either lease or purchase the Galápagos Islands from Ecuador between 1850 and 1950, largely for strategic reasons rather than for their unsurpassed natural history value. In the 1950s, the U.S. military even leased the nearby island of Baltra to get access to one of the Galápagos's two airstrips for its bombers. But feelings of sovereignty reign supreme in Ecuadorian hearts and have kept the Galápagos from becoming the fifty-first state, or, at the very least, Seward's Folly II. I pressed on. "You know, the government could receive all the profits from tourism, so there would be no economic losses. An agency with more resources and muscle to enforce the Special Law could ensure that these islands would return to the ecological state in which Darwin found them." I could see that Robert was more focused on keeping the Molotov cocktail–wielding fishermen from reinvading the field station. I soon realized that U.S. purchase of these islands was hardly any guarantee of their preservation. The current Bush administration would drill all over the Alaskan tundra if it could get away with it, and developers continue to pave over Hawaii. So I'm not sure, given its track record, that the U.S. government wouldn't make the Galápagos into a desert version of Bermuda or a Disney theme park.

Hopping around outside in the bushes was a small party of Galápagos finches. They were medium ground finches. Or maybe small ground finches. Or perhaps something in between. Normally, when you look at a new bird and consult the field guide, the longer you look, the more assured you feel of its proper identification. Watching finches in the Galápagos is reverse bird watching: The longer and more closely you look, the more confused you become. Some of the thirteen species found in the islands bring expert bird watchers to their knees. I suppose that the ambiguity of physical traits in Galápagos finches is demonstration of evolution at work. Among populations, variation in certain features piles up over time, confusing everything until a selection event sorts it all out, at least temporarily.

Roger and I rejoined the group and proceeded up to the highlands of Santa Cruz to visit giant tortoises and see the giant dandelion forests near the summit. Seven of the islands are high enough to support cloud forests of *Scalesia*, a relative of the common dandelion and sunflower. The patriarchs of the Galápagos Islands are the giant tortoises, but they don't live in the *Scalesia* forest. So we headed to a privately owned tortoise reserve in the Santa Cruz highlands to see them. The owner pointed to an abandoned field of fruit trees, strewn with lichen-encrusted boulders. The boulders, of course, turned out to be tortoises. These animals are the largest of their kind in the world, some reportedly reaching 630 pounds. Fueling such enthusiastic vegetarians requires a lot of plant matter. Tortoises consume at least fifty species of plants, of which two are particularly noteworthy. One is a tree that hugs the coastline, the toxic *manzanillo*, known in English as poison apple. Contact with any part of the plant causes severe burns to the skin, and visitors are warned to avoid it, like killer poison ivy. Manzanillo is a member of the spurge, or poinsettia, family, which contains some nasty toxins such as ricin, a poison from the castor bean plant.

How ghastly it must be to ingest the green fruits, something giant tortoises do regularly. The ability to detoxify manzanillo must be one of the great biochemical adaptations in nature. More understandable is the tortoises' fondness for the soft succulent pads of prickly pear cactus. In fact, a strong case can be made that tortoise nibbling on prickly pear has selected for distinctly different growth forms and plant armament on islands with and without tortoises. Where tortoises and cacti overlap, the cacti often grow as trees, with their green parts above the browse line of straining tortoises. Where the ping-pong-paddle pads grow low to the ground in tortoise country, they are defended by stout, strong spines. On islands that never had the lumbering cactus eaters on them, one can stroke the soft spines of the pads without fear of being punctured.

To some scientists, studying biological diversity is an ecumenical exercise. We should be as determined, as E. O. Wilson admonishes, to pay attention to the little things that run the world as to the more charismatic vertebrates. The number of species of insects, microbes, fungi, and nematodes may tally in the tens of millions when all are named. In contrast, there are only twenty-six thousand species of birds, mammals, amphibians, and reptiles known to science. There are now just two species of giant tortoise left on earth. Giant tortoises as a lineage will never match tiny parasitoid wasps and muck-dwelling nematodes in species richness, but sitting next to and stroking the carapace of an animal that might be 150 years old, I was overcome by the evolutionary exuberance of this noble creature. Stroking a wasp or a nematode, however egalitarian, would not be the same.

Our Galápagos interlude was nearing an end. After brief stops on Sante Fé and Plazas, we dropped anchor in Gardner Bay on Española, or Hood Island. The high point of our visit to this island was seeing the Hood Island mockingbirds and some large booby colonies. Galápagos mockingbirds also experienced an adaptive radiation, although not as intense as that of the finches. There are four species in the islands, and the Hood mockingbird is as unique to Hood as the Genovesa resident is to its namesake. Mockingbirds tend to be among the tamest of birds on the mainland, so out here they are cheeky beyond belief. They commonly steal food and nest material from tourists. There are reports that Genovesa birds move about by running on the ground. I suppose that if the lone predator, the Galápagos hawk, expresses little or no interest in them, there is no pressure to fly away. Perhaps if we come back to Genovesa in a thousand years, or even after a hundred generations, there will be a flightless mockingbird, the first of its kind. Even if Galápagos mockingbirds have not yet forsaken flight, they have lost their penchant for mimicry. Unlike the mockingbird on my street in Maryland (so named *Mimus polyglottus*), which imitates a tufted titmouse, Carolina wren, blue jay, and what sounds like a backhoe, Galápagos mockingbirds don't mimic anyone. The reason remains a mystery, but perhaps there is no pleasure or evolutionary advantage to demonstrating to other mockingbirds how well a male can imitate an atonal Galápagos finch or the nasal honk of a booby.

After a dawn circumnavigation of Kicker Rock (known in Spanish as *Léon Dormido*, or Sleeping Lion), we motored into the harbor at Puerto Baquerizo Moreno on San Cristóbal, the capital of the region, and headed to the airstrip to catch our flight to Guayaquil. As we drove in the bus to the airstrip, my mind somehow flipped from the Galápagos to Florence, Italy. I had now seen the pinnacle of a living museum of natural history to match the pinnacle of Renaissance art history. If only the world would treasure both equally.

I remembered the debate raging in Florence among Italian art curators and the art-loving public about what to do with Michaelangelo's *David* and thought of its relevance for the Galápagos. The giant statue is housed indoors in the Accademia Gallery to protect it from further environmental damage, but centuries of neglect had left it ill prepared for its five hundredth anniversary in 2004. There were three schools of thought on restoration: Leave it alone in its growing decay; give the famous statue a mild cleaning to wash away years of urban grime and pollution; or subject the statue to a complete cleansing to restore it to the condition when it was first unveiled. After I read about the controversy, I saw the struggle for the future of the Galápagos like that of the *David*. "Leave the islands as they are," advocate those who have their heads in the sand, or surf, as the case may be. "We are doing a fine job of managing this global treasure. Let's do a mild cleaning and restore a few islands and continue on our path," argue the incrementalists. I, and many other scientists that participated in our Galápagos vision workshop felt even more strongly about incrementalism being the path to doom. We needed to push conservation forward as fast as possible. And we needed to openly discuss what the incrementalists consider too controversial: the relocation of human settlements back to the mainland, paid for with incentive-laden reestablishment packages supported by conservation donors and major funding institutions such as the World Bank.

To move forward in conservation planning, however, one must first look backward. This is not a Zen koan but a founding principle in conservation biology. Most biological systems, apart from the Amazon or parts of the Congo basin, have been so altered by human activities that some degree of restoration is required to allow the native flora and fauna to regain their former prominence. But restoration to what? An old Missouri expression warns, "If you don't know where you are going, any road will take you there." To define what success would look like, we had to establish a benchmark that symbolized our end point. In biological terms, that meant selecting a period before intense exploitation began, when wildlife populations fluctuated naturally and before exotic species had become widely established.

But what date to choose as our beacon? The prewhaling days of the 1500s? That seemed truly preposterous. It will be centuries, if ever, before numbers of cetaceans and giant tortoises return to the glory of those days. But what about 1835, the year Darwin set foot in these islands? Some old hands who have worked for decades here would say that notion was also crazy, that we are asking the impossible. But imagine for a moment that it's the year 1960. John F. Kennedy is elected president of the United States and vows to put a man on the moon within a decade. Imagine the reaction to a molecular biologist stating in 1990 that it will soon be possible to decipher and map the entire human genome and display it on an invention called the Internet. The impossible often becomes possible much sooner than we think. It just takes a little imagination to do great things.

The Galápagos Islands are far more intact than most well-known tropical islands—Oahu, Bermuda, Guam, the Virgin Islands, Tahiti—to name a few. But, of course, there is trouble in this paradise, as well. Introduced plants such as guavas, quinine, *Lantana*, and a few others have overrun some areas. Introduced vertebrates—goats, pigs, cats, dogs, cattle, horses, burros, and black rats—are displacing the native biota and this change could be even more drastic, in the face of invading electric ants (also now introduced in New Caledonia) or introduced diseases. A biologist from New Zealand, an island nation plagued by exotic mammals and plants, was characteristically blunt when I spoke to him after visiting the Galápagos. "You want a fifty-year vision for this place? I'll give you one. At the rate you are going now, you have fifty years before these islands are completely overrun by exotic, invasive species. To think any differently is to ignore what has happened on other islands like New Zealand, Guam, Oahu, and to keep your head in the sand. It's your choice."

The route back to Eden is clear. We need to muster the courage to say what is obvious to most biologists who have set foot on the islands: A complete cleansing of exotic plants and animals and a systematic, generously funded program to resettle the human population from the islands should be our goal. The frigate birds, the boobies, and the penguins in the Galápagos seem so perfectly tuned to the world around them, as we are not. Excepting our species, selection in animals is to survive the moment; the best any sexually reproducing nonhuman species can do is to select a good mate to pass on its genes to its offspring. Our great and unique skill as a species is to design a happier life for future offspring, far beyond the next generation. We are the guardians of Darwin's legacy—the seabirds of Genovesa, the marine iguanas of Fernandina, even the crabby mockingbirds of Hood Island. We cannot fail them.

chapter eight

WHERE THE BUFFALO
STILL THUNDER

IN THE DESICCATING HEAT OF AUGUST, THE PARCHED LEAVES
and stems of blue grama grass crackle under our feet. Aside from
the endless vault of blue sky, only the yellow blossoms of gumweed
and prairie sunflowers lend color to this vast, thirsty landscape. Along
the roadsides, the cheery call of the western meadowlarks, the official
greeters of the northern Great Plains, and the raspy notes of vesper,
grasshopper, and savannah sparrows fill the air. Lark buntings, sporting their avian tuxedo plumage, mix with the more casually dressed
flocks of grassland sparrows.

Van Gogh would never have left Arles to paint this desolate scene.
But just over 150 years ago, there were endless waves of undulating
grass here, massive herds of thundering bison, and native peoples
whose patterns of life were closely tied to the rhythms of nature and
the seasons. And Montana's Great Plains inspired other artists. In the

early decades of the twentieth century, Charles M. Russell, one of America's foremost romanticizers of the Old West, captured the drama in his paintings, sculptures, and drawings of the wildlife, Native Americans, and cowboys of the region, a world that has vanished. Or has it?

From my first visit in August 2000 through a number of subsequent trips, I have come to view this place and a few other stretches of the northern Great Plains as providing a unique opportunity to restore the wild splendor of nature that inspired some of Russell's original canvases. Russell's unbroken horizon has been subdivided with barbedwire fences, speckled with domestic livestock. Widely scattered ranch houses give the land a more settled and tame appearance. But unlike other parts of the northern Great Plains, most of the prairie here in eastern Montana is still unplowed, with sod as intact as when wild bison roamed about in the nineteenth century. Cattle, whose presence is propped up by federal grazing subsidies, have taken the bisons' place. But the especially low rainfall (twelve inches a year) and the long distance to markets make this land actually better suited to bison and to a host of native species that flourished during the time of Lewis and Clark's 1805 expedition.

In the landscape created by European settlers and their followers, ranches and roads and barbed wire led to the removal or displacement of much of the native wildlife to the far margins of this region. But the original pieces of this ecosystem are all still here, waiting to regenerate. By uprooting a few fences, expanding prairie dog towns, replacing cattle with bison, and reintroducing the wolf's moonlit howl, we could rediscover the biological and spiritual heart of our continent.

A change of a different sort is already under way in the northern Great Plains, one so deep, widespread, and rapid that it may be as profound as the demise of the bison in the late 1860s. The change I am talking about is, at the moment, less ecological than demographic, social, and economic. It is being chronicled daily in the newspapers of the small towns that dot the northern Great Plains: a school closing here, another there, the cutoff of Greyhound bus service to a county seat. And something that only a local historian or regional demographer would notice at first: The human population in the region is shrinking rapidly. Ranching and wheat farming as livelihoods are declining in this and other locales in the northern prairies—it's too cold, too dry, and too far from the beaten track to compete with areas with better access to markets. Many young people of the region have migrated to the larger cities of the plains—Omaha, Rapid City, Cheyenne—or farther off, to Denver, Seattle, Spokane, where the prospect of jobs and an easier life beckon. Hardly a month goes by without an article in the *New York Times*, *Washington Post*, or other national journal cataloging the creation of new ghost towns, the hemorrhaging of the human population, and the stark reality confronting the region's politicians: If current trends continue, the northern Great Plains is likely to surpass Appalachia as the poorest section of America. Ironically, the only places on the northern Great Plains where population is rising are Native American reservations, fueled by indigenous growth and an influx of former residents seeking to reconnect with their cultures and roots.

In fact, a new chapter is just beginning, timed perfectly to coincide with the Lewis and Clark bicentennial, a chapter in which conservation could become one of the key elements in this remote region's economic revival. What if, in a few places, the wildlife populations of the Lewis and Clark era could be restored and with them the creation of the greatest natural history destination between Chicago and Yellowstone? Could a buffalo commons reappear in American history?

The concept of the return of the buffalo commons was already offered to an audience disinclined to hear it. In the late 1960s, Frank and Deborah Popper, professors at Rutgers University in New Jersey, put the Great Plains under the lens of cold logic and made a persuasive argument that it would be more cost effective and enviro-friendly to return the short-grass prairie to a bison ecosystem than to maintain it through a system of expensive ranching and farming subsidies that encouraged overgrazing of federal lands and paying farmers not to grow wheat when we had far too much in surplus. Safe when they made their argument in the halls of academe, the Poppers had to be escorted off the stage when they came west to play before a hostile populace.

Had the climate or the conditions the Poppers described changed much since they had introduced their unpopular vision for the northern Great Plains? I've made several trips to this prairie land over the past five years in the company of Jonathan Proctor of the Predator Conservation Alliance and WWF scientists, collaborators in initiating a prairie restoration project, to investigate how our organizations could hasten the recovery of a North American sacred landscape. It is one of those rare places in the world that move us spiritually as much as their ecology stirs us intellectually. Beyond bringing back bison and prairie dogs, the keystone species of this ecoregion, it is the spirits of these grasslands we are trying to reawaken.

If Florida's Everglades are described as the "River of Grass," surely the northern Great Plains deserves the designation of America's "Sea of Grass." Roughly 450 miles long and 200 miles wide, these plains extend from southern Alberta and Saskatchewan across eastern Montana, the western half of the Dakotas, and into northeast Wyoming and northwest Nebraska. They can be distinguished from the tall-grass and intermediate-grass prairies to the east by the much lower rainfall and, as a result, the shorter stature of the grass. "Old-growth" short grassland may be only a few inches high in places. Together with the southern short-grass prairie, this portion of our continent once contained one of the world's largest grassland ecosystems, rivaled only by the steppes of Russia and Kazakhstan and exceeding the more famous Serengeti grasslands, and the dry steppes of Patagonia and Mongolia. If you added up the weight of all the wild hoofed mammals this system once supported (termed its *wild ungulate biomass*), estimates from Lewis and Clark's era exceeded levels recorded in the African Serengeti, the most famous wildland on earth. Wolves and grizzlies, too, predators we typically associate with the Rocky Mountains, were commonplace on the northern Great Plains. Here they followed the bison migrations, feasting on the weak, the old, and the inexperienced, much like lions do today on the African savannas.

No species has gone extinct in the northern Great Plains, but the *abundance* of wildlife, the feature that once so characterized the ecoregion, has decreased dramatically. Nowhere is that more true than in two species on opposite ends of the mammalian spectrum—the American bison and the black-tailed prairie dog—and grassland birds.

Bison, often known as buffalo, once grazed and galloped across western America in herds numbering in the millions. Bison are the largest living mammals in either North or South America—an adult bull typically exceeds two thousand pounds—and they are as tough as they are massive. Unlike their distant relatives, domestic cattle, bison easily go for two or three days without drinking, and push through deep snow to find grass in winter. Most of the other megafauna disappeared in the Pleistocene extinctions. Bison, in contrast, are true survivors of the Ice Age, whose appearance, physiology, and behavior were shaped over the eons by the selective forces of blizzards, droughts, saber-toothed cats, and giant flat-faced bears. In short, they are one of evolution's tough guys.

Bison as a species are far from extinct. There are more than 230,000 individuals in the United States, but most are in tiny populations on small fenced ranches. They have become a fashionable "boutique" ungulate, like llamas. Even Ted Turner, the media magnate, has gotten into the game. He now owns the most bison in the country, numbering about 10,000 head. Turner's mission is not restoration, however, but to encourage Americans to eat more buffalo, among the leanest of meats.

In the ecology of the Great Plains, bison did more than serve as an understudy for domestic cattle, or a shaggier breed of charolais. They played a vital role in the prairie ecosystem that no domestic stock such as cattle can reproduce. Bison were what biologists call *ecological engineers*. Their grazing patterns in the prairie ecosystem, their fertilization of the ground through their dung and, when they died, their carcasses influenced the behavior, distribution, and ecology of many other species. If we want to bring back wild bison, there is a real urgency now of a different sort: Recent genetic studies on supposedly wild herds reveal that only a few populations are genetically pure; the remainder are contaminated with cattle genes. The job of recovering the fauna of this American Serengeti has become that much more difficult.

At the other end of the size spectrum is the black-tailed prairie dog, weighing between one and three pounds. The small size of these creatures in the ecology of the plains was offset by their extraordinary abundance, range, and impact on the native grasslands. Like the bison, black-tailed prairie dogs were everywhere. A hundred years ago, a naturalist described a prairie dog town in the southern Great Plains that covered roughly fifteen thousand square miles and contained an estimated 400 million prairie dogs. Numbers in the northern Great Plains might have been comparable. The animals' habit of closely cropping the native grasses and flowering plants of the prairie created space for those species that needed to nest in open clearings, like mountain plovers. Even more important, their burrows provided critical habitat for a wide variety of vertebrates, some of whom prey on the prairie dogs.

Black-tailed prairie dogs still perch at the edge of their burrows, whistling and chirping in their own rodent patois. But the size of their colonies is a far cry from a hundred years ago. There is not a single prairie dog town in the northern Great Plains larger than ten thousand acres. And the species range has been reduced by more than 95 percent. The crash in prairie dog numbers has also pushed the black-footed ferret, arguably America's most endangered vertebrate and an animal that preys almost exclusively on prairie dogs, to the edge of extinction.

The other group of vertebrates that has shown the steepest decline is the birds of the grasslands, now the most endangered group of birds in the continental United States. The continued conversion of grasslands to agriculture, the extreme fragmentation of what remains, and the heavy application of pesticides have caused grassland bird populations in this country to plummet precipitously. Conservation measures on the northern Great Plains, then, are about much more than bringing back the bison.

One vertebrate whose numbers in the region have increased greatly is domestic cattle of various breeds. Most ranchers hate bison and prairie dogs. Bison are of actual little worry because most are behind fences in well-maintained ranges, but prairie dogs are still relentlessly persecuted. Some cynics suggested that the 2004 senatorial election in South Dakota hung on which candidate could demonstrate the most commitment to exterminating this peaceful creature.

Elk and pronghorn still range freely on the Great Plains, as do three other large ungulates, bighorn sheep and two kinds of deer. But with a 70 percent dietary overlap with cattle, ranchers view elk as competitors, and so their numbers on the prairie are, for now, kept in check by hunting. Pronghorn, in contrast, as eaters of broad-leaved herbaceous and woody plants, have only a 5 percent dietary overlap with cattle and thus fare much better, though socially they tend to avoid big cattle herds.

Pronghorn are odd creatures. They can spring through the air as if equipped with pogo sticks, yet they prefer to run under barbed-wire fences rather than bound over them. They are also the most fleet-footed ungulate of the plains. No contemporary predator can catch them, but prehistoric cheetahs probably did. The pronghorn hardly seem to have lost a step, even with the extinction of the North American cheetah. Perhaps, as some sociobiologists suggest, pronghorn antipredator behavior—to run like the wind—is now a hardwired response selected for by a predator no longer in their midst. We all have our ghosts, I suppose.

Our journey to explore the potential for wildlife revival in eastern Montana began in earnest when Jonathan and I, along with two colleagues from WWF, Holly Strand and Kim Healey, headed north-east from Bozeman to the Charles M. Russell National Wildlife Refuge, the CMR, as locals call it, the third largest refuge in the lower forty-eight states. We descended Montana State Highway 191 from the west through cattle country—local private ranches and federal lands where cattle are permitted to graze for a small fee. The monoto-nous scenery changed with the passing of the last domestic herd. Up ahead were a line of bluffs capped with evergreens, a glimpse of the first wild real estate in seven hours of driving. We had just entered into the Missouri Breaks, a dramatic formation along the Upper Missouri River of upland plateau dissected by steep cliffs. As our truck snaked down the gorge, I had the overwhelming sense that I had been here before. Suddenly, it came to me. The scene in front of me bore a strong resemblance to East Africa's Great Rift Valley, a wide slash in the earth filled with large grazing mammals and the powerful preda-tors that ambush and eat them. The similarity must have been even greater at the time of Lewis and Clark's journey, when these grass-lands were teeming with big mammals. We spent the next three hours driving through the gorge and stopping to walk a bit. I imagined I was the naturalist accompanying Lewis, perhaps the day-dreaming one who was almost eaten by a hungry grizzly.

We then headed north, away from the river, and stopped in at the Matador Ranch, a sixty-thousand-acre spread purchased in 2000 by The Nature Conservancy (TNC). While the Matador may appear to be an ordinary ranch, it is potentially a vital corridor for movement of large mammals in this vast landscape. It abuts the southeast side of the Fort Belknap Indian Reservation and extends south almost to the CMR. The reservation is the home of the Gros Ventre and As-siniboine tribes, never friends or neighbors originally, but stuck on the same reservation as part of the grand scheme of some federal bureaucrat.

Brian Martin, the TNC biologist most familiar with this part of eastern Montana, was our host. He explained The Nature Conservancy's "good neighbor policy," which was to continue cattle ranching, at least for the time being, by allowing other ranchers to graze their cattle on the Matador in exchange for allowing more habitat on their properties to be managed for prairie dogs and other wildlife. This decision stems from a desire to show that ranching cattle and maintaining biodiversity are compatible goals, an idea that is anathema to some conservation biologists and not universally accepted within TNC. The position of TNC and the Matador's managers might change, however, if other conservationists purchase and reintroduce bison on key ranches in the corridor between the CMR and Fort Belknap.

We left the Matador and headed past a few ranches that border it and the CMR. There wasn't much moving. There wasn't much of anything in the foreground in the sweltering midafternoon except a group of excited prairie dogs unsure of our intentions. Unless you are a nature lover, a loner, or a hard-bitten cattle rancher, this is a godforsaken part of our planet. I can't even think of a town anyone would recognize to convey our latitude and longitude. But the vistas from the dog town! We could see thirty miles in every direction, buttes and mountains dominating the horizon. From the middle of a prairie dog colony where we now stood, it was one hundred miles west on mostly rough roads to the nearest hospital, grocery store, or espresso machine. There aren't many places in the lower forty-eight states so far from basic services and amenities. It's places like this that my biologist friends describe positively as the middle of nowhere because they are so rich in fascinating species, beautiful scenery, and endless sky yet so poor in human infrastructure.

On our way between the Matador and our next stop, UL Bend, we stopped to watch prairie dogs in one of the many small colonies along our route. As a mammalogist, I always felt uncomfortable about the classification of prairie dogs as members of the order Rodentia. They seem too collegial and far too adorable to be lumped in with the nasty wharf rat and the sullen Indian bandicoot. I had hoped that by now some geneticist would have announced that these social animals are actually closer to primates than to rodents. It was shocking to find out that local and national "Varmint Societies" have formed to make a sport out of blasting these poor creatures to smithereens. Every year, gun-toting enthusiasts migrate to the northern Great Plains and pay to shoot prairie dogs for the fun of it—sometimes even on public land. As monumentally barbaric as that sounds, consider that one arm of the U.S. government, the Department of Agriculture, is still poisoning prairie dogs at the behest of ranchers, even though another agency, the Fish and Wildlife Service, has for several years considered listing prairie dog species as endangered.

That prairie dogs still play their important ecological role is largely due to the efforts of Jonathan Proctor, our chauffeur and tour organizer. Despite his youth (barely over thirty), few biologists know more about prairie dog ecology than he does. For his master's thesis, he mapped the distributions of prairie dogs and created a predictive model for habitat suitability in the ecoregion. He combines the inquisitive mind of the field biologist with the missionary zeal of an Earth First member. It's in his pedigree: He hails from a deeply religious background and was a fundamentalist preacher for a time. Perhaps that's what gives him such courage to challenge management agency officials in public meetings when they try to bluster their way out of scientifically unsupportable positions. Like others scattered throughout the NGOs dedicated to northern Great Plains restoration, he works for peanuts. I was inspired to meet a young man more interested in the fate of the earth than in the status of his stock portfolio.

At the next prairie dog colony, we found a small flock of long-billed curlews. The Ichabod Crane of the bird world, these curlews seem 90 percent legs, with a decurved bill like a long hooked nose. I scanned the colony for other birds but wound up marveling at the congregation of curlews. At 120 individuals, I stopped counting. I had never seen so many in one place. Curlews utter among the most melancholy of calls, filling the prairie with their mournful lament, a striking contrast to the western meadowlarks, who release an ode to joy from their fence post perches every morning.

By late afternoon, we had reached UL Bend National Wildlife Refuge, adjacent to the Charles Russell Wildlife Refuge, hugging a famous stretch of the Missouri River where the "Mighty Mo" makes a U-turn through the Missouri Breaks. It's only two miles from one side of the bend to the other and twelve miles along the loop. In the old days, passengers taking the steamboat would disembark here and stretch their legs by walking across the U to meet the boat on the other side. We were to meet Randy Matchett, a U.S. Fish and Wildlife Service biologist who has been monitoring black-footed ferrets that were reintroduced in the region. He invited us to spend an evening with him to observe the elusive carnivores. His nocturnal ferrets are parts of a long-running and expensive experiment. For ten years, federal and state biologists have been trying, with little success, to reestablish wild populations of black-footed ferrets. As mentioned, the ferret is a predator that feeds almost exclusively on prairie dogs. By the 1980s, black-footed ferrets had become so rare that all of the remaining individuals were brought into captivity from the wild to prevent an immediate extinction, and research veterinarians tried to build up ferret numbers in carefully maintained facilities. Reduction in the number and size of prairie dog towns, combined with disease, had nearly caused biologists to write an obituary for this most elegant of weasels. Sylvatic plague, a flea-borne disease that wipes out prairie dogs and also affects ferrets, had been found on Fort Belknap, making the future of ferret reintroduction uncertain.

Matchett, whose cowboy hat and impressive mustache would blend perfectly into a Charles M. Russell canvas, met us at the UL Bend Ferret Research Station. The station was little more than an irregular row of house trailers adjacent to a large shed full of the paraphernalia of field biology: telemetry equipment, antennas, spare car parts, a retired oil drum rigged up as a barbecue stove, and a solar-powered water heater. We spent the next hour talking with Randy about the history of his decade-long project, the hopes and setbacks of reintroducing endangered species to the wild, and the idea of restoring this ecosystem on a grand scale. A few minutes into the conversation, I recognized in Randy a trait endemic to the best biologists: the capacity to allow a field research project to evolve into one's mission in life.

The only way to monitor the success of the black-footed ferret reintroduction is by keeping track of their numbers and locations. Randy and his crew often spend the entire night collecting these data, and tonight, we would accompany them on their search, using spotlights mounted on trucks. We would drive by and flash the beam on anything that moved in prairie dog town, trying to pinpoint the eyes of ferrets (which glow green in the spotlight) as they meandered between burrow openings. Randy advised us to get some rest before heading out, so we retreated to the guest trailers to cook dinner and relax. A few visitors had surely done the same earlier that summer, but the droppings of what must have been a Woodstock festival of field mice overshadowed any human evidence.

When night fell, we divided up into three teams and headed out in pickup trucks to specific neighborhoods of prairie dog town. As we gathered our equipment in the moonlight, I reminisced on my own nocturnal research history: the first time a vampire bat flew into a mist net I had erected over a stream in the Guanacaste lowlands of Costa Rica; my Ph.D. research on fruit bats in neotropical rain forests; calling for spotted owls in the Mount Baker National Forest in Washington State; spotlighting for black bears in Yosemite and for tigers along jeep tracks in Bardia National Park in Nepal. I remembered the practical advice of Jim Corbett, the famous hunter of man-eating tigers: one reflected red eye in the road and it's a nightjar; two red eyes and it's a tiger.

There are no tigers out here, but there are nighthawks, a cousin to the nightjar, and they, too, flash one red eye. There is also the eye shine of white-tailed deer (yellow and moving), coyotes (yellow and

low), burrowing owls (yellow and darting), and finally, the phospho-
rescent green headlights that signal ferrets. We drove for two hours,
accompanied by burrowing owls making unpredictable swoops in
front of the pickup, until two green dots, like flares, stopped us short
in our tracks. It was a female that had given birth to three kits that
summer. Randy knows all of the ferrets here, twenty-eight at the moment; each adult wears a radio collar and has an implanted microchip
to allow transponders to keep track of every individual. We learned
from Randy that after the initial failures of reintroduction—attributed
to unwary ferrets being eaten by badgers, coyotes, or great horned
owls—some of the original colonists had survived, and we were seeing
reproduction in the wild from ferrets that were born to captive-bred
parents. The annual reintroduction of ferrets has continued to build
the numbers rapidly and helped the ferrets escape the demographic
jeopardy that haunts small populations of endangered species. The
Fish and Wildlife Service even engages in predator control at the release sites by shooting all of the coyotes they see. Randy is opposed to
that practice, because he feels that eventually the ferrets are going to
have to get accustomed to living with, and avoiding, coyotes.

Then Randy shared with us a larger problem. It seemed that despite six years of reintroductions, predator control, and careful monitoring of reintroduced populations by extraordinarily committed field
biologists, ferret numbers still hover at depressingly low levels. Reintroduced ferrets *are* reproducing. But, at UL Bend, Randy ends up
with the same number of adults at the end of each summer (the
breeding season) as at the beginning—in the twenties. How was it
possible that ferret numbers failed to increase when many young ferrets are reaching adulthood?

The answer to the puzzle is obvious, and it transcends this particular
project and species: insufficient habitat. Black-tailed prairie dogs con-
stitute over 90 percent of the ferrets' prey. For the population of ferrets
to expand from its current level, it must have access to a complex of
prairie dog towns exceeding ten thousand acres. The biggest complex

in the area is no more than five thousand acres. Among the six sites in the western United States where ferrets have been reintroduced, only one, in South Dakota, has shown an increase in ferret numbers, and its prairie dog town exceeds the ten-thousand-acre threshold.

Proponents of captive breeding hold up the black-footed ferret program as a success story for how zoos can save an endangered species from extinction. Certainly, zoo veterinarians and keepers deserve a great deal of credit for rescuing a species on the brink. Yet the difficulty of the reintroduction effort provides a valuable parable for conservation: More than 90 percent of all the species on the U.S. federal endangered species list are there for one main reason—loss of habitat. No matter how much effort we devote to captive breeding and high-tech–assisted reproduction, we cannot put endangered species back into areas where their long-term habitat requirements are overlooked. Ten years of ferret recovery efforts will be pointless if we fail to expand the size of prairie dog towns. And that expansion will go nowhere unless enlightened landowners manage their properties for prairie dogs or conservationists purchase strategically located cattle ranches and allow prairie dogs to recolonize their homelands. It's that simple. If we did a cost-benefit analysis to find out how much has already been invested in ferret recovery, we would see that the cost of purchasing the nearby ranches, about $10–$15 million, is a bargain.

We saw only a couple of ferrets that night, but we were treated to two other memorable sightings: one earthly, one celestial. Sitting on top of a burrow, looking as menacing as Genghis Khan on the plains of Mongolia, was a large, ornery-looking badger. I had never seen a live badger before, and in the flesh at two in the morning, they are miniature monsters. This one held his ground as we approached within snarling distance. Respectfully, we retreated from his kingdom by hopping into the pickup and speeding off. Up the road, we stopped to stare at what seemed to be movie premiere lights beaming over the horizon. No Tom Hanks premiere out here; these were the northern lights. It's easy to forget how small we are on this planet, let alone in this galaxy. If the daylight vistas can't convince casual visitors to the northern Great Plains of their own insignificance, the northern lights are sure to humble them.

A postscript to our ferret watching appeared in the *New York Times* a few months later. For the first time in six years, the Fish and Wildlife Service decided not to release any more captive ferrets in this area until they determine how to deal with plague and the shortage of large blocks of prairie dog habitat. If there were still plenty of prairie dog habitat, it is unlikely that plague would be a major threat. Typically, epidemics become a serious problem only when natural populations have been reduced and remain at dangerously low levels. Ranch acquisition and better grazing practices by enlightened landowners—the remedy—went unmentioned in the short news story, but it may be all that prevents the tombstone being planted for this endangered species.

Our next stop on the ecoregion tour was Fort Belknap. On our way there, we did some "car birding" and came upon a scene that would warm any biologist's heart. Sitting on a tree stump was a splendid ferruginous hawk, a proud resident of the Great Plains and perhaps the signature raptor of the ecoregion. He was busily dismembering a ringnecked pheasant, a species introduced from Asia. After habitat loss, the introduction of exotic invasive species poses the greatest threat to biodiversity worldwide. We cheered loudly.

The sight of the hawk reminded me of another prominent avian resident of the Great Plains—the mountain plover. The fate of this bird, one of the region's most endangered species, is also linked with that of the black-tailed prairie dog. For endangered mountain plovers, black-tailed prairie dogs are essential real estate developers. They closely crop the vegetation in their colonies, leaving some parts of their towns looking like they have been sprayed with Roundup. That is just what mountain plovers need because they avoid areas where vegetation grows tall enough to hide nest predators. They require the golf course–like areas modified by prairie dogs to nest.

Successful invaders, like ring-necked pheasants, tend to have wide-spread distributions. At the opposite extreme, are endemic species, those found in only one place and thus vulnerable to extinction because of their restricted distribution. Endemic species help define the distinct communities of the ecoregion. Grasslands typically harbor many fewer endemic birds than other biomes, such as the celebrated tropical rain forests. Grassland birds are good fliers and dispersers, and the grasslands of North America are relatively young; that combination of features suggests a near absence of endemic birds in the ecoregion. Yet two species of longspurs, the chestnut-collared and McGowan's; Sprague's pipit; and Baird's sparrow are highly partial to the northern Great Plains. On a previous birding trip to the Great Plains, we tried to "bag" all four endemics in a single day. We struck out on pipits and Baird's sparrows but hit a home run on longspurs. We watched the McGowan's enact their wonderful courtship display, in which females fly low over a patch of prairie studded with territorial males. As the female flies by, the males shoot straight up in the air as if popped out of toasters, then flutter back down to their perches in the unique longspur language of love.

Bison are one of the few species for which we have a reasonable sense of what it will take to maintain a minimum population in nature. In a short unpublished paper titled "Trends in Bison Management: What It Means for the Species," coauthor Craig Knowles, one of the leading experts on bison, states: "The minimum herd size necessary to avoid inbreeding and to prevent genetic depletion is estimated at 580 adult animals." Unfortunately, few public bison herds exceed 580 adult animals. Average herd size for federally owned bison herds is 549, and only four out of eight herds exceed or approach 580. The average for state-owned herds is 254, and only two out of seventeen exceed or approach 580. Of six owned by nonprofits, none exceeds 580, and the average is only 222. We desperately need some big wild herds to maintain genetic viability and wildness, to say nothing of restoring large-scale ecological phenomena and processes. Their trampling, wallowing, defecating, urinating, and stampeding simply make a rebisoned grassland different for co-occurring species from one where domestic cattle graze.

So how big must a bison landscape be to permit sound genetic management, frequent roaming, and the occasional stampede? Knowles writes, "Genetic monitoring at Custer State Park in South Dakota has shown that a tightly managed herd of about 1,000 adult animals is not sufficient to maintain genetic diversity over the long term without genetic screening of breeder bulls." Later, he states, "In Montana, approximately 40,000 acres of grasslands are needed to provide for the year-long economy of a 580-head bison herd. This assumes that all 40,000 acres of grasslands are available to the bison during the entire year. If portions of the grasslands are blocked to bison access during winter months, additional acreage may be required for their health and well being. Historically, bison migrated to maintain constancy in habitat suitability." Thus, a population of two thousand adults, roaming over 220,000 unbroken acres, would provide for some margin of error (in terms of both genetic viability and stocking rates) and promote herd mobility, or as a Native American might say, allow the bison to go where their hearts lead them.

To some, the scientists' dream of several herds of more than two thousand bison populating vast landscapes of the northern Great Plains must seem like a Pleistocene pipe dream. As if a collection of normally sober ecologists had stampeded, without any prompting, over a buffalo jump of the senses. To some locals, it surely must seem like another intrusion of East Coast know-it-alls. Luckily, the conditions necessary for such a restoration are aligning like stars in the prairie night: the rapid exodus of human residents; the bankruptcy of the ranches surrounding the most logical targets in the United States for re-creating free-ranging bison populations; the availability of some of the cheapest real estate in the United States at $100–$200 per acre;

TNC's purchase of the Matador to start the corridor; the revival of bison culture on Native American lands; the strong coalition of science-based NGOs (including WWF) committed to developing a national constituency for this ecoregion; and the close scrutiny now being focused on farm and grazing subsidies in the West.

One of the trusted guides in our loosely based coalition to bring back this ecoregion is Curt Freese. Curt is a widely respected conservationist and a former senior vice president of WWF who paid his dues in D.C. trying to save the planet from inside the Beltway. At the end of an eight-year tenure, he followed in the footsteps of many dedicated conservationists and headed for the hills of Montana. His effective liaising among our coalition members and the spontaneous combustion created by the vision of a vast prairie reserve that could support thousands of bison has hastened the potential quilting together of a range of land-use designations into a single prairie conservation theme. Several families ranch cattle in what could become the greatest piece of conservation real estate in the region if it were used to create a bison-dominated landscape. There are many good reasons to believe this could happen. Several of the ranches are for sale, because the owners are retiring and their children are moving on in search of new opportunities. The tendency for sodbusting, or plowing up the native grasslands to plant wheat, persists, however, made economically feasible because of a massive government welfare system erected to maintain wheat farmers on the Great Plains. Subsidized or not, the going rate for these properties is $140 an acre for grazing land. And even as politically controversial as the issue of farm subsidies is, they will be scaled back someday as demands by wheat farmers in other countries for more equitable competition increase.

Currently, the wildest, most free-ranging bison in this potential landscape are on Fort Belknap Indian Reservation, where the return of bison is part of a cultural renaissance for local tribes. A similar "back to bison" movement is taking place on the Crow and Northern

Cheyenne reservations, and nearby Fort Peck Reservation has agreed to buy one hundred bison from Fort Belknap to start a herd.

At about two in the afternoon, we pulled into the parking lot of Fort Belknap Cultural Center. Fort Belknap is among the leaders in U.S. reservations for promoting restoration of endangered species. The swift fox, another endangered species, may be reintroduced to the wildlands here under the stewardship of aptly named Mike Fox, the chief wildlife biologist. In cooperation with the tribes, the Fish and Wildlife Service has designated this as another ferret reintroduction site. Sometimes, however, even the most ambitious visions are challenged by unforeseen and devastating events. Sylvatic plague arrived last year, and the prospects for further ferret recovery look bleak until a vaccine or other control mechanism is found.

We were met at Fort Belknap by Darrell Martin, the director of tourism and culture for the reservation. Darrell showed us the museum he had helped create, which features a series of beautiful old photographs of his ancestors in ceremonial dress, a stuffed bison, and essential and decorative items made from bison parts. All the while, he kept us entertained with a running commentary about his ancestors and the history of the reservation. Darrell is a mix of Gros Ventre and Assiniboine, like many on the reservation, with a touch of Crow thrown in. The Gros Ventre, or "Big Bellies," were so named by French trappers who came through the region and lived to tell about it. "We fought everybody," said Darrell with a sly smile. Now the Gros Ventre fight modern problems; 83 percent of the population of Belknap is unemployed, and the reservation struggles to find teachers who will stay in this remote area. A full college scholarship awaits any Native American student who graduates from high school, but few pursue higher education.

Darrell loaded us up in his van to take us to the bison herd of almost 450 that were grazing near Snake Butte. An important spiritual site for a number of tribes, Snake Butte is a massive piece of granite thrust up from the prairie. Tipi rings surround the butte itself, and there are petroglyphs on its flanks. As he drove at a rapid pace over the dirt roads, Darrell said, "The buffalo are our brothers. They know we revere them and are here to protect them. This is why we can approach so closely." We came within a few yards of the largest herd I had ever seen. The sheer size and power of the adult bulls were truly awesome.

We parked on the outskirts of a nearby prairie dog town. The sky was darkening ominously. A giant dust devil shaped like a miniature tornado was making its way toward us. In seconds we would be engulfed, so we scrambled into the car and shut all the windows. Realizing that traveling into the storm would be futile, Darrell turned the van around. I thought, What could be more dramatic than a dust storm on a hot summer day in the presence of a wild bison herd at the base of Snake Butte?

Darrell's friendly banter subsided when he looked north. What turned out to be the most violent hail and thunderstorm of the summer was just ahead. Darrell told us straight out, "We have to get back to the highway right now. These roads will turn to gumbo, and we'll be stuck up to the axles." During our travels out here, we had been warned of the dangers of "gumbo" roads, dirt tracks carved out of sticky clay soils that can immobilize even the most macho four-wheel-drive pickups. At UL Bend, Randy Matchett had once been stuck for two weeks until the rains had stopped and the roads became passable.

The peals of thunder grew more dramatic, and lightning crackled on the horizon. The storm was fast approaching, and we were still several miles from the main road. All of a sudden, the bison herd, as if sensing impending danger, began a stampede toward the safety of Snake Butte. I desperately wanted to ask Darrell to stop, if only for a moment, so that I could step out of the van and into this dramatic scene unfolding. I wanted to plant my feet on the prairie and feel the earth tremble from the pounding hooves of stampeding bison. But Darrell was determined to head in the other direction, so I kept silent and stared out the window at the spectacle shrinking from view as we sped away. I made these mental notes:

Many Americans love to claim that they are part Native American—"I'm actually one-sixteenth Cherokee," or "My great-great grandmother was kidnapped by an Apache warrior." I have not a drop of Indian blood in me. My only cultural link to buffalo is that during the Eastern European pogroms, my people fled to forests that held European bison (*Bison bonasus*), the slightly smaller cousin of the North American species. But Native American or not, I couldn't help being moved by what I saw and realizing that I had witnessed this wildlife extravaganza *without a passport*, without flying thousands of miles to East Africa. I was on the sovereign land of the Gros Ventre and Assiniboine and on the short-grass prairie of eastern Montana.

Watching the bison stampede to the base of Snake Butte, I felt for the first time the need to go beyond just conserving biological wonders. We must preserve and restore not just ecological and evolutionary phenomena such as intact large mammal migrations, but also the spiritual experience—the chance to observe vast aggregations of creatures undulating, flying, and running full tilt as far as you can see. I now had another reason to return to the Belknap and the Great Plains: to hear and see this spiritual phenomenon on a calm, dry day, when the rain, hail, and wind couldn't drown out the thunder of a herd of bison running pell-mell over the prairie. Observing spectacular wildlife aggregations reminds us of the most profound lessons we can learn in life: how small we are in the grand scheme of things, that we as individuals and as a species occupy but a moment on this earth, and that from these humbling insights spring the most vital of core values—a reverence for nature.

If we are ever to convince more than a fraction of the American population, let alone the world, that leaving behind a living planet should be more than a slogan, we must restore this reverence for nature, as rapidly and in as many hearts as we can. We need to restore free-ranging bison, not just because it's the appropriate ecological action but also because doing so will help to establish reverence for nature as a force in our decisions about how we use the earth, rather than an afterthought. Our ancestors have left a tragic emotional and ecological scar on our landscape that we have the collective power to heal.

I left the Belknap feeling as sure as I have ever felt as a scientist that my organization needs to play a central role in this grand effort, so that the restoration of bison becomes a touchstone for our work everywhere. We need to see curlews number in the thousands once again. And hear the wolves howling at the rising moon. Grizzlies will roam freely as the kings of the grasslands, digging up tubers and rolling in carpets of wildflowers, home after a long exile in the Rocky Mountains. A living prairie with all its species intact perhaps will inspire us Americans to appreciate the rest of our abundant natural bounty and set our sights on restoration in other parts of the nation. We can then speak openly with conservation-minded people in other nations about the mistakes we have made and the restoration we are undertaking to correct them, so that we can learn from each other. We need to play a major role here so that every American citizen can feel pride in the grand ecological revival, when, someday soon, vast herds of bison thunder across the northern Great Plains.

RE-TIGERING

THE ASCENDING SHRIEKS OF BRAIN-FEVER BIRDS AND OTHER agitated cuckoos dispelled the tranquility of my morning jungle walk. Up the trail, peacocks wailed from the safety of tree branches and gray langur monkeys coughed in warning. Red jungle fowl hens dashed for the cover of spiny palms. I looked down and saw fresh tracks in the mud. My biological acuity, dulled by urban living, sprang back to life, as it always does when I return to Royal Chitwan National Park in Nepal. And nothing heightens the senses more than knowing a wild tiger is stalking nearby. "It is the tigress of Baghmara. She has three young cubs," whispered Bishnu Bahadur Lama. Bishnu, our most experienced tracker, has photographed and identified the tigers and rhinos living in the Baghmara forest since its recovery under the protection of local villagers, beginning in 1993. Now in 2004, we were determining how successful the recovery had been in restoring Chitwan's tigers, rhinos, and other endangered wildlife in various habitats managed by local communities rather than government staff inside the park. The regenerated forest of Bagh-mara and this fresh tiger track were symbolic of our initial success in an even grander plan: to recover the charismatic large mammal pop-ulations in a whole network of reserves across Nepal and northern India. An experiment in re-tigering.

I placed my hand over the soft mud impression of splayed toes and footpad. We had missed her by mere minutes; if we moved carefully, we might catch a glimpse of black stripes on orange fur before she dis-appeared behind the curtain of the jungle. Tigers are the largest ter-restrial carnivores on earth, and those that prowl Chitwan in Nepal's lowland Terai region are among the grandest of all. I will never forget a tiger that lived near Baghmara (which means "site of a tiger kill" in the local Tharu language) that Bishnu and I once helped to tranquilize and radio-collar. He weighed over 560 pounds and exceeded ten feet from nose tip to tail tip, a good 100 pounds heavier and several inches longer than most adult males from this area. As far as I know, that record still stands among tigers of the subcontinent.

Tracking tigers through the forest or riding an elephant to follow radio-collared rhinos through twenty-five-foot-tall grass is a privileged occupation, but to save endangered species, the most important activ-ities are interactions with government officials and local communities, whether in Malta, Montana; Quito, Ecuador; or Nouméa, New Cale-donia. It is they who hold the fate of such species in their hands. While keen eyesight and tracking expertise are helpful, diplomacy is one of the most important strengths of the conservation biologist's reper-toire. Twenty-five years after my Peace Corps initiation, I had been in-vited back to Nepal, not to track tigers in Baghmara, but to address a conference near the capital of Kathmandu attended by the country's highest-ranking decision makers, foreign donors, village leaders, local politicians, development workers, and biologists. My assignment was to persuade them to endorse the Terai Arc Landscape—a massive habitat restoration program for tigers and other endangered wildlife that spans a 450-mile stretch of lowland jungle from southern Nepal west across the border through northern India—the largest and most ambitious wildlife and habitat recovery program of its kind in Asia.

Standing at the podium, I wanted to urge the members of that influential assembly to embrace endangered species conservation with the same fervor as they embraced the restoration of the holiest Hindu temples and Buddhist monasteries. I even considered starting my talk with the rallying cry of conservationists worldwide: that we must speak up for those species that have no voice in their own future. But I didn't.

In impoverished countries, wildlife conservation must be integrated with economic development to gain wide support. Fifteen minutes passed before I even mentioned the words *tiger* or *rhinoceros* in my speech. I first talked about the need for a continuous greenbelt of low-hill forest in Nepal and India's lowland Terai region to safeguard the watersheds and the productivity of South Asia's "rice bowl." I spoke, too, of the need to stop the tremendous amount of erosion that carries away farmers' hopes for a successful harvest. As someone once said, Nepal's greatest export is not Tibetan carpets or rice, but topsoil. Erosion is a natural process in the world's steepest, youngest mountain chain, where heavy rains are packed into a four-month monsoon, but it has greatly accelerated over the past four decades because of rampant clearing of forest in the outermost foothills, known as the Siwaliks, and behind them the first true range of the Himalayan mountains, the Mahabharat chain.

I described to the Terai conference attendees how biologists and progressive economists have urged accounting for the subsidies that nature provides us through what are termed *ecological services*— natural irrigation and water purification, prevention of soil erosion through forest cover, flood control, pollination of crops by wild honey bees, to name just a few—the goods we get for free by conserving the natural habitats adjacent to agricultural areas and rural settlements.

Then I posed a series of questions to my audience that addressed that concept. What if the governments of Nepal and India had to pay the real costs of maintaining clean and abundant water, soil fertility, pollination of crop plants, and the extraction of natural products upon which millions of people depend in the Terai? What if all forests above the parks and in protected floodplains inside the parks were cut down? What would it cost to create water diversions and dams to minimize catastrophic monsoon floods that often result in massive siltation, extensive soil erosion, and refugee crises? Wouldn't it be far cheaper to invest in forest conservation to save precious topsoil, human lives, and livelihoods? Local farmers realized from painful experience that if they cut down the Terai forests lying above the floodplain, they exposed the stony soil, known as *bhaber*, which has poor water-holding capacity. Low retention means more unpredictable floods, lower water tables, and lower crop yields. For those reasons, a significant portion of those forests remains.

All of these vital natural resource conservation goals underpinned the Terai Arc project. I didn't have to convince the wildlife hotel owners and senior employees attending that the Terai Arc program goes beyond an agricultural conservation program to embrace wildlife conservation and nature tourism, which makes up a surprisingly large fraction of Nepal's GDP. They were already part of the converted.

It was not until I made those arguments to the conference participants that I presented a scientific rationale for the Terai Arc Landscape. I distilled thirty years of radiotelemetry research and natural history studies of large mammals supported by the government of Nepal, WWF, and the Smithsonian Institution into a few key points that I hoped would hold the attention of even the most biologically disinclined listener. Biologists knew that even though tigers prowl over large territories of 4–40 square miles, move 12 miles in a single night, and are powerful swimmers, they are remarkably poor dispersers. If tigers reach the edge of a jungle separated by more than 1 mile from another forest, they hesitate to cross the intervening area of human habitation. Even more important, we discovered that no single reserve in Asia was large enough to ensure the survival of its own healthy tiger population over the long term. The only solution was to embrace a bold vision: to fashion a network of connected reserves where tigers could be managed as a single population linked by dispersal—what biologists call a *metapopulation*. To make that vision a reality would require restringing a green necklace of eleven parks, from Parsa Wildlife Reserve east of Chitwan across Western Nepal's jungles to Rajaji National Park in India. Government forests, community forests, and buffer zones would form the corridors to reconnect the reserves, and local villagers would be encouraged to play an active role. Local peoples had lived with tigers as neighbors for millennia. The Terai Arc program was the first, though, to give them economic incentives to encourage and maintain such proximity. If we could zone the most productive lands for agriculture and ensure adequate watershed protection and flood control, the possibility of a healthy future for farmers would be greatly improved, as well as a chance for tigers and other charismatic species to greet the twenty-second century. The Terai Arc Landscape, along with a few other examples in Asia and Africa, I predicted, would shatter forever the belief that ambitious wildlife restoration programs are incompatible with rural development in the poorest countries.

Fortunately, this jungle landscape is a forgiving one. The tall, riverine grassland habitats preferred by tigers and rhinos are so resilient that they recover within a year or two of protection from domestic livestock grazing. The formula for restoring wild tiger populations is simple: Stop the poaching of tigers and the wild animals they eat, protect enough of their habitat, and provide enough surface water for drinking. Do all that, and tiger numbers would rebound at an astonishing speed. After all, tigers are one of two large predators (the other being wolves) that breed faster than their prey. Back in the winter of 1937–38, when Chitwan was a royal hunting reserve, the ruling family of Nepal and the viceroy of India bagged 120 tigers and 38 rhinos in the grasslands and forests of Chitwan. While the total number of trophies was staggering, the population remained stable—a testament to how resilient these large charismatic mammals can be when they are fully protected.

When we embarked upon the Terai Arc project, my Nepalese and Indian colleagues and I had to rethink how to approach the conservation of large mammals. The most challenging task was to make tigers worth more alive than dead to poor villagers. We began by lobbying for policy changes that would directly benefit impoverished residents. First, new legislation passed in 1991 allowed local village groups in Baghmara and across the Nepalese Terai to manage certain government lands in buffer zones around parks. Villagers would be allowed to harvest firewood, grasses, timber for building, and other forest products and grow native hardwoods in tree plantations if they let a large part of the land under their protection naturally regenerate to restore wildlife populations. An even more groundbreaking act was passed in 1993, requiring that 50 percent of the revenues generated by tourism in Nepal's nature reserves be returned to village committees residing in the buffer zones. Overnight, villagers once arrested as park intruders became guardians of endangered species and architects of habitat restoration. The relationships were clear: The more wildlife in the parks and buffer zones, the greater the number of tourists. The more tourists, the more money generated by park entry fees and hotel stays, which meant more money for the local communities. Visitation to Chitwan soared through the late 1990s, generating $500,000 annually for local development in the buffer zone. That amount dipped as a Maoist-like insurgency in Nepal hurt the tourism sector of the country. By the time I addressed the Terai conference in 2004, however, tourism appeared to be on the rebound, and residents had begun to understand clearly that the funds available to finance development efforts were coming from conservation. At last, wild tigers and rhinos in the backyard had become an economically valuable presence rather than merely a threat to human welfare.

I concluded my remarks to the conference by pointing out that the birthplace of the Buddha at Lumbini, Nepal, is within the Terai Arc Landscape. It seemed fitting for the most enlightened wildlife recovery program I had ever witnessed to be born in the same habitat that gave us the most enlightened being. Harmony between man and nature is part of the Buddha's teachings, I said, and by implementing the Terai Arc, we were following the noble path. Let these good works spread, I urged.

I returned to Chitwan the day after that Kathmandu meeting. Bishnu and I entered the community-managed forest. When we had first erected the fences to keep the cattle out of the forest, some villagers had wanted the fences removed. But after a single monsoon, they realized that the increased growth of thatch grass and firewood in the fenced-off areas was available to them, reducing the need to travel far for those essential items. And the wildlife rebounded almost immediately on these once degraded lands. An unanticipated benefit early on was community-based ecotourism, as the charismatic species such as tigers and rhinos that tourists come to see crossed over the river and took up residence in the buffer zone habitats. We had thought that even with the improvements to the habitat in the buffer zones, tigers and rhinos might not become residents but rather remain transient visitors. We were wrong; the tigers and rhinos created new home ranges in the buffer zones, and the enterprising Baghmara forest committee rented domestic elephants, established foot trails, and built treehouses suitable for overnight stays so that adventurous tourists could get to see them. Within weeks of starting operations, these outfits were profitable.

The village committee had asked Bishnu and me how to improve Baghmara for wildlife viewing. I suggested that they leave all of the standing dead trees rather than cut them down for firewood, as is done illegally inside the park. The trees were valuable foraging and nesting habitat for woodpeckers, whose nest holes were subsequently used by other endangered bird species. From that moment on, not a single standing dead tree was cut in Baghmara. We were rewarded for our recommendations by hearing lesser flamebacks and yellow-naped woodpeckers hammering against the dead standing trees at the start of the trail. And the villagers were rewarded by more tourists generating income for local activities.

We came to a wetland in the heart of the forest, where four greater one-horned rhinoceros were submerged up to their nostrils and fabled horns. The villagers wanted to attract more rhinos to Baghmara, so Bishnu and our staff had suggested creating wallows. During the monsoon, rhinos are semiaquatic, wallowing up to eight hours a day to cool off in the humid weather. The villagers' excavations exceeded a few wallows; they created shallow lakes filled with aquatic vegetation preferred by rhinos, and the giant herbivores settled in. We watched the rhinos blow bubbles in the water. Despite periodic poaching events, such as in 2002, when more than 35 animals were killed, the strong recovery of rhinos in Chitwan over the past three decades enabled us to relocate the rhinos from Chitwan to other reserves where the species once flourished. We have moved over 100 individuals to three of the other nine parks that had lost their own populations. The capture of rhinos has become so routine that Bishnu, along with Nepalese biologists, has shipped up to five rhinos in a single day from Chitwan to new destinations. The translocation plans for the Terai Arc Landscape do not stop with rhinos. Gharial crocodiles, swamp deer, and wild water buffalo, to name a few, are next on our list of endangered species to transplant and restore to their former haunts in Chitwan and in other Terai parks and reserves as their recovering numbers permit. Beyond the adventurous aspects of these maneuvers is a fundamental scientific principle of endangered species management: to create at least ten populations of one hundred individuals each to ward off the dangers of species extinctions—the idea of not putting all of your eggs in one basket. If the protection of rhinos holds, thousands of animals could be flourishing in the Terai Arc reserves within three decades. This seemed a mere pipe dream when we started, but then, as a local wildlife official once astutely observed, "In Nepal, the impossible is possible, but the possible is often impossible."

Restoration of tiger habitat cannot come soon enough. I once overheard at a scientific meeting that there are more tigers in the state of Texas than in the wild. At first, I considered that tall Texas talk, but today in the wild, tigers are widely but thinly distributed from India northward to Nepal and Bhutan, across parts of Indochina, and south toward Sumatra. One population roams much farther north, the fabled Amur, or Siberian, tiger. This vast range suggests that the total wild population should exceed ten to twenty thousand animals, but the best guess of field biologists puts the number at fewer than six thousand individuals, less than the total estimated in private hands in the Lone Star State.

The tigress eluded us that day in Chitwan, so we headed for the Khagady River, where boatmen were waiting for us. By now the sun was high in the sky, and the marsh mugger crocodiles would be out sunning themselves on the riverbanks. We greeted the boatmen and sat down in the dugouts, and they poled us into the gentle current. A few years ago, these boatmen were fishermen, plying the Khagady and the Rapti River with nets to catch fish, which they would sell in the market. When the villagers started managing the Baghmara forest area, they banned fishing in the rivers but offered the fishermen a deal: Stop fishing and instead take bird watchers and other nature-loving tourists for rides down the river. They agreed, and within a year of the fishing ban, fish populations rebounded, and the crocodiles returned in numbers. We floated to within a few feet of a ten-foot-long marsh mugger completely undisturbed by our presence and photographed five others at close range. Along our route, we saw five species of kingfishers plunge into the water. The fish had returned, and the food chain was reviving. It was after a ride down this river that George Schaller called the Terai Arc program the most impressive wildlife restoration effort he had seen in Asia. Even the poorest villagers are conservationists at heart, I mused. We just need to offer the right incentives to align their livelihoods with nature protection.

Nepal is not the only success story. In a variety of other places, optimistic plans for conservation that were met with cynical disbelief are now materializing with diligent work.

In Costa Rica, where I overcame my bat phobia and fell hard for the tropics, a WWF team led by George Powell developed a vision for conserving the cloud forests from Monteverde southeast to the Talamanca Mountains. That vision for filling out the reserve network—by including more underrepresented mid-elevation reserves and corridors linking lowland and high-elevation sites—has been adopted by a number of groups, such as The Nature Conservancy, Conservation International, the Wildlife Conservation Society, and many local conservation nonprofits, and work is already under way to achieve it. In the Himalayas, thanks to Helen Freeman, Rod Jackson, Mingma Sherpa, and Joe Fox—champions all of snow leopard conservation—the amount of snow leopard habitat under formal protection in the Hindu Kush and the greater Himalayan range has trebled since our initial trip to Kashmir in 1983. In New Caledonia, new initiatives are now beginning to protect rare tropical dry forests. Across the Amazon, a bold new plan sponsored by the Brazilian government, the World Bank, WWF, and the Moore Foundation is being implemented with the intention of saving 75 percent of the remaining forest cover of the richest rain forests on earth. The largest terrestrial reserve in the world, Tumucumaque National Park, twice the size of the state of Massachusetts, was created in 2004 under this new plan. The Orinoco basin, where we searched and found giant river otters, is now the subject of a project sponsored by WWF and its companion Venezuelan organization, Fudena, to develop extensive plans to conserve that still intact tropical wilderness. Even the black rhinos of Africa are rebounding, thanks to increased vigilance by the wildlife departments across southern Africa. I wish Henri Nsanjama could have been with me in Etosha National Park in Namibia in September of 2003 to see one of his dreams fulfilled. With the vital support of the Namibian government and financial help from WWF, there are now five hundred black rhinos in Etosha, and translocation to other reserves is under way.

In the American West, an almost inconceivable breakthrough is still possible. In the northern Great Plains of eastern Montana, conservation efforts to recreate an American Serengeti, a landscape rich with diverse plant and animal species, are moving forward. In January of 2004, American Prairie Foundation with WWF support purchased its first ranch to connect the Fort Belknap Indian Reservation with the Charles M. Russell Wildlife Refuge. It will become a beachhead for prairie restoration. In October 2005, a herd of buffalo will be released on the property, the first step in rebisoning. After several ranches are purchased, this new landscape of private and public land could support the largest free-roaming bison herd in the world. A civilization of prairie dogs will be reborn, numbering in the tens of millions, to be hunted by a resurgent population of America's most endangered species, the black-footed ferret. Someday, vast herds of bison, and smaller groups of pronghorn, elk, deer, and bighorn sheep could dot the plains where cattle once grazed.

Not everywhere does the future seem bursting with optimism, however, and in several places conservation is still on the defensive. At the time of this writing, the Galápagos conservation program is mired in Ecuadorian politics. The federal navy has taken over patrol of the marine reserve from the Galápagos National Park Service, but illegal fishing inside the marine reserve is still rampant. The world has not come to the rescue of that iconic desert archipelago or its wild inhabitants. This must be a top priority for world leaders—to work with their Ecuadorian counterparts to return those islands to their former grandeur. I would like to report that New Caledonia has emerged in the public consciousness as the other Madagascar, which recently has benefited by a decision of the current Malagasy president to triple the size of the national protected areas system. New Caledonia deserves the same special treatment.

I could list other setbacks or places where conservation seems to be stalled around the world. Its greatest success, however, is right here in the Terai, in my eyes. In February of 2004, the government of Nepal officially adopted the Terai Arc Landscape as its blueprint for conservation for the region. A vision for the future of Tigerland has become the official national plan. The Indian government has also pledged to increase the connectivity of reserves on its side of the border with Nepal. A long list of international donors, including the Save the Tiger Fund and ExxonMobil Foundation, WWF, the Smithsonian's National Zoo, the United Nations, and several European nations, have pledged support to restore wildlife corridors through community forestry programs. Tigers have already responded. The same month the plan was formally adopted, three individual tigers had taken up occupancy in a reconnected corridor between Royal Bardia National Park in Nepal and Katarniaghat Wildlife Reserve in India.

My emotional connection to Tigerland is hardly camouflaged. In my house just outside Washington, D.C., I grow indoors a species of *Murraya*, also known among gardeners as the orange jessamine tree, which covers the understory of Chitwan. When its night-blooming flowers fill the air with a sweet citrus aroma, I am transported back to Nepal. Sometimes I relive the most memorable moment of my years there. In April 1987, I was camped out in the middle of Chitwan with my staff and the five elephants that enabled us to photograph and count the rhinos in the park. After a simple meal of rice and lentils and stories around the campfire, everyone had gone to bed. The full moon shone through my tent. My eyes snapped open when I heard a deep familiar moan. AAAAAWWWWRRRR! AAAAAWWWWRRRR! I unzipped the fly and crawled out.

If a tiger wanders through a camp, its unexpected appearance can spook the elephants and create bedlam as they trumpet in excitement. But this tiger was too far away to interrupt the snores of our sleeping elephants and the raspier sawing of their drivers. The trackers and elephant crew had bedded down under a long lean-to fashioned expertly from thatching grass and tree branches. Nearby, four elephants lay sprawled on their sides. Only our noble pachyderm Chanchal Kali, the sixty-year-old matriarch of our stable, stood awake in the moonlight. Together we listened to the catcalls on a hot spring night. Rumbling softly, as if she were telling me to stay calm, Chanchal held out her magnificent ears in response to the sounds of the tiger searching for a mate. I cannot adequately describe the sensations of that moment, the primal moan of the tiger, the nocturnal fragrance of the *Murraya*, the reverberated knocking sounds of large-tailed nightjars—and the quiet, confident voice from deep within: to see my chosen direction with renewed clarity. Those sensations reaffirmed my life as a guardian of wild places and wild things.

ACKNOWLEDGMENTS

MY UNLIKELY EVOLUTION AS A CONSERVATION BIOLOGIST would never have happened without many amateur and professional naturalists guiding my way. Rene Fabricant and Duncan MacElfresh stimulated my budding interest in birds and wildflowers on a farm in Lake Bluff, Illinois, that has long since disappeared. May that special green heron rest in peace. Jim Newman, my advisor at Huxley College, encouraged me to undertake fieldwork, and Duncan invited me to join him on a study of black bears in Yosemite that I will never forget. Claire Dyckman inspired me to join the Peace Corps, and my fellow volunteers in Nepal—Will Weber, John Lehmkuhl, Paul Wilson, Cliff Rice, Tom Dahmer, Luke Golobitch, Kathy Johnson, and Brot Coburn—shared what became the formative experience of our lives, one I would not have survived without the guardianship of Gagan Singh.

Richard Taber, Gordon Orians, Jill Zarnowitz, Holly Dublin, and Nat Wheelwright made graduate school at the University of Washington a remarkable learning experience; and Jill, Nat, Bill Haber, Gary Hartshorn, Robin Foster, Richard LaVal, and Frank Bonaccorso helped make the tropics and its nonhuman inhabitants come alive for me. Two Georges, George Schaller and George Powell, inspired me as a young field biologist by their examples, and still inspire me today. Helen Freeman, Joe Fox, and Rodney Jackson taught me about snow leopard biology and conservation. Chris Wemmer allowed me to return to Nepal under the sponsorship of the Smithsonian Institution's Conservation and Research Center of the National Zoo to study rhinos and became my mentor; Hemanta Mishra, perhaps the most innovative Asian conservationist of my lifetime, became my counselor and project director, and my fabulous staff of trackers and elephant drivers taught me how to be a real junglewallah during our many nights camped out in the wilds of Chitwan National Park.

During one of those outings, in 1986, I was joined by Kathryn Fuller, who for sixteen years served as CEO of World Wildlife Fund–U.S. After counting rhinos for four days and camping out in the forest, she returned to Washington but gave me her t-shirt with Dürer's rhino stenciled on it, a shirt I coveted, and three years later, a job at WWF, a gift I valued even more. I am indebted to her, Jim Leape, Ginette Hemley, Diane Wood, and my extraordinary staff in the Conservation Science Program for allowing me to state unequivocally that I have the greatest job in the world. It has allowed me to travel to the best places on earth, work with dedicated individuals who are their defenders, and in some small way, try to tell their story. To count as colleagues so many outstanding conservationists within my organization is a privilege and an honor I have never taken for granted. Generous support from the Armand G. Erpf Foundation, Jeffrey Berenson, and Elizabeth Ruml over the years has allowed me to be an advocate for tigerlands.

ACKNOWLEDGMENTS

I thank Arnaud Greth for bringing me to New Caledonia and David Olson and Linda Farley for sharing with me their love of the Caura and its giant river otters. I was lucky to work in partnership with David for almost eight years, and I learned more natural history from him than anyone I have ever met. Henri Nsanjama was an inspiration to those who knew Africa and to novices like me. I thank Max Morgan-Davies for showing me how to break in a Land Rover and the ways of an African field hand. Roger and Vicki Sant invited me to the Galápagos for the first time, and the penguins, finches, tortoises, and dramatic landscapes have kept inviting me back since; I wish that I could do more to save that treasure. Curt Freese and Steve Forrest have been partners and schemers, along with Sean Gerrity, Kyran Kunkel, Elizabeth Ruml, in plans to bring back the American Serengeti. Anil Manandar, Arun Rijal, Narayan Dhakal, Anup Joshi, Chandra Gurung, Mingma Sherpa, and Eric Wikramanayake have been inspirational collaborators in re-tigering the Terai Arc.

The chapters benefited from critiques by many of the naturalists listed above. Others whom I wish to thank for critiquing early drafts of the manuscript include John Lamoreux, Colby Loucks, Minette Johnson, Michele Rekstad, Robin Abell, Meghan McKnight, Holly Strand, Jonathan Adams, Eric Wikramanayake, Nancy Sherman, Karen Ross, Ute Moeller, and Holly Dinerstein; and for critiquing the final draft, Andrea Brunholzl, who also taught me much of what little I know about writing. Meseret Taye and Danielle Miranda helped in preparation of the final drafts.

David Wilcove suggested the title "Re-Tigering" for the epilogue, and, even more important, he and Kent Redford introduced me to Jonathan Cobb, executive editor of the Shearwater Books imprint at Island Press. Shearwaters are mostly widespread and common, but there are a few rare ones, just as Jonathan is a rarity among editors, one who reads every word and considers the emotion and passion behind it. He is everything an editor should be: enthusiast, cheerleader, defender of the lay reader, and the best guide to clear writing any novice or experienced author could ask for. Emily Davis, also of Island Press, made excellent suggestions and helped to give the book its shape.

This book is dedicated to my mother, Eleanor, and sister, Holly, who were a constant source of encouragement and gentle nudging to write this book, especially when my confidence flagged. They have always supported my pursuit of an unusual career path, though I have not been as good about sharing some of my most important experiences with them. And finally, to Ute and Declan, for allowing me to continue to lead a charmed life.

INDEX

INDEX

INDEX